Civil Society and Democratic Theory

The idea of civil society is gathering momentum today as the search continues for forms of political action outside of what is often seen as a discredited state. But what can we really expect from civil society? In particular, could citizen self-organisation 'beneath' the state provide for the democratic self-determination that so many feel is lacking in modern society, despite promises to the contrary from liberal democracies?

This book explores these pressing and topical questions by introducing radically alternative models of civil society that have been developed outside the liberal democratic frame of reference, models which suggest that civil society *does* offer new and non-statist democratic possibilities. Drawing on a wide range of civil society theory–practice from anti-authoritarian struggles in Eastern Europe and Latin America (including the Zapatistas in Mexico), and from visions of global society too, this book is uniquely positioned to consider the questions posed by these alternative voices for democratic theory and practice.

- Are there alternatives to the liberal democratic vision of civil society?
- Is democracy located in civil society rather than the state either possible or desirable?
- Can global civil society further the struggle for democracy initiated by national civil societies?

Gideon Baker is Lecturer in Political Theory in the School of English, Sociology, Politics and Contemporary History at the University of Salford. He has published on the theory-philosophy of civil society in a wide range of journals.

Routledge Innovations in Political Theory

1 **A Radical Green Political Theory**
Alan Carter

2 **Rational Woman**
A feminist critique of dualism
Raia Prokhovnik

3 **Rethinking State Theory**
Mark J. Smith

4 **Gramsci and Contemporary Politics**
Beyond pessimism of the intellect
Anne Showstack Sassoon

5 **Post-Ecologist Politics**
Social theory and the abdication of the ecologist paradigm
Ingolfur Blühdorn

6 **Ecological Relations**
Towards an inclusive politics of the earth
Susan Board

7 **The Political Theory of Global Citizenship**
April Carter

8 **Democracy and National Pluralism**
Edited by Ferran Requejo

9 **Civil Society and Democratic Theory**
Alternative voices
Gideon Baker

10 **Ethics and Contemporary Political Theory**
Mark Devenney

Civil Society and Democratic Theory

Alternative voices

Gideon Baker

Routledge
Taylor & Francis Group
LONDON AND NEW YORK

First published 2002
by Routledge
11 New Fetter Lane, London EC4P 4EE

Simultaneously published in the USA and Canada
by Routledge
29 West 35th Street, New York, NY 10001

Transferred to Digital Printing 2003

Routledge is an imprint of the Taylor & Francis Group

Typeset in Baskerville by
Prepress Projects Ltd, Perth, Scotland
Printed and bound in Great Britain by
TJI Digital, Padstow, Cornwall

British Library Cataloguing in Publication Data
A catalogue record for this book is available from the British Library

Library of Congress Cataloging in Publication Data
A catalog record for this book has been requested

ISBN 0-415-25418-3

Contents

Acknowledgements

The research upon which this book is based began back in 1995, in pursuit of a doctoral thesis. For the three years thereafter, my academic supervisors – David Beetham and John Schwarzmantel – were a great support to me: offering regular, invigorating feedback and generally helping keep the research project on track. I am indebted to them for this, and also for their commitment to me ever since.

I would also like to thank my partner, Kate, and to acknowledge the sacrifice that she has made in making allowances for me at my most preoccupied – when working on this book! Without her companionship, this period of research would have been very one-dimensional indeed.

Finally, my thanks go to my father, Bruce Baker, who has been a highly valued and thought-provoking 'fellow traveller' on this venture from the very beginning. Although I know that he shares many of the sentiments contained in these pages, it has never stopped him being challenging and controversial in all of our many discussions, stimulation for which I am very grateful. I would like to dedicate this book to him.

Though the argument in this book is new, elements of the material contained in some of the chapters is reworked from previously published work: 'The changing idea of civil society: models from the Polish democratic opposition', *Journal of Political Ideologies* 3, 2 (1998), published by Carfax; 'From structuralism to voluntarism: the Latin American left and the discourse on civil society and democracy', *Contemporary Politics* 4, 4 (1998), published by Carfax; 'The taming of the idea of civil society', *Democratization* 6, 3 (1999), published by Frank Cass; 'Civil society theory and republican democracy', *Critical Review of International Social and Political Philosophy* 4, 2 (2001), published by Frank Cass.

Introduction

The concept of civil society is gathering momentum today as the search continues for forms of community and political action outside of what is often seen as a discredited state. But what can we really expect from civil society? In particular, could citizen self-organisation 'beneath' or outside of the state provide for the democratic self-determination that so many feel is lacking in modern society, despite promises to the contrary from liberal democracies? Liberal democratic theory complacently assumes that civil society should act merely as a support structure for democracy 'proper' at the level of the state – shaping parliamentary deliberation by providing a voice to public opinion, educating citizens in democratic values, and generally acting as a 'watchdog' over those in power, but otherwise leaving the 'real' business of democracy to representatives. Are there, though, alternative visions of civil society to this domesticated liberal democratic one? In particular, is a democracy located in civil society rather than the state desirable or even possible? And can the slogan 'civil society first', involving turning our backs on the state, continue to be a meaningful mode of democratic organisation today, even after the events of 1989 appeared to signal its redundancy? Remarkable as it may seem more than a decade after the triumph of liberal democracy supposedly ushered in the 'end of history', some still answer yes to these questions – but why and in what ways? And can such sentiments ever be other than utopian?

This book seeks to shed light on these questions by offering a new and critical perspective on the now extensive debate concerning the relationship between civil society and democracy.[1] This perspective involves providing a wider and more inclusive picture than has been taken previously. By wider I mean wider in two dimensions. On the first dimension I seek to include not only the Western canon of political theory on the topic of civil society and democracy, but also voices from Central–Eastern Europe and Latin America. On the second dimension, I consider newly emergent calls for 'global civil society' and for global action in civil society as a possible alternative for democratic theory and practice to the historically exclusive focus on the state–civil society relationship. I make no claims to be comprehensive in my treatment of these 'alternative voices', for my purpose is not merely descriptive but analytical – seeking to chart the ways in which the resurgent idea of civil society has been, and continues to be, articulated in radical ways which require us to reflect more fully on our taken-for-granted understanding of civil society and also on the possible outline of a form of civil society different from that which currently predominates in theory and in practice.

This process of reflection involves demonstrating that the hegemonic liberal democratic perspective on civil society is one singular point of view rather than a universally accepted one. The reverse side of this process involves uncovering aspects of the emergence and formation of the *particular* liberal democratic perspective on civil society so as to historicise a concept that is more often reified. In this aim I loosely follow Foucault's genealogical method, in as much as this seeks to question concepts 'as to their use in practical systems [and] for the ways in which they constitute and circumscribe our capacities to act'. Civil society, as with any other such concept, should therefore 'be interrogated for the ways in which it structures and delimits our political imaginations'. This is a project in tune with Foucault's wider call for a form of liberation that involves thinking that 'that which exists is far from filling all possible spaces' (Ashenden 1999: 158; Foucault 1989: 208):

> The role of the genealogist is to draw attention to the way in which dominant discourses conceal the emergence and effects of the practices they sustain. It is only by tracing out the genesis of these discourses and practices, and by contextualising them in relation to other practices and discourses, that other possibilities foreclosed by dominant interpretations can be reactivated and possibly pursued.
>
> (Howarth 2001:18)

In particular, the alternative readings of the relationship between civil society and democracy that I include in this book (in order to open up this discursive space) have a common orientation towards locating democracy primarily in civil society itself. The vision of a 'democracy of civil society', as we might term it, is of a very different type to the democracy that we actually have, where 'people power' is read as primarily a mechanism for selecting the people's representatives in the state. In this democracy, civil society is largely instrumental. The question posed by the alternative voices considered here is: could it be other than this?

However, the purpose of this book is not to offer up a new model of civil society for democratic theory. With its critical project in mind, and considering the alternative theories that are its primary focus, it does consider what the democracy of civil society might look like by way of a reconstruction of an ideal-type democracy of this sort. But this is provided because of the heuristic value of working with an ideal-type that makes explicit the implications of valorising the democracy of civil society. For unlike much radical civil society theory, which tends instinctively to assume that 'more power to civil society' means more democracy, a more systematic and questioning approach is required if we are to make a meaningful assessment of the extent to which the democracy of civil society represents a coherent alternative for democratic theory and practice.

The structure of the book is as follows: in parts I and II I explore models of civil society and democracy from Eastern Europe and Latin America respectively. The alternative discourses treated here are primarily from the 1970s and 1980s and were articulated under conditions of authoritarian state repression. In their different yet complementary ways, theorist-activists in both regions turned to the idea of civil society in the face of what they saw as the moral and political distortions of statist politics. 'Civil society first' is the leitmotif here, and I analyse the ways in which this was understood to promise a radically new approach to the theory and practice of democracy centred on civil society.

In part III I chart the eclipse of the radical approach to civil society – as introduced in parts one and two – by the liberal democratic model of civil society during the 1990s.[2] I do this by focusing on academic debates about democratisation in the same two regions (Eastern Europe and Latin America), where the radical reading of civil society emerged most powerfully. What becomes apparent is the essentially statist and instrumentalist reading of civil society by an academe within which, post 1989, liberal democratic categories are hegemonical to the extent that alternative readings of civil society are largely forgotten or rendered invisible.

In part IV I continue the task of considering alternative visions of civil society and democracy by looking at more recent challenges to the liberal democratic model. These include, first, the 'global civil society' approach, which is imparting a growing sense of democratic possibility to the increasingly transnational actions of new social movements and other non-state associations with global ambition and reach (human rights and environmental movements, for example). Second, I reflect on the theory–practice of democracy as global resistance within civil society that is being worked out by the Zapatistas (along with their global coalition) in Mexico today. The model of civil society to 'power' articulated under the shadow of the authoritarian state in the 1970s and 1980s might have been eclipsed, but can these new global perspectives recover the significance of 'civil society first' for our times?

In the final part of the book, in order to bring together my reflections in a more wide-ranging discussion, I first reconstruct an ideal-type model of a democracy based in civil society such as appears to be pre-figured in the alternative readings of civil society considered throughout the book. I provide this model as a *reconstruction* of key features of the radical approach because, to reiterate, I do not want to suggest a new approach myself, but rather to ask some hard questions about the democracy of civil society in order to contribute one answer to the question: what can we reasonably expect from such a democracy? The answer that I give, to state it only crudely here, is that the theory of the democracy of civil society recovers crucial insights from what we might term the republican tradition in democratic theory –

aspiring to autonomy and self-rule where these values have been downgraded in liberal democratic thought through its uncritical adherence to statism. However, I also show that it falls well short of being a fully developed theory of democracy.

I conclude by shifting focus from problems in theory with the democracy of civil society to the role of this ideal as a self-definition of radical political *practice* over the last twenty years. I take from these various actor-centred articulations of the democracy of civil society a powerful argument against the axiomatic treatment within liberal democratic theory of the legitimacy of the state. I suggest that the idea of a democracy of civil society is a necessary reminder to students of democracy that, instead of seeing the legitimacy of self-organisation in civil society as requiring justification, we should shift the burden of proof to those (liberal democratic) theories and practices which assume that the state can be effectively democratised and then that this is all democracy is. For in turning away from the state to civil society, the idea of the democracy of civil society encourages us to redirect our political efforts towards more local, particular and self-determining manifestations of democracy, and this may indeed be it's most significant achievement.

I now devote the remainder of this introduction to a brief history of the idea of civil society, in order to situate the contemporary debates with which I am concerned in some wider historical context.

The history of a concept

The idea of civil society was articulated first by the philosophers of the Scottish Enlightenment.[3] These philosophers were able to posit the universality of civil society (commercial society within a framework of law), as a solution to the particularity of the market sphere that was increasingly redefining the estates system of feudal society. This particularity, which for Adam Ferguson represented a serious threat to civic virtue, arose out of the increasing thirst for private wealth, which turned people away from 'affairs of state' while also escalating the state's role in upholding security. The very real threat of despotism followed from this, according to Ferguson (Ferguson 1966: 261).

The concern, first, with the rising tension between individualism and community life, second, with the need to check the power of the state, and, third, with the need to rediscover some kind of republican virtue or public spirit represents enduring concerns for theorists of civil society to this day. However, in its Enlightenment form such thought was arguably not yet fully modern; for Ferguson because, although he is able to identify associationalism as important to the resolution of the problems named above, this is not defined as activity outside of the state. Ferguson is still thinking in the classical terms of an essential unity between civil society and the state (Keane 1988a: 44). A less than fully modern approach to civil society is also characteristic of the theorists of the Scottish Enlightenment more generally. They, particularly Adam Smith, posited civil society's 'solution' to the problem of the greater good in society as arising from the natural sympathy or moral sentiment displayed within it. This was a quintessentially eighteenth-century notion, shaped still by Christian and natural theology, which suggested that a transcendental mutuality was implicit in the recognition by individuals of other individuals in the arena of exchange (Seligman 1992).

The Scottish Enlightenment's idea of civil society then travelled to Germany by way of the translation of Ferguson's *Essay on the History of Civil* Society (1767) and Smith's *The Wealth of Nations* (1776–8) (Ashenden 1999: 145). Thereafter, Hegel was the first philosopher to begin to develop a recognisably modern notion of civil society in his *Philosophy of Right*, written in 1821. Although Hegel articulated the same tension between individual autonomy and community as the philosophers of the Scottish Enlightenment, he did this without reference to an ethical unity from without. Instead, Hegel sought to resolve the contradictions that existed in civil society as a result of its particularity by reference to the universal state. It is only at this point, then, that the idea of civil society is first concerned with the proper relation between the state and civil society as separate spheres. However, Hegel's theory of civil society also gave the concept a pejorative hue for the first time. The state, in order to realise its universality, requires the creation through civil society of individual freedoms and the ability to satisfy needs. Yet by this very process of development, civil society is increasingly characterised by chaos and inequality that undermines ethical unity. Such ethical unity is found only in the universal state, which, although it should not abolish civil society, should rule and guide it.

For Marx, going further than Hegel in criticising the atomisation unleashed by an unfettered civil society, any separation of spheres between state and civil society had to be overcome entirely. Marx also rejected Hegel's account of the supposedly impartial, 'universal' state ruling over civil society; as far as he was concerned, this state actually furthered the dominance of the bourgeois class over subordinate classes in civil society. Thus, although Marx retained Adam Smith's identification of civil society with economic interactions through the mechanism of the market, he was decidedly less sanguine than Smith about the possibility of the 'greater good' emerging from the sum total of these transactions. The formal 'freedoms' of civil society were for Marx a sham masking the deep structure of class inequality that defined this sphere in the first place. Real political freedom could only be attained if the working class took over state functions which, in being alienated from civil society, reinforced the latter's individualistic, egoistic and therefore socially atomising character (see Marx 1977). In this moment of revolution, 'particularistic' civil society itself would be abolished by the universal rule of the proletariat. Marx's damning critique concerning the alienation and exploitation supposedly to be found in the sphere of civil society contributed thereafter to its significant decline as a field of study. More generally, the growing dominance of the modern state from the second half of the nineteenth century led anyway to declining interest in the sphere of civil society.

It was nearly a century after Marx's critique that Antonio Gramsci, an Italian Marxist, isolated civil society as a category of importance in its own right. Gramsci characterised civil society as the realm of culture and ideology, or, more concretely, as the associational realm (made up of the church, trade unions, etc.) through which the state, under normal circumstances, perpetuates its hegemony or achieves consent. However, precisely because this associational realm represents a non-state *and* a non-economic sphere, Gramsci, contra Marx, saw it as having the potential for dual autonomy from both the state and market relations. He was therefore the first to articulate the idea that civil society, in a moment of counter-hegemony, could actually be resistant to state power as, in his well-known phrase, so many 'earthworks and buttresses' (Gramsci 1971: 238). The voluntarism of Gramsci's account of civil society contrasts, of course, with Marx's structural determinism. Rather than political change being dependent on the unfolding of the laws of history within the deeper structure of production upon which civil society rests, action in civil society itself is made possible. Gramsci's more political or agency-centred emphasis is reflected in most contemporary accounts; civil society is therefore used to identify a sphere of willed action, rather than an 'unwilled, non-purposive, arena of human interaction' such as the early moderns had in mind when they coined the term to describe the operation of commercial societies (Pearce 1997: 58).

How did this new emphasis within civil society theory arise? It appeared first with the re-emergence of the concept in communist Central–Eastern Europe.[4] Democratic opposition movements in this region (especially in Poland) used the idea of civil society in theorising their struggle to create a protected societal sphere separate from the official sphere of the all-embracing party-state. Indeed, accounts of the history of the idea of civil society itself have been rewritten to some extent through the influence of these discourses. Alexis de Tocqueville (1805–59), for example, despite his infrequent use of the term itself, has recently emerged in academic consciousness as a key civil society theorist. This is at least in part because of the compatibility of his observations with those arising from the Central-Eastern European opposition movements; that is, he was the first, in *Democracy in America*, to articulate the need for strong, independent associations – *'corps intermédiaires'* as he terms them – to stand between the individual and the state.[5] For Tocqueville, looking in bewilderment at the totalitarian implications of statist, centralising and, as he saw it, potentially stifling and conformist developments in post-revolutionary France, and for the Central-Eastern European oppositionists considering their weakness in the face of even greater 'totalisation' from above, the importance of the 'self-defence' of society against the state must have been equally apparent.

Robert Fine differentiates this new approach to civil society (what he terms 'civil society theory', which he also claims emerged during the 1980s in connection with the political struggles in Central and Eastern Europe) from the concept of civil society that we inherit from the 'classical' theory (Fine

1997: 9). For Fine, what sets current civil society theory apart, 'is that it *privileges* civil society over all other moments or spheres of social life, on the ground that civil society furnishes the fundamental conditions of liberty in the modern world ... ' (1997: 9). This was not the case for the earliest theorists of civil society, who saw the emancipatory potential of civil society in more limited and historicised terms: as the role of private property in freeing 'humanity from the personal dependencies, status inequalities and other injustices associated with the old political order' (Fine 1997: 16). As far as Fine is concerned, the new situation in civil society theory of the privileging of this sphere over all others is a shared feature of otherwise very different approaches to using the concept. Indisputably, civil society is now central to democratic theory, as will become clear from the following review of its current uses in the field.

Starting on the left of the political spectrum, it might be imagined that leftists would be given to recalling Marx's critical analysis of 'bourgeois' civil society. Yet, on the contrary, increasing numbers of left-leaning theorists seem to be abandoning any reservations that they once had about the category of civil society. This is especially true of the New Left. Many New Left or post-Marxist theorists find insights within the idea of civil society which are seen as crucial in coming to terms with two admitted areas of weakness in their earlier accounts. The first of these is the supposed failure of orthodox leftism to recognise the threat to democratic self-organisation posed by modern state bureaucracies. The modern state, it is argued, based largely on the experience of state-socialism, but also of welfare statism, has a deadening tendency to subordinate ever more areas of social life to its control regardless of whether it has been captured by and seeks to 'represent' previously oppressed classes (Lefort 1986: 280). The second alleged mistake was the left's class objectivism, involving the downplaying of the 'fact of pluralism' characteristic of modernity and an adherence to vanguardist strategies now invalidated by the acceptance of such pluralism. This error is seen to require some kind of separation of spheres between state and civil society in order to preserve both an open, uncoerced public sphere and also a personal private sphere from the intrusions of state power (and, ultimately, from totalitarianism).

These are the problems facing a previously authoritarian left from the standpoint of democracy, but for the New Left civil society represents their solution.[6] For Jürgen Habermas, the most influential of New Left theorists, civil society is the source of self-reflexivity in society, without which democracy itself dries up. That is, the institutions of civil society must act to protect the autonomous development of public opinion in the public sphere from being undermined or colonised by state bureaucracy – the system of power – and by the economic power of the market – the system of money (Habermas 1992: 444). In particular, Habermas has identified new social movements as attempts to hold back the incursions of this instrumental or self-steering 'system' of power and money into the non-instrumental or goal-orientated 'lifeworld' of civil society. However, contra republican readings of civil society, and broadly in line with liberal thought on the topic, Habermas wants to preserve – make normative even – the separation of spheres between state, civil society and economy. For Habermas argues that civil society, given the complexity of modern decision-making and the need to protect certain levels of efficiency, cannot govern, but can only 'influence' or 'sensitise' the state through democratic will formation. Thus he states that 'the public opinion that is worked up via democratic procedures into communicative power [in civil society] cannot "rule" of itself, but can only point the use of administrative power in specific directions ...' (Habermas 1994: 9–10). That is, the pure republican formations of political will by elements of the public sphere, constituted through civil society, are 'only *catalysts* and not the end results of political action' (Ely 1992: 178); or, as Habermas puts it:

> [L]egitimate law reproduces itself only in the forms of a constitutionally regulated circulation of power, which should be nourished by the communications of an unsubverted public sphere rooted in the core private spheres of an undisturbed lifeworld via the networks of civil society.
>
> (1996: 408)

Yet the New Left are not alone in redeploying the concept of civil society for their own purposes. Within mainstream political science, the concept seems to have taken off as an explanation for the collapse of communist – and other authoritarian – regimes, through the apparent resurgence of independent associational life as a basis for popular political resistance. Here the term civil society becomes central to the vocabulary of analyses of the so-called 'third wave' of democratisation since the 1980s, especially in Central–Eastern Europe. As Schwarzmantel observes, this mode of thinking about civil society actually places the concept in a line of thinking about totalitarianism, and resistance to it, which traces back to theorists such as Hannah Arendt. Here, the antithesis between civil society and 'rude society' identified by the Enlightenment theorists is replaced by a new binary opposition between civil society and totalitarian society (Schwarzmantel 1996: 7). In other words, the norm of associability which the term civil society was originally used to deploy in critiquing 'barbaric societies' is now used in contrast to the atomisation of society under total state control. For theorists such as Arendt, totalitarian regimes obliterated the groups and associations which were all that stood between the power of the modern state and the weak, isolated individual. This understanding of civil society, as a bulwark in the face of the state leviathan, is now the commonly accepted one in accounts of the 'third wave' of democratisation. It turns the civil society 'solution' away from problems posed to society arising from 'below' (i.e. untrammelled individualism) and exclusively towards threats from 'above'.

Thus, Ernest Gellner (1995) states that 'civil society is that set of diverse non-governmental institutions which is strong enough to counterbalance the state [and which] can prevent the state from dominating and atomising the rest of society'.[7] Diamond, who agrees that civil society is defined in its relation to the state, writes that he conceives of it 'as the realm of organised social life that is voluntary, self-generating, (largely) self-supporting, autonomous from the state, and bound by a legal order or set of shared rules' (1994: 5). Diamond's definition is not merely descriptive (as no account of civil society, however crude, can be), but contains also a clear normative agenda. Indeed, Diamond identifies this for himself. It includes, first, that civil society is concerned with public not private ends; second, that it does not seek power in the state; and, third, that its associations are themselves pluralistic and diverse (1994: 6). In some senses the concept of civil society, so interpreted, returns to pluralist thinking on the character of liberal democracies – where these are understood as possessing multiple centres of power with no one set of interests predominating (since membership of groups is cross-cutting) and with influence, broadly speaking, moving from civil society to the state, which acts as a mere facilitator for, and adjudicator of, social demands. Of course, theorists of civil society, given their awareness of the role of civil society against the state under authoritarianism, should be less optimistic than pluralists that the state always acts as a neutral referee and that it has no interests of its own. Yet in relation to liberal democracy this rosy picture does seem to be accepted for the most part, if only implicitly in the sense that their telos of 'civil society against the state' outside the liberal democratic world is clearly that it becomes part of that world.

With this essentially liberal focus, premised upon the notion of a separation of spheres with civil society programming the state in society's interests, we come full circle back to Habermasian approaches to civil society that are common currency for the New Left. For whether it is articulated in the form of a liberal counterweight to state power, or as a 'lifeworld' outside of the state for the generation of a critical public sphere, few commentators would now disagree with Habermas that:

> the now current meaning of the term 'civil society' ... no longer includes a share of an economy ... and thus differs from the modern translation, common since Hegel and Marx, of '*societas civilis*' as 'bourgeois society' ... However, this much is apparent: the institutional core of 'civil society' is constituted by voluntary unions outside the realm of the state and the economy ...
>
> (1992: 453)

This, then, appears to be the dominant paradigm for understanding civil society today. But recall: Habermas, in elucidating this paradigm, does not see civil society 'ruling' itself in any sense. Thus civil society, although crucially separate from the state and the economy, must still be placed within this overarching tripartite schema, without which it is nothing. Separate, on this account, does not mean self-governing in any way and involves significant surrendering of popular control to spheres of administrative and economic expertise. Crucially, the suggestion here, as for theorists of the 'third wave' of democratisation, is that the civil society we find within liberal democracy is broadly the civil society of our normative ideal-type. Yet surely this stance should cause alarm, given how effectively critique is marginalised when real and ideal are conflated, resulting in their being no place from which to argue outside the dominant paradigm. It is all the more necessary, therefore, to ask the question: Can civil society be more than this? *Must* it continue to act within the constraints set down by the state and the market under liberal democracy? Some rather different answers to this question from the liberal democratic one form the subject of the chapters to come.

Part I

The parallel polis

Central–East European models of civil society

1 'The self-limiting revolution'

Polish voices

Despite its Western European pedigree, we must look outside West European thought to account for the re-emergence of the idea of civil society in recent years. This re-emergence had much to do with the events surrounding Solidarity, the independent trade union, with its unique activities in communist Poland during 1980–81, and thus also with the theoretical–political models worked out by the Polish democratic opposition during and even before this period.

As early as 1956, nationwide strikes saw Polish workers abandon the communist party trade unions for their own local and autonomous trade councils based in the factories. Although this instinct for self-organisation was subsequently suppressed by the Polish communist party-state, a precedent was set for the remarkable birth of Solidarity following on from the strike at the Lenin shipyard in Gdansk in July 1980. Striking in support of the Gdansk shipbuilders, workers across the country were, in their turn, supported by the Gdansk caucus, who now called for their strike to continue until all factories' demands were met. As ever-increasing numbers of factories joined the subsequent Inter-Factory Strike Committee (MKS), the list of demands to be met if work were to be resumed also grew. The first and most significant of these, by now highly political, demands was that the communist government must accept 'free trade unions independent of the Communist Party'. Faced with a crippling general strike, the Party had little choice but to accede to these demands. Following the Gdansk Agreement, as it came to be known, the creation of the free trade union, Solidarity, took place through the amalgamation of over thirty regional unions in September 1980. Although it was only to last until December 1981 (at which point, under threat from the Soviets, martial law was declared and Solidarity crushed – its leaders imprisoned), Solidarity was seen as a beacon of hope for all of communist Eastern Europe in one sense in particular: it appeared to participants and observers alike to herald the rebirth of civil society there.

At stake, then, in detailing the Polish discourse on civil society is a proper understanding of the recent history of the concept. Indeed, Andrew Arato helped to restart the debate on civil society in the West with his 1981 analysis, in the then left-wing journal *Telos*, of the Solidarity events according to the model 'civil society against the state' (Arato 1981). Arato was thus the first to use a previously contextualised Polish debate about civil society as a category of political theory generally – that is, as connected to notions of the public sphere allegedly applicable to all societies (Ely 1992: 176). The considerable influence of Arato's work on civil society theory therefore constitutes, at least in part, the popularisation of the 'Polish model' of civil society.

Yet the architects of this model sought originally to articulate their ideas with specific reference to what they saw as the uniqueness of the Polish context. As Arato wrote in his 1981 essay, reviewing these thinkers and their models, 'The categories of civil society are not extraneous to the Polish events' (1981: 23). At stake for Polish theorists was not a generic account of democratic opposition in the realms of theory, but the discovery of a model of democratic practice that could take account of the constraints of their situation. It was in developing this practice that they came increasingly to rely on the idea of civil society.

Encapsulating this union of theory and praxis was the idea of the 'self-limiting' revolution. First explored by Polish theorists before 1980, it came also to characterise something of the character of Solidarity: 'Solidarnosc sought neither to form a political party nor to "capture" state power. It sought neither the restoration of capitalism nor the withering away of the state. Rather, it pursued a self-limiting "evolutionist" strategy' (Keane 1988a: 5).

This undoubtedly strategic approach to opposition may appear to have signalled the abandonment of more substantive political values. Yet the tactic of the peaceful transformation of society towards self-organisation – which would 'hollow out' and eventually transform the institutional arena[1] – although undoubtedly pragmatic in its recognition of the limits to action posed by Soviet power in the region, was not by any means purely instrumental. This ideal of 'self-limitation', of autonomous self-organisation outside the official and state sphere, was understood as an end in itself. As a value that came to prominence within the Polish civil society debate, but which is now a significant component in much civil society theorising of a more general nature, 'self-limitation' is illustrative of the significance of this debate:

> The self-limiting revolution avoids the total destruction of its enemy, which would inevitably mean putting itself into the place of the sovereign, thereby depriving society of its self-organisation and its self defence ... The common core of all the interpretations [of self-limiting revolution] ... is the concept of civil society, or rather some of the components of this concept. All agree that civil society represents a sphere other than and even distinct from the state.
>
> (Cohen and Arato 1992: 74)

I proceed in this chapter by looking, first, at the origins of thinking about civil society in Poland in the formative years 1976–81. In the section 'Civil society and totalitarianism', in order to establish a broader theoretical context to these developments, I outline the importance of the totalitarian paradigm to the new thinking about civil society. In 'The politics of civil society' I highlight the distinctive elements of the 'Polish model' and the political debates contained within it.

Content, context and timing

Ideas that after 1980–1 fall under the rubric of civil society are expressed by three main thinkers (Leszek Kolakowski, Adam Michnik and Jacek Kuron) in essays from as early as 1971. All of these men were Polish, seeking to develop new approaches to political opposition in the wake of the failure of two major challenges by workers to the communist system in 1970–1 and 1976.

In 1976 the Workers' Defence Committee (KOR) was formed, in which Polish intellectuals, including Michnik and Kuron, re-established close ties with the workers' movement. In the same year, Michnik's highly influential essay 'A New Evolutionism' was published (see Michnik 1985), which built on earlier work by Kolakowski, an exiled philosopher. Before 1980 and these developments, the term civil society had been used in only a number of isolated places: by Smolar in the preface to *Une societe en dissedence* – a volume of writings by Polish dissidents published in 1978; and by Rupnik, following Kolakowski, as a term for the new 'post-revisionist' opposition strategy (Arato 1981: 23). Yet by 1982, a series of lectures under the title *Power and Civil Society* given by Leszek Nowak – a philosopher and Solidarity activist – to his Solidarity co-internees is orientated entirely around the concept of civil society, defined as 'the sphere of civil autonomy' (Nowak 1991: 29).

Kolakowski, although in exile, set this process in train as early as 1971. In his essay 'Hope and Hopelessness' (1971), Kolakowski distanced himself from the prevailing pessimism concerning the likelihood of democratic political change in Eastern Europe following the Soviet 'normalisation' of Czechoslovakia. Despite the willingness of the Soviet Union to use overwhelming force in the region when processes of reform from within ruling communist parties went too far (as in Czechoslovakia in 1968), Kolakowski believed that Soviet-type systems could nonetheless be reformed 'from below'. Because the party-state could only retain its control by suppressing all dissent, Kolakowski called for the reconstruction of the social sphere through resistance. This resistance was not to be aimed at overthrowing or substantially reforming the communist regime directly, but at creating a growing societal realm free from party-state control. As Kolakowski put it, oppositionists should look for a reformist orientation 'in the sense of a belief in the possibility of effective, gradual, and partial pressures, exercised in a long term perspective of social and national liberation' (1971: 42).

Stimulated by Kolakowski's ideas and, further, by the failure of recent workers' strikes, the new political thinking inside Poland came to hinge on two key themes: the interrelated oppositional strategies of 'evolutionism' and putting 'society first'. The former strategy was outlined originally in Michnik's essay 'A New Evolutionism'. The idea of 'evolutionism' was intended as a critique of revisionism in that, like Kolakowski, although Michnik thought it only realistic to accept the limits imposed by Soviet power in the region for revisionism itself, he did not see this as imposing limitations on action as such. 'For me', he wrote in this essay, 'the lesson of Czechoslovakia is that change is possible and that it has its limits ... [R]evisionists ... believed in having concessions and rights "granted" from above rather than in organising pressure from below' (1985: 139–40).

Parallel to these intellectual developments, Michnik was also part of a movement seeking to put them into practice – the 'organisation of pressure from below' taking the form of the KOR. 'To offer solidarity with striking workers', he wrote in 'A New Evolutionism', '... is to challenge the intraparty strategy of the revisionist[s] ... Social solidarity undermines the fundamental component of [reformist] strateg[y]: acceptance of the government as the basic reference point' (1985: 142). As will become apparent, this link between theory and praxis was to be characteristic of the Polish model.

However, if reformism would not work, then the idea of 'evolutionism' accepted that neither would revolution:

> The dilemma of nineteenth-century leftist movements – 'reform or revolution' – is not the dilemma of the Polish opposition. To believe in overthrowing the dictatorship of the party by revolution ... is both unrealistic and dangerous. As the political structure of the USSR remains unchanged, it is unrealistic to count on subverting the party in Poland.
>
> (Michnik 1985: 142)

Eschewing violent revolutionary action was not mere pragmatism, since Michnik denied wholeheartedly that the Leninist vanguardism required for such actions had any legitimacy. 'Given the absence of an authentic political culture or any standards of democratic life, the existence of an underground would only worsen the illness and change little ...'(Michnik 1985: 142).[2]

What, then, was the evolutionary strategy to consist of?

> In my opinion, an unceasing struggle for reform and evolution that seeks an expansion of civil liberties and human rights is the only course East European dissidents can take. The Polish example demonstrates that real concessions can be won by applying steady public pressure on the government ... To draw a parallel with ... the Spanish model ... [evolutionism] is based on gradual and piecemeal change, not violent upheaval and forceful destruction.
>
> (Michnik 1985: 142–3)

Nevertheless, as Michnik (1985: 146) made clear when he ruled out the idea that reformers in the party could be political allies, putting pressure on the government to concede civil liberties and human rights was a hoped for byproduct of 'new evolutionism', not its *raison d'être*:

> what sets today's opposition apart ... is the belief that a program for evolution ought to be addressed to an independent public, not to totalitarian power. Such a programme should give directives to the people on how to behave, not to the powers on how to reform themselves. Nothing instructs the authorities better than pressure from below.
>
> (Michnik 1985: 144)

This 'society-first' strategy, as it has been termed, was at the heart of the new civil society approach for other Polish theorists too. Bernhard gives the example of Kuron's changing political thinking at the time, which reveals a similar trend. In the mid-1960s Kuron, along with most other dissidents, still addressed his grievances to the party; in this way, the final legitimacy of the party was not called into question. For example, Kuron's 'Open Letter to the Party' (co-authored with Karol Modzelewski) from this period advocated a programme of socialist self-management that, despite its plea for decision-making to be decentralised to the workers and the peasantry, was, according to it own title, self-evidently not intended primarily for this wider audience (Bernhard 1993: 313). Yet, like Michnik, by the mid–late 1970s Kuron was looking towards 'society' as the locus of political change rather than the party-state. This can be seen from his 1976 pamphlet on oppositional strategy, which Arato claims was the first to outline 'a systematic programme for the reconstitution of civil society through the re-establishment of the rule of law, an independent public sphere and freedom of association' (Arato 1981: 28). And in 1981, intimating once again his departure from conventional state-directed dissidence, Kuron wrote, 'of course it would be better if the party mustered up enough strength for an inner reform. But I know too little about that and have no way of influencing it. I have to think in terms of my own categories' (1981a: 95).

Kuron also shared Michnik's view of the need for an evolutionary process of change, for 'self-limitation' by the organised forces of pressure from below. Indeed, the 'self-limiting revolution' was a term first coined by Kuron during the Solidarity period. 'Let me express the conviction', he stated, 'that in the interests of the Polish nation, and all other nations of the Soviet bloc, that these changes are accomplished in an evolutionary manner' (cited in Hankiss 1990: 150). Elsewhere, in a 1980 edition of an opposition information bulletin, Kuron also called for a path to democratisation that would 'safeguard national security by not overstepping [its] boundaries' (1981b: 37). Then in a 1981 interview, even at the height of Solidarity when so much seemed to have been achieved, he re-emphasised how vital it was 'not to lure the [Soviet] wolves out of the woods' (Kuron 1981a: 94). Again, it is important to see the normative, rather than purely tactical, nature of this emphasis on 'self-limitation'. In 1982, despite the defeat of Solidarity's self-limiting strategy after the imposition of martial law, Nowak addressed his Solidarity co-internees in continuing support of this strategy, 'according to a well-known saying, "the revolution devours its own children" ' (1991: 57):

> [Revolutionary] utopia does not offer any guarantee of universal freedom, equality, and fraternity, except for one: the good will of the revolutionaries ... Therefore [revolutionary] utopia expresses the interest of the oppressed, but it does so only so long as the social system against which it has turned lasts.
>
> (Nowak 1991: 97)

Recognition of the futility of replacing one absolute power in the state with another led the 'society-first', or civil society, theorists to deny interest in state power as a *permanent* feature of their political programme.[3] In this sense, the Polish model of civil society, as Arato for example has always claimed, did implicitly advocate the separation of spheres between state and society as more than merely strategic:

> While the full range of meanings in the concept of self-limitation was never fully articulated ... the notion ... meant not only the need to avoid the transformation of the movement of society into a new form of unified state power, but also that one will not attempt to impose the logic of democratic coordination on all spheres by suppressing bureaucracy and economic rationality. Movements rooted in civil society have learned from the revolutionary tradition the Tocquevillian lesson that such fundamentalist projects lead to the breakdown of societal steering, productivity, and integration, all of which are then reconstituted by dramatically authoritarian means.
>
> (Arato 1990: 26)

However, despite their undoubted acceptance of the necessity of an autonomous societal sphere (which is how they defined civil society in the first place), there is considerable evidence that Arato is incorrect in describing the Polish theorists as advocating a strictly delimited and tripartite separation of spheres (a polity within which civil society only exercises *indirect* democratic control). First, these theorists did see a market sphere as necessary to reducing 'totalising' bureaucratic control by centralised state mechanisms,[4] so this sphere can be seen to hold some kind of separateness for them; but it is not clear that market rationality was seen as sufficient for the coordination of this sphere as some kind of separate 'sub-system'. Second, with regard to a state separated out from civil society: while such was clearly the mainstay of their political programme,[5] this was much more for the sake of self-management in civil society than in order to establish the state as a distinct system with its own administrative rationality (which is anathema to self-management). Kuron and Michnik's emphasis, as will become clear, was in fact on the transformation of the societal sphere – including the economy – through local self-management; and they also talked very little about a substantive role for the state in democratisation, although it was recognised that the state was unlikely to simply wither away.[6] A quote from Kuron indicates well both these points: first, that the desired autonomy of civil society from the state was not intended to countenance the state monopolising sovereignty and, second, that although the economy was to be taken outside state control and marketised, this was not to preclude local democratic control of the economic sphere either:

> [W]e have to bring ourselves to inject our independence into dependent state structures. Now is the time for what I call the 'interdependent economy'. It is time to form self-management workers' councils in factories, to make state enterprises autonomous, to replace administrative control with the market.
>
> (interview with Luczywo, in Rupnik 1988: 285)

In fact, the key to understanding the earliest versions of the civil society model in Poland, as will be explored more fully below, is that the theorists concerned wanted some form of self-managing or council democracy. Arato has glossed this over in retrospect in his 1990 article, although he saw it at the time. Given his own Habermasian project, everything has come to rest upon the tripartite separation of spheres. However, it is necessary to see the emergence of the civil society concept in Poland in its proper context – neither the wholesale post-Marxism nor the systems theory that Arato ascribes to the 'Polish model' really belong to this context.

Democratisation, these Poles suggested, necessitated not only changes in the overall structure of society but also the rebuilding of autonomous social structures from below. This self-organisation, which was seen as representing a nascent civil society, became a desired end in itself – not just the hoped for byproduct of a more conventional reformist or revolutionary process of political change:

> A system for society to function must be worked out ... It is a matter of a system in which the social structure can be established from below, from the populace, which is increasingly well organised ... [and] which demands more pluralism, more democracy.
>
> (Kuron 1981a: 95)

It is in this sense that the term civil society itself started to be used around 1981. Michnik wrote at this time, describing the Solidarity accords:

> For the first time organised authority was signing an accord with an organised society. The agreement marked the creation of labour unions

> independent of the state which vowed not to attempt to take over political power. The essence of the spontaneously growing Independent and Self-governing *Solidarity* lay in the restoration of social ties, self-organisation aimed at guaranteeing the defence of labour, civil, and national rights. For the first time in the history of communist rule in Poland 'civil society' was being restored ...
>
> (1985: 124)

As Arato pointed out, observing these events as they developed, there was in fact a consensus among Polish theorists that this 'civil society building' strategy was the only way forward. Yet, far from seeing this solely as a constraint they 'settled on a path to social transformation that began and ended with the reconstruction of civil society' (Reidy 1992: 169).

Civil society and totalitarianism

The intellectual ground that the new idea of civil society took root in was prepared initially by the re-emergence of thinking about totalitarianism. The rediscovery of the totalitarian paradigm in the 1970s was a specifically Central-Eastern European innovation. Indeed, within the Western academic community theories of totalitarianism had long since given way to apparently more realistic accounts of the quasi-pluralism extant in communist regimes in the post-Stalin era. Neither, according to Rupnik, was 'the rediscovery of the concept (and realities) of totalitarianism a return to the American political science of the 1950s. It was a completely new attempt to redefine the concept in the light of the system's evolution and the new methods of Communist rule' (1988: 267).

Western political science in the 1950s had defined totalitarianism according to criteria such as charismatic leadership, mass terror, the 'permanent purge' and ideological mobilisation (Rupnik 1988: 271). The Polish theorists, differently, did not emphasise the role of personal leadership or terror and purges, since these categories were not so directly relevant to their situation. Yet, despite this change of emphasis, the Poles' version of the totalitarian paradigm was still, contra Rupnik, built upon elements of theorising carried out in the 1950s, specifically on the key role of ideology in totalitarianism. Thus, in repudiating newer Western theories of a *post*-totalitarian order, which they acknowledged had some purchase on the changing nature of the communist regimes, but which missed the remaining 'totalising' tendencies of a system in which the state sought to control all areas of human activity (Keane 1985: 8), the Poles adopted a more orthodox account of the totalitarian properties of the party-state mechanism. This was mainly because of the state's central role, as Kolakowski put it, in ensuring the supremacy of ideology as the 'institutional lie', which 'is the great cognitive triumph of totalitarianism. By managing to abrogate the very idea of truth, it can no longer be accused of lying' (cited in Rupnik 1988: 269).

This account of totalitarianism focused upon the totalitarian power's ability to manipulate information so that the very basis of 'truth', and with it the moral and political resources necessary for social autonomy, are destroyed. Here there was certainly continuity with earlier work from the 1950s, particularly Arendt's, where both the Poles and Arendt looked not so much on the strength or violence of totalitarian regimes, but on the ideology that usurps moral considerations. As Arendt saw it:

> The point ... is not the use of violence per se, not even on an unprecedented scale, but that 'totalitarian indifference' to moral consideration is actually based upon a reversal of all our legal and moral concepts ... In other words, the peculiarity of totalitarian crimes is that they are committed for different reasons and in a different framework which has a 'morality' of its own. Th[is] morality is contained in the ideology ...
>
> (1958a: 78)

The theme of the central role of the 'lie', and of resistance to the 'lie', under totalitarianism was to be most fully developed by the Czechoslovakian thinker Václav Havel. The Poles were generally more directly programmatic in their thinking than Havel, yet they too sought to couch their resistance to totalitarianism in moral terms. Michnik for example, along with Arendt, sees the totalitarian power's ideological hegemony as more pernicious than its coercive properties:

> I ... believe that totalitarian dictatorships are doomed ... They still have the power to jail and kill, but almost no other power. I say 'almost' because (alas) there still remains their ability to infect us with their own hatred and contempt. Such infection must be resisted with our whole strength, for of all the struggles we face this is the most difficult.
>
> (Michnik 1985: xix)

Thus Michnik apparently shared Arendt's fear that 'totalitarian movements conjure up a lying world of consistency which is more adequate to the needs of the human mind than reality itself ...' (Arendt 1958a: 353).

The importance of the totalitarian paradigm to the Polish model of civil society lies here. So-called 'convergence theory' in the West saw the modernisation of Soviet-type societies as leading inexorably – via the stage of 'welfare state authoritarianism' or 'institutional pluralism' – to liberalisation in all spheres (Ekiertz 1991: 292). Yet Polish theorists recalled elements of more long-standing accounts of totalitarianism to account for the fact that basic features of the system had *not* changed (even after the upheavals of 1956 and 1968), and also that they were not likely to in the foreseeable future. This led in turn to a model of democratisation – the 'society first', or civil society strategy – that took this analysis as its starting point.

Kolakowski's model of totalitarianism as a society deprived of all social self-defence encouraged a proactive oppositionism that did not expect 'modernisation' to weaken the authoritarian system, but which sought itself to 'defend' society against the state. This in fact was the reasoning behind the establishment of the KOR by Michnik and Kuron *et al.* in 1976, as a statement from Kuron in 1980 made clear: 'The general direction of th[e] [democratisation] programme has been worked out some time ago by various groups working with KOR ... It is a programme of social self-defence ...' (1981b: 37).

Yet the specifically Polish strategy of building 'civil society' to counter 'totalitarianism' was in some ways a contradictory thesis. As Kolakowski had identified it, societal self-defence was necessary because with resistance the 'system' could never be totalised (Arato 1981: 28). Thus although the idea of totalitarianism provided the driving force for the new civil society strategy, it was accepted that, *de facto*, totalitarianism did not exist. Michnik seemed to acknowledge this when he conceded that 'the communist powers in Poland ha[ve] learned to coexist with independent bodies – for instance, with the powerful and independent Catholic church'. But he then goes on to say, 'All this allows me to believe in the viability of a hybrid system in which the state's *totalitarian organisation* could be combined with democratic institutions in the society' (1985: 110, emphasis added). Similarly, Kuron made the seemingly self-contradictory observation in the 1980s that 'Today Polish society is outside the totalitarian system ...' (cited in Rupnik 1988: 285). Arato was therefore surely right when he observed that:

> the reintroduction of the totalitarian thesis [was] primarily for polemical rather than theoretical reasons. As long as one seriously expected the system's liberalisation, the totalitarian thesis remained unacceptable. For critical East European intellectuals its acceptance would have meant the end of one strategy before the birth of a new one.
>
> (1981: 29)

There is no doubting the utility of the concept of totalitarianism to the Polish authors of the new idea of civil society. In effect, it significantly strengthened the case for an evolutionist strategy that did not expect too much too quickly and which turned to 'society first' for results. As Milosz comments in his introduction to a volume of Michnik's work:

> In th[e] deep reach of totalitarian government into daily life, which is usually seen as its source of strength, KOR discovered a point of weakness: precisely because totalitarian governments politicise daily life, daily life becomes a vast terrain on which totalitarianism can be opposed.
>
> (1985: xxvii)

After the suppression of Solidarity this orientation to daily life became even more pertinent. A strategy intended to allow society to provide 'self-defence' even without direct confrontation with the state could now turn instead to private, informal and familial groupings. As Arato described the civil society thinking behind this response to 'totalitarianism':

> Circles of family and friends protect the private sphere from an administered public one. They permit the defence of ... society, its customs, mentalities, its national and local identities. The reconstruction of society is possible because the foundations are there. Only more complete social ties have to be reconstructed.
>
> (1981: 29)

The politics of civil society

The issue that dominated the Polish opposition's debate during the years 1976–81 concerned the relationship of the new thinking on civil society to the socialist tradition. How, if at all, was it possible to reconcile socialist solidarity and self-management with pluralist interest representation and formal–legal political democracy? This discussion was too wide-ranging for it to be covered exhaustively here, but our two key theorists, Michnik and Kuron, will form the focus of attention, as above. The Solidarity-linked philosopher Nowak will also be included because of the detailed theoretical contribution that he made to the debate on the character of civil society.

The KOR theoreticians Michnik and Kuron described themselves in our period as democratic socialists, and their goals as compatible with socialism. Their emphasis was on worker self-management, on forms of council democracy for the working class. Parliamentary or procedural democracy, as Arato observed, was hardly mentioned in their deliberations (1981: 46). In 1980, Kuron, for example, called for the establishment of a 'mini parliament' described as a council 'elected by all the employees of any given enterprise' (1981b: 38). The emphasis on economic democracy and on changes to the organisation of the sphere of production illustrates Kuron's socialist priorities. Michnik concludes his influential 1976 essay expressing similar sentiments: 'Every act of defiance helps us build the framework of democratic socialism, which should not be merely or primarily a legal institutional structure but a real, day-to-day community of free people' (1985: 148).

As we have seen, this emphasis on local self-management over formal–legal political democracy was central for Kuron too:

> [The state's] powers ought to be as narrowly circumscribed as possible, limited by the right of those affected to appeal to court, to challenge censors ... [But any guarantees so won] are significant only when they are connected with social organisations independent of the state. These organisations are the decisive thing, the key to it all.
>
> (Kuron 1981a: 97)

Nowak also privileges direct action in civil society over institutional mechanisms for preserving political accountability in the state. Wherever 'the mechanisms of political competition' extend their scope beyond that which is indispensable for society to function, he writes, it is enough for the 'civil masses' to step in: 'The commonness of revolutionary attitudes among the citizens and the resulting tendency of the citizens to control the authority are sufficient to guarantee that the sphere of regulation does not reach beyond the range of administration ...' (Nowak 1991: 64).

All three thinkers seem at first sight to possess a model of decentralised self-management – implying only a minimal state administering 'things rather than persons' – reminiscent of libertarian-Marxist or even anarcho-syndicalist approaches. Indeed, Wojcicki (1981) (a Solidarity-linked Catholic intellectual contemporary of the KOR theorists) accused these theorists of retaining Marxist ideology, 'of advocating the repoliticisation of society, the vanguard role of the working class and a council democracy comprising the unions' independence' (Arato 1981: 35). The first and the last of these charges stand to some degree as we have seen, and Michnik in *A New Evolutionism* had also based his strategy on 'faith in the power of the working class' (1985: 144). Yet what sets the KOR theorists apart from previous experiments in council democracy – 'where it is a question of rebuilding a monolithic order from the ground up' (Arato 1981: 34) – is their attentiveness to questions of pluralist interest representation. The crucial difference, then, is that although Kuron, Michnik and Nowak emphasised self-managing forms of democracy, they did not see this as exhausting democratic politics (Arato 1981: 29). Indeed, their characterisation of the problem of interest representation as a problem at all points to an ultimately liberal conception of politics as involving competition between various pre-given interests: 'Democratic equilibrium is the result of a continuously renewed compromise between the various elements of society', states Michnik (1981: 75) along these lines, '[t]he government must realise that the institutionalisation of conflict and compromise is the only way to base public life on the principle of social accord' (1985: 105).

Given this understanding of politics, any notion of a vanguardist identification of society's universal interests is dropped from Michnik's account of democratisation:

> It seems to me that the underground today does not need the moral principles and organisational structures of an army of the Leninist kind. What it needs is the bond of shared aims and solidarity in action. And respect for individuality. And consent to plurality. It seems to me that the underground should not promise a world devoid of conflict.
>
> (1985: 62)

Similarly for Kuron, although 'the accommodation of different interests and divergent points of view can be accomplished only by social movements' (1981b: 39), differences in interests are accepted nonetheless. Thus although state functions should be socialised and civil society should be politicised – practising genuine self-management instead of acting merely as a means to interest representation in the state – civil society must also be conceived pluralistically:

> As Kuron put it, the movement of industrial workers now institutionalised as *Solidarity* has brought about a new level of independence of civil society. But what role should it play? Is it to be (1) *the* alternative power bringing about the further legal and institutional power of civil society; or (2) one of the *many* alternative powers to do so?; or (3) one form of interest representation under the new situation? Kuron himself says he has moved from (3) to (2).
>
> (Arato 1981: 34)

This insight into Kuron's thoughts is revealing. First, he does not 'seek to remythologise the workers as a universal subject' (Arato 1981: 34), and neither did the KOR as a whole, which changed its name from KOR (an acronym for Workers' Defence Committee) to KSS-KOR (Social Self-Defence Committee – KOR) in order 'to indicate its support for *all* initiatives' for interest representation (Arato 1981: 23). Evidence of this shift can be found elsewhere, when Kuron accepts that union representation does not exhaust the range of legitimate interests: 'Solidarity must push through the concept of self-management, but as an institution it must be absolutely independent of the unions ... Because it is impossible to occupy simultaneously the employer's and the employee's standpoint' (Kuron 1981a: 96). Second, in Kuron's view Solidarity's *raison d'être* is not to give voice to 'society', understood as some undifferentiated whole, but rather to defend the autonomy of various social groupings: 'I am not just thinking of pluralist unions ... I am thinking of a democratic pluralist society, i.e., pluralism on the level of corporations, cooperatives, consumer associations ... different cultural associations ... (etc.)' (1981a: 95).

On the basis of evidence such as this, Arato described KOR at the time as *post-* rather than *neo*-Marxist (1981: 35). Post-Marxist they might have been, but although the KOR theorists advocated pluralism on a societal level it is not clear that they agreed with liberalism, which believes that the crucial thing is that such pluralism is represented in the state. In fact, in contrast to Michnik, the idea of the state as a mere facilitator of society's otherwise self-managing components remained alive in Kuron's accounts. As Arato (1981: 36) himself pointed out, Kuron bypasses the issue of the vertical structure of compromise within which his pluralist society would, in the liberal view, need to be integrated. Kuron calls vaguely for 'institutional forms to be created to enable these pluralist movements to organise and cooperate. A system for society to function must be worked out' (Kuron 1981: 95). Yet it is not clear how this relates, if at all, to state design or function. Kuron's faith seems to rest entirely with civil society, as is illustrated when he writes that 'the interests of society will emerge from discourse and compromise' (1981b: 39). Arato (1981: 39) ended up categorising Kuron's thought as 'syndicalist'.

The difference with Michnik's approach was that while Michnik too talked mostly of pluralism merely on a societal level, this was clearly because his thesis built pragmatically upon the likelihood of an authoritarian state existing into the foreseeable future. Michnik does not downplay the role of the state in a democratic polity to the same extent as Kuron (Arato 1981: 38). Indeed, in an underground debate, carried out in the *Biuletyn Infomacyjny*, Michnik criticised Kuron for focusing only on the formation of autonomous institutions. It was as if Kuron's strategy, in looking no further than the self-organisation of civil society, predicted over time the 'withering away of the state': 'In Kuron's thinking the movement for independent institutions [alone] can be classified as political opposition. In our opinion these independent institutions form [only] a part of the broad movement aiming to make our society democratic ...' (Michnik 1985: 150)

Nowak, meanwhile, in theorising the relationship of political power to civil society, is more akin to Michnik in his emphasis on the dangerous utopia of a stateless society:

> It is not so that the authority is merely the enemy of the society ... as anarchism claims. Nor is it so, however, that the authority is an institution established by society for the common good, as the ruler's ideologists claim.
>
> (Nowak 1991: 39)

However, if the state, as with any authority system, 'is a class system that generates enslavement [and] enslaves civil society' (Nowak 1991: 39), what useful role can it really play in democracy? Must we not return to decentralised forms of self-managing democracy? Nowak's answer, tempered by realism, is as follows:

> The only systematic form that the civil masses can influence permanently is [political] democracy ... Democratic administration represents a compromise between authority, which is forced to be democratic, and civil society, which is forced to obey the state authority ... Political democracy [thus] becomes an arena of the already legalised pressure of the civil masses to institutionalise the autonomous sphere of social life.
>
> (Nowak 1991: 81–2)

Nowak's model of civil society thus has something in common with post-Marxist thinking in the West (as Arato has always claimed the Polish model did generally), but with some different emphases that deserve notice. First, democracy is seen to require as much citizen participation as possible in the public spheres of civil society, although this is articulated, significantly, more in terms of self-management in Nowak's account. Second, Nowak nevertheless shuns antistatist utopias – which reject any form of centralised political power – for being unable to secure the conditions necessary for their own survival. That is, without the state, it is suggested, the settled structure of rights necessary for the ongoing reproduction of a free civil society can never be guaranteed. However, again there is a difference of emphasis with the New Left: Nowak is much more reluctant to see the state as integral to a democratic polity, talking of the need for a compromise between democracy (as self-management) and the state in which civil society 'forces' the latter, which is external to democracy, to abide by democratic principles. Third, a further reason why this compromise is necessary is that the utopia of the purely socialised state – as a mere administrator of things – is understood to miss the anti-democratic implications of bureaucratic power in any society. Since the state will inevitably 'rule' in some sense, therefore, formal political democracy is essential in order to ensure some measure of popular control over it.

In addition to the debate about civil society and self-management, the Polish theorists were committed also to working out the implications of their model of civil society for political practice. There is a link in all the different formulations of civil society between theory and praxis – which usually takes the form of facing up to the tension between articulating normative ends and analysing practical possibilities: 'In searching for truth, or, to quote Leszek Kolakowski, "by living in dignity", opposition intellectuals are striving not so much for a better tomorrow as for a better today' (Michnik 1985: 148).

Most of Michnik's essays, and this was true throughout the democratic opposition, are addressed to ongoing situations in Poland at the time and to reflecting upon other relevant Central-Eastern European experiences (especially Hungary, 1956, and Czechoslovakia, 1968). Michnik's most famous piece, *A New Evolutionism,* is entirely devoted to tactics. Elsewhere, in *On Resistance*, his strategic orientation is again made clear:

> The institutional form of Solidarity must be left open ... No nation has ever been given human rights as a present. These rights have to be won through struggle. The question is: how should this struggle be conducted? ... I know that no generalised moral values can replace political perspectives.
>
> (1985: 55)

Concerning this practical perspective, how significant was the new thinking about civil society in shaping Solidarity's theory–practice in the period 1980–81? The KOR, of which Michnik and Kuron were members, was linked to Solidarity in an advisory role from the beginning. Its influence in this capacity is indicated by the attempts of the communist authorities, once they started negotiating with Solidarity, to make the expulsion of the KOR committee of advisers a condition of these negotiations (Swidlicki 1981: 119).

Elements of the then unique Solidarity strategy were undoubtedly influenced by KOR thinking. The most striking of these influences can be seen in Solidarity's explicit denial of any interest in 'political' power (by which they meant power in the state). Lech Walesa, Solidarity's leader, went so far as to call Solidarity an apolitical movement in order to reinforce this point, as would the Czechoslovakian dissidents who also took inspiration from the KOR. Here the strategy of self-limitation, first outlined in Michnik's *A New Evolutionism*, is taken on board.

Solidarity also shared the KOR's orientation towards self-management or council democracy. As we have seen, Michnik, Nowak and especially Kuron prioritised this form of democracy, and it is present in Solidarity's declarations also, for example at their 1981 Congress, which enshrined the idea of the 'self-governing republic'. This was articulated in council-democracy terms – as involving the transference of factories from state control to self-managing units with democratically elected workers' councils. But Solidarity's plans for 'social ownership' did not stop here, since 'self-management was to be introduced into education, culture and mass media. The residual legal and financial powers of the state in these fields were to be controlled by democratically elected 'national' or 'social' councils' (Pelczynski 1988: 375).

These various connections between the analyses provided by KOR thinkers and Solidarity theory–practice have led many commentators to adopt a rather one-dimensional understanding of the relationship between the Solidarity movement and the 'Polish model' of civil society. Yet it is clearly a mistake to see Solidarity as the practical outworking of the theorists' vision of civil society in any straightforward sense. First, Solidarity was influenced by values other than the libertarian-socialist ones of the KOR. Lukes describes an 'amalgam of the ethical teachings of Catholicism, of Polish Nationalism, of liberal democratic values and of a basic egalitarianism ... [but] with no particular links with socialism, even with a human face' (1985: 15). Indeed, in 1981 Walesa terminated KOR's advisory role, a clear indication that the close relationship between the two bodies and their respective political thought can easily be overstated. And Michnik and Kuron were not uncritical of Solidarity themselves. In 1982 Michnik wrote, 'I do not want to idealise Solidarity, its actions, or its activists. I know about the demagogy and baseness ... ' (1985: 51). Earlier, in 1981, he had stated:

> Solidarity ... has for a year now been the *guarantor* of the growing Polish democracy. But it is still too soon to draw up a balance sheet of its bright and dark sides ... [It] combines the cult of its leader with a democracy that reaches pathological proportions; and that joins an astounding wisdom with a rare naiveté.
>
> (1985: 130)

One of the characteristics of Solidarity that has frequently drawn criticism to the Polish model of civil society (which it supposedly encapsulated) was its tendency to view Polish society as a unified whole. 'Eastern European intellectuals tended to develop civil society as a new *Weltbild* of a highly integrated society without major factions', as one commentator put it, with Solidarity clearly in mind (Von Beyme 1994: 106). Such accusations are not made without reason. For example, the National Congress in 1981 declared Solidarity's activities as those of a 'self-governing Republic' in the following terms:

> Our union sprang from the people's needs ... It is the product of the revolt of Polish society against political discrimination. Thanks to the existence of a powerful union organisation, Polish society is no longer fragmented, disorganised and lost, but has renewed strength and hope. There is now the possibility of real national renewal. Our union, representing the majority of workers in Poland, seeks to be and will become the driving force of social renewal.
>
> (cited in Pelczynski 1988: 370)

Yet in contrast to this view, as has been shown, Michnik and Kuron saw the idea of civil society as implying societal pluralism; and they viewed Solidarity's significance in this light too. As Kuron put it, 'What we are dealing with is a tremendous social democratisation movement in all possible strata. The independent self-managed union Solidarity is just part of this movement and at the same time its symbol' (Kuron 1981a: 94). Michnik also denounced 'the idea for a "centre" and a front for national reconciliation [which] are typical products of wishful thinking. I do not believe in the Poles' "moral-political unity" ' (1985: 111).

'Civil society against the state'

The Polish opposition's discourse on civil society was clearly central to the re-emergence of the concept in Eastern Europe and beyond during the 1980s, especially by way of Arato's characterisation of the Polish theory-praxis as 'civil society against the state'. As a category that had previously been seen to lack any significance in situating a radical, transformatory politics, the putative significance of civil society within the Polish context – as the site of political opposition and democratisation – gave the concept a new lease of life in political theory. The more Gramscian sense – though without Gramsci's Marxist teleology – of civil society as a potentially autonomous sphere inhabited by counter-hegemonical forces began to appear everywhere from this point on. Subsequently, popular conceptualisations of the concept also shifted. Denoting originally an unwilled, non-purposive arena of human interaction within commercial society, civil society had been reborn as the political, agential locus of change familiar to students of the concept today.

At the time, as Arato concluded in his original analysis, it appeared that 'the Polish democratic movement had placed the programme of a *socialist* civil society, suspended as a result of 1968, back on the agenda of Eastern European alternatives' (Arato 1981: 47). Yet the socialist character of the Polish theorists' model was, unsurprisingly in the context of Soviet empire, never unambiguous. Undoubtedly they *were* socialist in orientation – hence the equation of civil society with self-management, with democratic control of all spheres of social life. Yet there was clearly also a strong liberal strain to the theorists' civil society, which sat uneasily with the self-management project overall. This was evident particularly in their acceptance of the inevitability of societal conflict, following on from the denial of any general will, which seemed to imply, if only by default, some kind of 'refereeing' role for a limited, liberal state. It is also apparent in the absolute primacy given to societal autonomy from 'totalising' politics, which, in the final analysis, implicitly privileges the liberal separation of spheres over all attempts at overcoming the alienation of political power through the complete re-socialisation of state functions.

As it turned out, the apparent failure of the original 'Polish model' as a consequence of the crushing of Solidarity in 1981, as well as the continuing stalemate in Czechoslovakia, led to Polish conceptualisations of civil society in the 1980s becoming less 'political' and more concerned with private life and the symbolic. In general terms, the negative version of civil society – as simply anti-authoritarian – began to triumph over the earlier, more positive, model which had aimed at mobilising forces for societal self-management (Bibic 1994: iv). This is illustrated by claims in this period by a number of theorists, including Michnik, that political distinctions between left and right no longer held any meaning for them (see Michnik 1985; Havel 1988). Thus the socialist analysis of civil society provided originally by Kolakowski and then by Kuron and Michnik went into significant decline. Michnik, for example, as Scruton points out, talked far more in non-socialist terms after 1983 – as his defence in 1987 of the Polish church as the foundation of Polish civil society illustrates. As Scruton noted at the time, 'In his change of attitude, I believe, one can see the birth of a new, more sombre, but more realistic assessment of Socialist Europe' (Scruton 1988: 645).

Yet despite its ambiguous relationship to socialist thought, an interesting feature of the Polish model of civil society is that, taken as a whole, many of the themes reworked by the post-Marxist or New Left in the West in the same period are present. Indeed, the impetus for this wider shift on the left was stimulated, *inter alia*, by Polish developments. Much like the Western New Left, the Polish theorists developed a model of civil society that was differentiated from the classical model based exclusively upon a society of bourgeois property owners (a feature illustrated by the Polish sense of civil society as 'citizens society') *and* from the Marxist conflation of civil society with the capitalist economy. Cohen and Arato commented upon this distinction when they over-optimistically characterised the Eastern European opposition as nothing less than the 'creation of a post-bourgeois, democratic, civil society' (1984: 266). Analysts writing in German had to transpose the now different sense of the term into the German debate by introducing *zivilgesellschaft* to replace *burgerliche gesselschaft* (bourgeois society) – the latter being 'semantically bound' to the capitalist economy (Krizan 1987: 100). In other words, the Polish version of civil society was meant to imply a society of free citizens, rather than a society of economically 'free' property owners in the market sphere (von Beyme 1994: 104).

The Polish debate has fed into New Left thinking on the relationship of civil society to the state in other ways too. A number of complementary themes are worth pointing out. First there is now a general acceptance on the left that genuinely transformatory movements cannot be successful merely through the popular seizure of power, since in this case there is nothing to prevent the emergence of a new ruling class as repressive as ever before. Neither is the revolutionary replacement of the dominators by the dominated seen to herald the possibility of the dissolution of the state, since the abandonment of the utopia of a revolutionary end to power signifies an acceptance of conflict at the heart of politics. Thus even if statist forms themselves are normatively rejected, they are no longer expected to 'wither away' in a movement from the management of people to mere things. Second, if revolution is eschewed, then so is an uncritical adherence to its classical alternative, reformism. Reformism, like revolution, focuses upon the state instead of seeking decentralised and self-managing forms with which the citizen body can maximise its democratic power. Civil society, in this schema, is an end in itself – committed to the autonomy that would be denied to it by any state-centric strategies, be they exclusively party-based, reformist or revolutionary.

The significance of the Polish theorists' model of civil society, then, especially in its recovery of the totalitarian paradigm, was that it helped to conceptualise and apply to political practice a critique of state dominance that sought to radicalise the insights of liberalism. This, as Lefort observed at the time, was much needed on the left:

> Why, I asked, was the Left reluctant to employ the concept of totalitarianism? ... I would now dare to say: because the concept is political and the Left does not think in political terms. Socialists are determined advocates of state intervention in every domain of social life in order to diminish or suppress the inequalities that arise in the context of civil society.
>
> (Lefort 1986: 277)

This attitude towards civil society, as Lefort saw it, was where the left became blinded to the essence of totalitarianism, 'to the idea of a state that aspires to be omnipresent through its bureaucratic network' (1986: 281). It was the contribution of the Polish theorists of civil society to bring this analysis of totalitarianism to bear on traditional left-socialist categories. For them, civil society did not constitute the realm of unfreedom and inequality to be abolished by a proletarian state, as Marx had originally described it. Turning Marx on his head, civil society came instead to represent the realm of freedom which the very annexation of civil society by the state, and the subsequent 'totalisation' of power, had precluded. The Marxian defence of the oppressed of civil society through the state had become the defence of the state-oppressed through civil society.

2 'The independent life of society'

Czechoslovakian and Hungarian voices

Czechoslovakian voices

> Charter 77 [is] ... a free, informal, open community of people ... united by the will to strive, individually and collectively, for the respect of civic and human rights in our own country and throughout the world.
>
> (declaration of Charter 77, January 1977)

Unlike their contemporaries in Poland during 1976–81, the opposition intellectuals connected to Charter 77, the Czechoslovakian human rights group, were never able to pursue a directly political programme. That is, a programme for the construction of an autonomous civil society as occurred in Poland was simply not feasible in their circumstances. The weakness of the Czechoslovakian opposition movement resulted from the effective repression pursued by the Husák regime after the 'Prague Spring' of 1968. This repression isolated dissidents from the general population – Charter 77 never had the opportunity to link up with a mass movement in the way that the intellectuals of the Polish KOR cooperated with Solidarity. In Czechoslovakia, then, the interaction between political theory and collective action was generally confined to the symbolic (Jorgensen 1992: 46):

> In Czechoslovakia too, thinking about totalitarianism and civil society reflects a specific situation. In the face of the apparently unending 'normalisation', considerations tend[ed] to focus on the 'metaphysics' of totalitarianism: on spiritual and cultural resistance to the totalitarian language and mode of thinking relentlessly imposed by the system on the society.
>
> (Rupnik 1988: 285)

Characterisations of the Czechoslovakian opposition discourse such as this appear to be based on the assumption that it was relatively apolitical (or antipolitical, where this is understood to mean the same thing). Václav Havel, the best known of the oppositionists from this period (and it was Havel who wrote the first draft of the Charter's declaration), certainly adopts a more lyrical prose in much of his writing, as might be expected from a playwright. Yet Havel's thinking is seriously misrepresented if it is conveyed as essentially apolitical. Indeed, the Czechoslovakian approach to civil society in general was much more political than it has been given credit for.[1] The message of antipolitics was most certainly not an apolitical one.

I seek to demonstrate as much in this chapter by reconstructing the Charter 77 'model' of civil society from an analysis of the collection of eighteen essays – with Havel's *The Power of the Powerless* forming the centrepiece – which were published in 1979, in *samizdat*, under the title *On Freedom and Power*. The Chartists do not yet, except in a few instances (see Hejdánek 1985: 149; Battek 1985: 101; and Kusý 1985: 155), use the term civil society, which re-emerges fully only during the Solidarity period in Poland. Nevertheless, the ideas that came then to fall under this rubric are expressed in the same terms (only as yet without the title) by the Chartists too.[2] Indeed, *On Freedom and Power* was intended as a joint Czechoslovak–Polish venture – a collection to include contributions from both Charter 77 and KOR (however, owing to arrests, the Czechoslovakian papers had to be rushed into publication separately). Furthermore, the Warsaw Solidarity leader, Zbigniew Bujak, remarked in 1981 that Havel's contribution to this collection 'gave us theoretical backing, a theoretical basis for our actions' (cited in Lukes 1985: 12), just as the 'Polish model' was profoundly influential on the Czechoslovakian Chartists in turn (cf. Havel 1985: 60, 67; Uhl 1995: 194–6). It is therefore no sleight of hand to reconstruct Czechoslovakian Chartism retrospectively as, among other things, a discourse on civil society. As Keane makes this point in relation to Havel:

> [T]he cultivation, from below and against all odds, of institutions that can develop 'the independent life of society' and thereby empower the powerless [was Havel's vision]. Tentatively, and in clumsy language, Havel called this new and desperate possibility 'social self-organisation'. With greater confidence and precision – and political implications of the most dramatic type – it would soon be called *civil society*.
>
> (1999: 286, original emphasis)

Charter 77 is remembered primarily for the terms of its resistance, which involved seeking to hold the communist party-state to its endorsement of the Helsinki Accords on human rights – in the process pointing out 'the discrepancy between law and reality in socialist Czechoslovakia' (Keane 1999: 244). The Charter movement is not usually associated with any distinct theoretical–political models, which is unsurprising, given that the Chartists appeal variously in their essays to Czech national tradition; ethical teachings from Czech history; non-Marxist social democracy; Catholicism; lay Protestantism; and neo-Trotskyism (Lukes 1985: 13). As well as varying ideologically, the Chartists also disagreed on how to interpret the political context that they found themselves in. In particular, what could not be agreed on was how totalitarian the party-state system was:

> For Havel, the system is 'post-totalitarian'; for others [e.g. Battek] it is still 'totalitarian'; for Uhl it is bureaucratic centralism (from an economic point of view) and bureaucratic dictatorship (from a political point of view) – a view that Havel directly contests.
>
> (Lukes 1985: 17)

Yet remarkably, given these seemingly irreconcilable political differences, there emerges within *On Freedom and Power* a recognisably distinct and unanimous approach to the question of how to pursue political opposition and also of some of the desired ends of opposition. It is this, largely overlooked, accord that I draw out below. As will become clear, such agreement is also best understood in terms of a specific approach to the category of civil society.

Neither reform nor revolution but civil society

The Chartists were agreed upon the inadequacy of reformism. Along with the Polish theorists they repudiated conventional, party-state-directed dissidence for leaving initiative in the hands of incumbent elites. Battek, for example, wrote, 'What must become fundamental for us is *initiation*, not *dissidence*. That is, we should consider ourselves first and foremost as initiators of future possibilities ... We should transform our *opposition* into an increasingly clear *position*' (Battek 1985: 104). More broadly, reformism *and* revolution, given their state-centrism, were seen as sharing the same limited horizons; the 'new politics' as Benda put it, echoing the Poles, involved putting 'society first'.

The Chartists also agreed on the importance of non-violence and on the need for the self-limitation of the popular forces, which should not seek state power. The Charter itself stated clearly that Charter 77 was not to be understood as a revolutionary organisation 'planning and plotting to seize state power, by cunning or strength. Charter 77 would instead aim to function as a citizens' initiative' (Keane 1999: 245). Besides, revolutionary violence was seen as self-defeating since the Chartists endorsed, as would Nowak in Poland, Danton's warning that 'the revolution devours its own children'. In Havel's words, violent revolution would 'fatally stigmatise ... the very means used to secure it'. However:

> this attitude should not be mistaken for political conservatism or moderation. The 'dissident movements' do not shy away from the idea of violent political overthrow because the idea seems too radical, but on the contrary, because it does not seem radical enough.
>
> (Havel 1985: 71)

Other Chartists emphasised their commitment to non-violence in different ways. Echoing the Polish concern with a sustainable evolutionary strategy in which gradual pressure from below is preferred to direct confrontation, Cerný, for example, wrote that 'the Charter is not a resistance movement, it is a pressure group' (1985: 129). Vohryzek, though advocating 'civic resistance', also claimed that 'violence as a form of civilian resistance has lost its human dimensions ... [since] all [violent] groups ... degenerate morally' (1985: 200). For Hejdánek too, the opposition struggle could 'only be jeopardized by political agitation, organisation, coercion and violence' (1985: 150), since 'whenever the settlement of social demands has been violently divorced from its democratic roots ... socialism has entered a historical blind alley' (1985: 144). Indeed, this emphasis upon non-violence was shared even by the quasi-revolutionary theorist, Uhl, who called for a form of revolution 'which ... will limit violence to a minimum' (1985: 197).

The imperative of non-violent resistance was also part of a wider rejection of the revolutionary vanguard, since '[a] violent *coup d'état* could just as easily replace the mass discrimination of today with a new wave of discrimination ...' (Vohryzek 1985: 198):

> Conspiratorial methods ... considerably slow down the evolution of alternative projects like the parallel *polis*. The principle of operating in the open, which Charter 77 established to a broader extent, must be strengthened and extended ... In the past, the avant-garde, usually a revolutionary party, has assumed the role of organizer. However ... this party always becomes the cradle of a bureaucracy.
>
> (Uhl 1985: 194, 197)

Yet behind the abandonment of the revolutionary vanguard lay the still more ambitious refusal of the project to seek power in the state even through non-violent means. Just as Solidarity theorists were later to deny any interest in formal political power whatsoever, Cerný similarly claimed that Charter 77 'does not aspire to power' (1985: 128). Jirous also averred that 'the parallel polis does not compete for power. Its aim is not to replace the powers that be with power of another kind, but rather under the power – or beside it – to create a structure that respects other laws ...' (in Benda *et al.* 1988: 227). Havel meanwhile, adding his voice to the Polish call for a strategy for societal 'self-defence', proclaimed 'the purely defensive character' of the various national dissident movements 'as their greatest strength' (1985: 69). Hejdánek in particular grappled with the seeming contradiction of seeking to develop opposition as a permanent political project, denying that Charter 77 considered itself a conventional political opposition, and that it had 'any intention of constituting the first rung on the ladder for some alternative power bloc'. However:

> The political role of such groups is obvious: they hold a mirror up to the

> face of the regime ... By playing this role, they might indeed begin to represent an opposition-in-formation ... In the long term, however, the principle of keeping at arms length any pretensions to power ... opens up a new dimension of political, or should we say 'apolitical' public activity ... As soon as the opposition wins power, its criticism of injustice, illegality, etc., ceases to be functional ... Without the background of a vigorous 'alternative' cultural front independent of state structures, the activity of the defenders of human rights and freedoms would inevitably atrophy and decline.
>
> (Hejdánek 1985: 145–6)

What Hejdánek is seeking to articulate here would no doubt be seen today as a commonplace call for a civil society, separate from the state, to act as a 'watchdog' for abuses of state power. Indeed, Hejdánek goes on to say that the '[i]nternational understanding of a non-governmental and extra-governmental character is becoming absolutely vital' (1985: 148). Uhl similarly talks of what would now be termed civil society when he writes that 'For the future, we must also be thinking about "initiatives" like independent trade unions, political discussion clubs and parties. [However] the term "citizens' initiative" ... unfortunately does not express the lasting nature of the alternative associations' (1985: 196). Yet as we shall see below, it would be mistaken to think that a civil society limited to a regulatory role *vis-à-vis* the state is all that the Chartists had in mind.

Civil society as 'antipolitics'

For Hejdánek, Uhl, and the other Chartists, there was a more radical, or certainly less instrumental, reason behind their denial of interest in state power. Their programme for democratisation was about more than the growth of non-state associational life, being concerned also with the development of a new form of politics that switched focus away from the state entirely. As Keane has characterised it latterly, the *Power of the Powerless* 'necessarily involved a challenge to the whole of modern political thought's preoccupation with the sovereign power of the territorial state. Without saying so in exactly these words [it] proposed lopping off the head of sovereign power' (1999: 283). As the Chartists expressed these sentiments at the time: 'The way forward must consist chiefly in providing tangible proof that the state and political power are not the supreme expression of the life of societies ... and, indeed, that [they] will have to play an increasingly minor role' (Hejdánek 1985: 148). 'Anti-political politics ... is possible and can be effective, even though by its very nature it cannot calculate its effect beforehand. That effect, to be sure, is of a wholly different nature from what the West considers political success' (Havel 1988: 397).

Such comments have been interpreted as expressing an antipathy to politics per se. Yet this reduces politics to the state, which seems absurd.

'Antipolitics' in this connection was not meant to imply, as some commentators have assumed, that regime opponents advocated some privatist retreat into the microsphere of friends and family networks. Albeit that it *was* envisaged on a local level, this was instead a call for the recovery of a more self-determining and less alienating political order as an antidote to bureaucratised, statist politics. As Havel put it:

> I believe in structures that are not aimed at the 'technical' aspect of the execution of power, but at the significance of that execution in structures held together more by a commonly shared feeling of the importance of certain communities than by commonly shared expansionist ambitions directed 'outward' ... Any accumulation of power whatsoever (one of the characteristics of automatism) should be profoundly alien ... They would be structures not in the sense of organisations or institutions, but like a community.
>
> (1985: 93)

The other Chartists shared Havel's vision of 'a future form of politics ... light years away from politics in the present sense of a struggle for power'. For Benda, resonant with Havel's republican sentiment, politics should instead be about a 'playful and sacred concern for the affairs of the polis' (Benda 1985: 122). For Hejdánek too, the domination of 'the life of society' by coercive, bureaucratic state mechanisms is a worldwide problem, 'which is why it will take a worldwide programme to halt or suppress it' (1985: 148).

This 'antipolitical' message then, when explored further, reveals a decidedly political sub-text, namely antistatism, an attendant emphasis on self-management and a vision of a 'new politics' beyond that of both East and West. The Chartists' antistatism, therefore, although this has been largely forgotten since the watershed of 1989, was not just a critique of 'real socialism' but of the authoritarian centralism and deadening bureaucracy seen as characteristic of statist politics *either* side of the iron curtain. Hejdánek, for example, claimed that thoroughgoing democratisation is impossible 'without the emancipation of the overwhelming majority of the lives of societies and individuals from the clutches of *dirigisme* and control by the machinery of the state' (1985: 150). Kusý, who interestingly retains a Marxist notion of civil society (as 'a product of the bourgeois revolution'), also sees socialism as 'a movement from civil (*étatist*) society to a society that is genuinely human ... [So,] just as Marx's socialism is a negation of civil society ... real socialism is a negation of that negation, a return to *étatism* (Kusý 1985: 155). Although Kusý still holds to a pejorative notion of civil society, it is in the sense of seeing civil society as the outcome of human worth submitted to reasons of state. Marx's utopia of a state-free, communist future is employed here against that approach to socialism seen as destroying social self-management. In other words, Kusý's argument is similar to that made by many of the Chartists, who see civil society positively, only the Marxist antipathy to the term is not yet abandoned in Kusý's account. This basic affinity can be seen by comparing Kusý's antistatist vision to one provided by Uhl. Uhl has the same revolutionary (though non-violently so) ends in mind as Kusý, only he has stopped using Marxist language to express them:

> It is utopian to assume that society will 'merge' with the parallel polis, thus causing the withering away of the state and its bureaucratic machinery ... It is only during the revolutionary process that [this polis] will rapidly 'absorb' society, which will create, on islands of alternative associations and activities, a polis which is no longer parallel, but an authentic polis of free people.
>
> (Uhl 1985: 195)

Civil society as self-management

For the Chartists, then, antistatism flowed from their emphasis upon self-management, rather than being antecedent to it. The imperative of self-management was indisputably central for most of the Chartists and was central to their call for a completely new form of politics. Havel set the tone in his essay when he wrote that 'the classic impotence of traditional democratic organisations' (which he elsewhere specifies as parliamentary democracy) can only be overcome through the formation of structures that 'naturally rise from *below*' as a consequence of authentic 'self-organisation' (1985: 93). Indeed, for Havel, non-bureaucratic modes of self-management were so important that, once specific needs had been met through particular instances of self-organisation, the structures in question 'should also disappear' (1985: 93).

Other Chartists were equally unambiguous about the need for self-managing forms of democracy. Battek called for 'social structures [to] be democratized by expanding the elements of self-management, limiting institutional growth ... and strengthening direct democracy' (1985: 108). However, despite his call for 'the bureaucracies ruling society [to] shrink to assume merely compliant roles', Battek went on to 'shun those fascinating social utopias with their visions of the elimination of power, government and the state ... Given the complexities of modern social structures, power cannot be eliminated, just as the state form of social organisation cannot be done away with' (1985: 108). Yet the acceptance of the state as a problem for democratic theory and practice was not meant by Battek to imply that the model supplied by 'modern democracies' is thereby sufficient for the democratic organisation of society. Although he conceded that liberal democracies have many important insights to bestow, Battek had in mind 'the future democratic, self-managing socialist society', a society needed throughout 'the world of today' given the 'unjustified, unwarranted class privileges' that obtain in both East and West (1985: 108). What then, exactly, does liberal democracy have to contribute to this vision of a 'third way'? Battek, representatively of Chartism at this point, was somewhat vague here. The closest he comes to endorsing liberal democracy is when he apparently concedes the need for some form of separation of spheres, although this is by no means unambiguous:

> Every proposed organisation of society, even one with a maximum of self-management, will need to be balanced by extra-governmental, extra-managerial, extra-organisational activity on the part of the voluntary associations established for the widest variety of short-term and long-term needs and purposes ... Hope ... lies ... [in] the realization of a social order in which the formalized and functionalized structure of society will be regulated and controlled by this 'newly discovered' spontaneous civic activity, which will be a permanent and essential source of social self-awareness.
>
> (1985: 108)

Battek's desire to move 'beyond' statist, representative institutions towards more self-managing forms of democracy is widely shared by the other Chartists. Hájek also calls for 'radical changes in the systems either side of the dividing line in Europe' along the lines of the experience of the Paris Commune (1985: 138). Hejdánek, although he accepts the need for some form of 'central control', also argues that 'the dangers inherent in this can only be avoided by a thorough-going democratization, i.e., the establishment of self-managing bodies at every level ... It is also clear that a similar solution is called for in other parts of the world' (1985: 149). From an even more radical standpoint, Uhl claims that parliamentary government 'does nothing to develop forms of direct democracy which can help emancipate society and individuals and overcome alienation' (1985: 190). Indeed, 'social self-management is not a panacea: it is only worthy of support if it guarantees the continual expansion of direct democracy in favour of the gradual dismantling of representative democracy' (Uhl 1985: 191).

Another noteworthy feature of the Chartists' emphasis upon self-management is that it represents to varying degrees the continuation of a socialist project. Lukes observes in his introduction to *The Power of the Powerless* that:

> None of these essays is explicitly unfriendly to the socialist ideal or socialist principles. None advocates a return to capitalism or even to liberal democracy; and none is touched by the various forms of the free market ideology that have since become dominant in the West. Most engage in the 'immanent critique' of so-called 'real socialism' for failing to live up to its principle, which none explicitly rejects. With the exception of Uhl, and in a different way Hájek, these authors have no particular attachment to the Marxian socialist tradition, but they do not reject it

> either ... The socialist tradition, in one form or another, still haunts these essays.
>
> (1985: 14).

This claim is true even for Havel, whose political writings came to represent the antithesis of socialist thought for some commentators. For example, Havel calls for the principle of self-management to be applied to the economic life of society, seeing this as achieving 'what all the theorists of socialism have dreamed about, that is, the genuine ... participation of workers in economic decision-making ...' (1985: 94). As for the other Chartists: Cerný and Hájek talk of the fundamentally democratic character of socialism (Cerný 1985: 131; Hájek 1985: 134); Hejdánek looks to the coming 'post-capitalist' society (1985: 142) – since 'socialism is democracy taken to all its conclusions in every field' (1985: 144); and Uhl, calling also for an anti-capitalist project, envisions 'a democracy of the productive forces' in which 'democracy means a system of workers' councils, horizontally coordinated ...'(1985: 191). Indeed, Uhl is directly critical of what is seen in liberal democratic theory as one of civil society's most important functions: its role as a 'safety valve' to siphon off social discontent. Uhl's 'alternative associations', by contrast, 'nurture the critical spirit that can influence the whole of society'. Finally, as if to make his point of difference from the civil society project in the West as clear as possible, Uhl claims that 'Charter 77 has no equivalent in the bourgeois democracies' (1985: 192).

Civil society and pluralism

However, in agreement with their Polish allies, the Chartists' desire to see democracy socialised was matched by a new awareness of the need also for the rights-based political democracy that offers protection from public power. This lesson from liberalism is clearly expressed by Hájek in the following proposition:

> While it is true that people cannot be really free unless they enjoy the right to work, education and social security, it is equally true, and experience in the socialist countries has proved it, that these eminent social, economic and cultural rights are not worth the paper they are printed on ... if there is a failure to guarantee and implement those 'classic' civil and political rights and freedoms ...
>
> (1985: 140)

Even Hejdánek, despite his acknowledged desire for a 'post-capitalist' system, begins his essay with a statement made on behalf of all the Chartists: '[W]e are now seeing a convergence of emphasis on political democratization, which is viewed increasingly as a *sine qua non* of a developed socialist society' (1985: 141). Benda too, despite his concern with the 'worldwide crisis of politics' (1985: 112), is convinced of the importance of the limited, liberal democratic state:

> [T]he 'new politics' ... should ... involve people up to their necks ... Yet it should not tie one down: a state ... may be perceived as a useful factor in limiting evil, but it must never become an instrument for creating a 'heaven on earth'. It should be a politics in which human rights and the rules of a parliamentary democracy ... are all a matter of course ...
> (Benda 1985: 123)

So, despite their ongoing commitment to radical political forms over liberal democracy, a noticeable feature of all the Chartists' essays is the concern with the rule of law, pluralism and systems of rights advocated by liberals. The notion of legality implied operating publicly and openly in the face of the arbitrary abuse of power, and was therefore seen as a mainstay of the opposition programme (Havel 1985: 69). The rule of law was also perceived as limiting political power. In Hejdánek's words, 'The purpose of human rights campaigns [in the socialist bloc countries] was, at the outset, to establish the bounds beyond which *all* state and government intervention ceases to be legitimate and legal' (1985: 148, italics added). Also, for Hejdánek (1985: 141) and the other Chartists, despite their radical critique of liberal democratic forms, human and civil rights were not bourgeois mystifications, but rights of an 'inalienable' citizenship.

With regard to pluralism a broad consensus emerged, as in Poland, that there was no possibility of reforming the artificial and oppressive unity of 'real socialism' through the imposition of yet another monist view of society.[3] Thus Battek, for example, writes that '[e]fforts to democratize any totalitarian system only make sense when the ground is laid in society for a free choice between options' (Battek 1985: 107). Similarly, Ruml bemoans the fact that some within the democratic opposition 'have apparently not yet broken old habits of "united fronts", so that they still confuse personal responsibility with military discipline' (Ruml 1985: 184).

Engagement with questions of pluralism was clearest in the role in securing privacy (and thereby, implicitly, difference and diversity) that the Chartists wanted civil society to play in addition to its public duties. Indeed, the Chartists' notion of civil society is of a sphere that is at once public and private: public in the sense of its facilitation of self-management, private in its provision of a non-state sphere by which (state) 'politics' could be strictly delimited:

> [There is] a tension between two attitudes in the same individual – between his or her attitude as a person ... and as a citizen (the individual's position in civil society). Essentially, it is tension and conflict between

> the private and the public, the individual and the collective, the non-political and the political, the personal and the social ... [However,] [t]hese two categories (of being human and acting as a citizen) *are neither exclusive nor separable*.
>
> (Battek 1985: 101, emphasis added)

Totalitarianism: 'the system of the lie'

The Chartists' emphasis upon the sphere of civil society both as a site for opposition and as an end in itself, was, as for the Poles, intimately connected to their analysis of the system within which they lived. Thus Tesar, for example, stated, 'if the totalitarian system ... arises[s] more easily in an environment where the structure of "civil society" is not sufficiently formed, then the most reliable means of preventing [its] genesis is to encourage the development of that civil society' (Tesar 1981: 85)

As Tesar's analysis indicates, along with the Poles many of the Chartists persisted in seeing state-socialism as 'totalitarian'. In a similar manner to Michnik of the Polish KOR, who understood totalitarianism as encapsulated in the 'system of the lie', Kusý wrote:

> In its entire spirit and thrust, real socialism is an ideology ... of *as if*: those who preach it behave *as if* the ideological kingdom of real socialism existed in 'what we have here now' ... the nation behaves *as if* it believed it ... This *as if* is a silent agreement between the two partners.
>
> (1985: 164)

Through this all-embracing language, real socialism politicises and ideologises 'the totality of life. It is total politics and total ideology' (Kusý 1985: 159):

> What is the source of this total politicization of real-socialist life? Unquestionably, it has to do with the very essence of the totalitarian regime. For what is specific about real socialism is that once it has started that kind of idealization of reality it cannot stop halfway ...
>
> (Kusý 1985: 160)

Kusý was not alone in persisting with the claim that for these reasons real socialism was most adequately characterised as totalitarian. Battek also wrote about the 'totalitarian political structure', wherein 'just about every facet of human existence is politicized' (1985: 104); Cerný, rejecting reformism in favour of speaking 'the truth about the way things are', announced that 'it is folly to rely on totalitarian power' (1985: 130); and Vohryzek, describing 'the totalitarianism of today' as demanding 'a total vacuum of civic will, a *perpetuum silentium*, passivity and quiescence', claimed that 'silent disagreement is one of the pillars of totalitarian power' (1985: 200). Benda, closest to the Poles in his analysis, called for radicals to adopt an understanding of totalitarianism and argued that Western leftists, in as far as they did not do this, were inaccurate in their reading of 'real-socialism':

> The western Left, in the widest sense, may be right a hundred times over in their critical assessment of politics in their own countries, but as long as they fail to understand the vast differences between totalitarianism and democracy (and the Left does *not* understand them, and clearly, for very basic reasons, does not even want to) ...
>
> (Benda 1985: 111)

Havel's contribution to the debate about totalitarianism in Central–Eastern Europe is clearly the most central here. In his earlier work, including *The Power of the Powerless*, Havel's injunction to 'live in truth' stands not only as a moral imperative, but also as a political project. In short, Havel sees 'living in truth' as 'a way of denying the legitimacy of a public realm that rested on the forced acceptance of an official definition of reality' (Smolar 1996: 26). Some, such as Roger Scruton (1988: 457), have seen the undoubtedly individualistic emphasis in this and other essays by Havel as symptomatic of the strength of New Right thinking in Czechoslovakia at the time. However, it is worth noting that in *The Power of the Powerless* Havel sees 'living in truth' as including 'any means by which a person or group revolts against manipulation: anything from a letter by intellectuals to a workers' strike ...' (1985: 43).[4] Thus it is less that Havel's political philosophy is methodologically individualistic, and more that his analysis of totalitarianism brings to the fore the responsibilities it places on individuals in a context where collective action is largely precluded. Besides, collective action is not the only or even the most important sight of struggle since, according to Havel, totalitarianism works primarily at the level of the individual. Through outward semantic conformity to official ideology, individuals

> *live within a lie*. They need not accept the lie. It is enough for them to have accepted their life with it and in it. For by this very fact, individuals confirm the system, fulfil the system, make the system, *are* the system ... [Thus the] line of conflict ... in the post-totalitarian system ... runs de facto through each person, for everyone in his or her way is both a victim and a supporter of the system.
>
> (Havel 1985: 31, 39)

It is this insidious characteristic of state-socialism that leads Havel to adopt the phrase 'post-totalitarian', not because 'the system is no longer totalitarian; on the contrary, I mean that it is totalitarian in a way fundamentally different from classical dictatorships, different from totalitarianism as we usually understand it' (1985: 27). To reiterate, crucial to this distinctiveness for Havel, as for the Poles, is the central role of ideology within the 'system of the lie', ideology that creates 'a bridge of excuses between the system and the individual' (Havel 1985: 30). Totalitarianism as the rule of the ideological lie is new in the sense that as individuals outwardly conform to it they actually produce the discourse of the lie themselves and are thus implicated in their own oppression.

Yet civil society can play a role in offering resistance here. For it provides a space for free and open expression in which people cease reproducing the ideological lies that perpetuate totalitarianism. This free expression, in turn, forces the regime to confront its illegitimacy, for now it ceases to be a pure totalitarian order in which the exercise of power does not need 'to be legitimated because nobody is capable of speaking and interacting with others' (Keane 1999: 179). Civil society has changed all this as a sphere of speaking the 'truth'. As such it is the key to a post-totalitarian order, to shaking off totalitarian ideology's presence within each individual and to calling the lie to this ideology so that the emperor is seen to have no clothes (Keane 1999: 270–2).

'Civil society first'

The Chartists' dialogue about the nature of civil society was clearly very similar to the discussion being carried out in Poland at around the same time. Like the Polish theorists the Chartists were still, at this stage, sympathetic to socialism and consequently understood self-management in all spheres as the essence of a democratic society. Also compatible with the Polish theory, this emphasis upon self-management led to a widespread ambiguity towards the state and, subsequently, there was no great enthusiasm for liberal democracy, with its concentration upon interest representation in the state. Yet despite saying little directly in favour of liberal democratic institutions, the majority of theorists accepted something of liberal politics – that is, pluralism and the separation of spheres. This, again, represents common ground between the Chartists and the Poles.

Where there were differences between the Chartist and the Poles, this was more a matter of emphasis. Probably reflecting the more limited room for manoeuvre in Czechoslovakia, the Chartists' model is more guarded – the Chartists do not reflect much upon the long-term prospects for the democratisation of the state apparatus, as for example Michnik and Nowak do in Poland. In this sense, the Chartists advocate to an even greater degree than the Poles the strategy of 'civil society first', particularly in terms of their enthusiasm for self-management in civil society.

The analysis of totalitarianism as involving the capillary penetration of the ideological 'lie' is central to the Chartists' call for a sphere with complete autonomy from the official or state one. Essentially, what is provided within *On Freedom and Power* is a model outlining the parameters of a counter-hegemonical struggle. Although the Chartists do not refer to Gramsci's theory of hegemony, their analysis is close to elements of his in terms of their understanding of the obstacles to political change. Thus there is a keen sense in *On Freedom and Power* that systemic control is not all, or even primarily, about the coercive power available to the party-state. What really matters is the power of dominant ideology to instil unquestioned conformity and quiescence. Thus civil society represented the space of autonomous self-organisation where it was hoped that ideological 'lies', even more than enemies in the party-state, could be resisted and eventually replaced by forms of free and open communication. Yet 'living in truth' in this way was not to be directed at power as 'a thing to be grasped or abolished' (Keane 1999: 273); for, unlike previous generations of radicals, the Chartists refused an exclusive orientation to the state whether in terms of seeking its seizure or its abolition. The power of the powerless begins and ends in civil society.

Hungarian voices

In Hungarian, the phrase which is translated into English as 'civil society' refers generally to that which is not of the state, as 'something akin to the English word civilian (but while civilian in English is distinguished primarily from the military, here it is distinguished from all occupants of state office)' (Seligman 1992: 202). As elsewhere in the region, the Hungarian theorists of civil society came from a reform-communist or revisionist background, in the Hungarian case from the so-called 'Budapest School'. However, even as early as 1978, the philosophers János Kis (the leader of the Hungarian democratic opposition centred around the *samisdat* journal *Beszelko*) and György Bence shared with KOR and the Czechoslovakian Chartists the post-reformist belief in the importance of a 'society first' programme: 'Even those people who have criticised the policies of the apparatus in the name of the working class', they wrote, 'have in fact addressed themselves to the apparatus and not to the working class itself' (Kis and Bence, cited in Bernhard 1993: 312).

Assessments by Hungarian dissidents of the Solidarity experiment illustrate the influence of the Polish civil society theory-strategy in Hungary also. For in addition to rejecting reformism, the Polish idea of 'self-limitation' as both a political strategy and a normative imperative is also endorsed:

> After 1976, the Polish democratic opposition invented a new formula which was, from a certain viewpoint, the opposite of the old one. It was no longer a question of clinging to a great democratic transformation: it was necessary to be resigned to seeing the existing, essentially anti-democratic regime be perpetuated. But within this framework, it is possible to be assured of an area for democratic autonomy ... [However], I think that it is not just under constraint and in a spirit of compromise that they invented this formula and that they really do *not* intend to intervene in decisions and their implementation. They seem to be saying to the government and to the party, 'Do your work, since it must be, but

> do it well, since we will no longer accept being its victims.' Certainly, that is politics, for to have a policy presupposes that one occupies a position of power. But, in reality, this power is a counter-power: the free unions do not want to replace the party and government.
>
> (interview with Bence, *Telos* 1981: 145)

> I think that at the present time the road opening for Eastern Europe to move toward democracy is passing between the two historical impasses; on the one hand, the total challenging of the authority of the regime in power; and, on the other, the acceptance of reforms imposed from above. This narrow road consists in promoting limited changes sustained by autonomous organised forces independent of power. This has been the tactic of the Polish opposition since 1976; this is the development which is becoming reality in Poland.
>
> (interview with Kis, *Telos* 1981: 146–7)

However, if some of the key players in the Hungarian democratic opposition initially endorsed the 'Polish model', others sought to modify it to fit Hungarian circumstances. After 1987, the Hungarian opposition finally consolidated their activities into a network of independent initiatives (the Democratic Forum) such as the Poles had done a decade previously. Subsequently, Janos Kis and his team (especially Koszeg and Solt) revised the Polish model of democratisation with the idea of the 'Social Contract'. As with the Polish oppositionists, this model represented an attempt to marry theory with the exigencies of political practice specific to the country in question. Thus the Social Contract, in contrast to the Polish model, involved the Hungarian opposition more in party-state-directed political action (Jorgensen 1992: 46). This befitted a weaker and less broad-based opposition in a context in which pragmatic segments of the party-state apparatus were themselves initiating a reformist programme. Here, precisely because of these developments 'from above', the 'two society' model based on the Polish experience had begun to lose its relevance (Hankiss 1990: 111).

The influence of the 'Polish' model

Yet despite the difference in operational emphasis between the Hungarian Social Contract and the Polish model of civil society, there remained fundamental points of agreement between the two models. Scruton, for example, although he acknowledges that the Social Contract idea was representative of the Hungarian tradition of liberal constitutionalism, also points to the Social Contract's 'more socialist-seeming values', such as the down-playing of private property and the separation of powers (1988: 649). And, for Cohen and Arato:

> The 'Social Contract' retained an important link to the Polish politics of

> the 'new evolutionism' by maintaining, against other approaches of the time that still addressed the regime or its reformist elements, that groups, associations, and indeed movements outside the official institutions would have the primary task of pushing the reforms through. In Hungary, though, the idea was paradoxical, given the absence of anything resembling the Polish level of societal self-organisation.
>
> (Cohen and Arato 1992: 64)

Similarities with Polish thinking were also evident in the Hungarian opposition's debate about the extent to which the creation of a 'parallel polis' could do away permanently with the need to secure interest representation in the state. For the philosopher Hegadus, a democratised Hungary:

> would be a pluralist society in which, on the one hand, power would tolerate different non-integrable movements, organisations and tendencies; on the other hand, the forces controlling power – forces representing diverse social interests – would not seek to undermine power by insurrectional means, nor to constitute themselves as a political party in order to take over the direction of the state by means of parliamentary elections.
>
> (interview with Hegadus, *Telos* 1981: 144)

As early as 1977, Kis and Bence had criticised Hegadus for this approach (as Michnik criticised Kuron in Poland), for not seeing the achievement of representation in the state as one means of bridging the democratisation of society *and* state:

> The [existing Eastern European opposition] movements are both stronger and weaker than Hegadus wants. Stronger [because] whether they can realise their goals does not depend on the power structure's good intentions. Weaker, because they cannot replace independent institutions of representation.
>
> (Kis and Bence, cited in Arato 1981: 31)

At the time, Arato saw this debate between Hegadus and Kis and Bence in Hungary as akin to the Polish one between KOR and the reformists. Kis and Bence, he believed, took a KOR stance – whereas Hegadus, hence his suspicion of parliamentary forms of democracy, moved only from a classic reformist position to a 'half-way' civil society model of 'reformism from below' (Arato 1981: 31).

Yet Hegadus, in as much as his focus is not on democratising the state but on the creation of some form of 'parallel polis', is not unrepresentative of the Hungarian opposition, or, as we have seen, of wider oppositional discourse in the region. Arato reads the model of civil society in Eastern Europe at this time as prioritising conventional, state-directed democratisation every bit as much as self-management. Yet the key theorists behind this model all expressed their dissatisfaction with statist, representative democracy. The Hungarians were no exception here. The philosopher György Konrád, for example, in his influential book *Antipolitics* (1984), is also explicit about the need for local – including economic – self-management over 'mere' parliamentary democracy:

> In Eastern Europe today, self-management is society's prime demand ... It is a matter of common observation that the workers don't want to exchange their government-appointed managers for capitalist owner–managers ... Workplace and local community self-government, based on personal contact, exercised daily, and always subject to correction, have greater attraction in our part of the world than multiparty representative democracy because, if they have their choice, people are not content with voting once every four years ... That somehow seems very little when people hope that, by taking a part in the affairs of the community, they can gain a voice in their own destiny ... When there is parliamentary democracy but no self-administration, the political class alone occupies the stage.
>
> (Konrád 1984: 137)

> Clearly, the democracy that exists where I am means more to me than the democracy that exists someplace where I am not ... Self-management means that representative democracy spreads from the political sphere to the economic and cultural spheres as well.
>
> (Konrád 1984: 139–40)

Konrád adds that these sentiments are not to be taken as a rejection of the importance of multiparty, parliamentary democracy, which, much like the Poles, he understands to be a condition for society's self-defence (1984: 138). However, taken separately, '[t]he notion of self-governing factories and cities, not subject to Party authority, is at least as attractive as that of a division of the political class into two or more party leaderships ...' (Konrád 1984: 138). Indeed, such is Konrád's commitment to local self-management that he goes on to wonder whether a Solidarity-style 'self-defence organisation on a nation-wide scale (actually mirroring the articulation of the state administration itself) ... is capable of self-management? If it is not centralised there is no coordination, and if it *is* centralised there is no self-management' (Konrád 1984: 142). This, then, is the importance of civil society: as an autonomous societal sphere outside the state wherein self-management can be worked out. 'Antipolitics is the ethos of civil society, and civil society is the antithesis of military society', as Konrád summarises it (1984: 92).

'The social way'

Despite their greater emphasis upon a quasi-reformist strategy, Hungarian interlocutors to the debate on civil society substantially agree with their Polish and Czechoslovakian counterparts. The same core theme remains: self-management in civil society. The greater flexibility of the Hungarian party-state when compared with Poland and especially Czechoslovakia demanded that attempts be made, as just one part of an otherwise 'society-first' opposition strategy, to achieve concessions 'from above'. But the recomposition of self-organisation 'from below' was the mainstay of Hungarian hopes for democratisation.

The liberalisation of the market sphere characteristic of Hungarian developments was seen as providing useful space for the development of autonomy from the party-state, but not as an essential precondition for democratisation itself, as this has come to be accepted in liberal democratic theory. Thus when oppositionists such as Konrád advocated the Hungarian 'social way' over the Polish 'political way', this was intended to suggest different strategies for democratisation. But democratisation itself was still understood as growing self-management.

This model of civil society appears to have remained uppermost for the Hungarian opposition even until 1988. The advocates of 'civil society first' – arguing for 'a slow maturation process and the postponement of party formation' – were only at this point sidelined by those who sought to replace 'movement' with 'party' politics. By then, however, 'While one group emphasised the re-politicization and self-management of society and the elimination of existing power, the other one had already shifted the stress to replacing it' (Bozoki and Sukosd 1993: 229–30).

Part II

Democracy at the grass roots

Latin American models of civil society

3 'We need to build civil society because we want freedom'

The Latin American left's discovery of civil society

Also turning to the category of civil society at around the same time as the Eastern Europeans, yet quite independently of them, were many Latin American radicals. For, again as in Eastern Europe, the Latin American discourse on civil society took place originally on the left. As well as throwing light on how and why the civil society concept emerged in this region, this chapter is therefore also about the central part played by this concept in the transformation in leftist thinking there. This transformation, from an orthodox Marxist left for whom democracy and 'civil' society were a bourgeois sham, to a 'new' left in which democracy and civil society were embraced as ends in themselves, has been much discussed by the Western leftists in relation to their own interlocutors, yet has been largely overlooked in its parallel importance elsewhere.

Specifically, this chapter outlines how, for sections of the Latin American left, the idea of civil society lost the negative connotations it had inherited from classical Marxism and attained a central place in their new radical-democratic theory. This conceptual shift saw elements of the Latin American left abandon their previous statism and begin to articulate the importance of the self-organisation of the 'grass roots' over the Leninist vanguard's seizure of power. It also entailed turning away from a structural-determinist account of action in civil society in favour of a voluntaristic or agency-centred interpretation. This, in turn, opened up space for a more broad-based conception of popular resistance. Although these theoretical developments form the focus of this chapter, we shall see in Chapter 4 their importance in stimulating a completely new approach to the practice of political opposition in the region during the course of the 1980s.

The traditional antipathy towards democracy and civil society

The near total dominance of Marxist theory among Latin American intellectuals during the 1960s and 1970s ensured that there was little attention given to the idea of civil society in the region, except in a pejorative sense. That the 1980s saw the concept take on a totally different, and this time favourable, meaning for many of the same intellectuals is a remarkable feature of the debate on civil society in Latin America.

The Latin American left's commitment to Marxism–Leninism did not endear it to democracy since, for such revolutionaries, democracy as a means of will formation was redundant where (socialist) ends were already known. The real problem was thus one of tactics and strategy, not democracy (Barros 1986: 54). The success of the Cuban revolution was also hugely influential for the radicals of the 1960s in terms of demonstrating that armed revolutionary strategies were achievable. Furthermore, before the 1980s, the stark but apparently realistic choice between either violent socialist revolution or 'fascistic' and imperialistic capitalism did not encourage the Latin American left to take the idea of a democratic alternative seriously anyway. Latin American dependency theory, highly influential during the 1960s and 1970s, appeared to demonstrate that the level of penetration of international capital in the region had precluded the emergence of a relatively autonomous 'progressive national bourgeoisie' which could foster the first (bourgeois–democratic) stage of the development towards socialism. As Dos Santos, one of the key dependency theorists, put it:

> Since 1966 we have defended the thesis that the dominant pattern of economic development in Latin America, characterised as dependent, super-exploitative, monopolistic, centralistic, exclusionary and marginalising is not compatible with bourgeois democracy.
>
> (1979: 43, translated in Barros 1986: 54)

Less in the theoretical foreground, but perhaps as important to this rejection of democracy, was the Latin American experience, before the authoritarian era, of oligarchic and exclusionary parliamentary regimes – of 'the very real limits of democracy' (Castaneda 1994: 340). What was the point of pursuing a parliamentary path to reform when previous parliamentary regimes had proved so unwilling to seriously challenge Latin America's vast inequalities of wealth and power? For Latin American leftists, the contradiction between formal political equality and the gross inequalities of peripheral capitalism rendered actually existing democracy just as hollow as it had appeared to Marx when he criticised formal 'bourgeois' democracy in *On the Jewish Question* over a century earlier.

The historical inability of 'democracy' in the region to be substantively reformist, never mind radical, was a point eclipsed anyway by the supposed impossibility of returning to parliamentary democracy, even if this had been seen as desirable. Dependency theory had already suggested the basic incompatibility of 'bourgeois democracy' with dependent development. Hence the arrival of military regimes across Latin America in the early 1970s (following the Brazilian military coup of 1964) seemed an even clearer indication that the evolving imperatives of capitalist accumulation in the region, specifically the exhaustion of import-substituting industrialisation, now required the absolute dominance of capital over all popular sectors and classes. This was the conclusion of Guilermo O'Donnell's seminal book *Modernization and Bureaucratic Authoritarianism* (1973); and it was a conclusion shared independently by most Latin American Marxists, given their belief that the state was merely an agent of class power. On this analysis, the question of democracy 'is transformed into a problem whose realisation is exhausted by a transformation of productive relations subsequent to the seizure of power' (Barros 1986: 57).

Unsurprisingly, one implication of the dominance of Marxist theory for the Latin American left was that their understanding of civil society was similarly Marxist. For example, even as late as 1983, by which time he had moved away from orthodox Marxist analyses in most areas, the Brazilian social scientist and left politician (and now President of Brazil), Cardoso, retained a negative Marxist perspective on civil society.[1] This is apparent when he criticises the 'theory of the gap' between state and civil society:

> By postulating this kind of dynamic, what was clear in Marxist theory about civil society is hidden – that it is ruled by *domination* – and that – taken by themselves alone – civil society and democracy have nothing to do with each other as such, given that the democratization of society requires struggles among competing classes and the overcoming of the contradictions between the exploited and the exploiters.
>
> (Cardoso 1989: 312)

Yet in the very same article Cardoso begins to embrace a new, more positive, approach which is in some tension with his residual Marxism – characterising civil society as a potentially participatory public sphere within which the popular sectors can resist the otherwise all-powerful state (Cardoso 1989: 324). This apparent tension is illustrative of the traditional dominance of the Marxist understanding of civil society (as the realm of unfreedom and exploitation) as well as its re-evaluation at this time. O'Donnell, who was later to become one of the leading proponents of the importance of civil society to democracy and democratisation, similarly identified civil society solely with the private sphere in a 1979 article entitled *Tensions in the Bureaucratic–Authoritarian State and the Problem of Democracy*. Though he soon abandoned completely this Marxist equation of civil society with the privatised market realm of capitalist social relations, O'Donnell, like Cardoso, was already moving away from a Marxist understanding of civil society. This is revealed, as Cohen and Arato point out, by his more Hegelian focus overall on the mediations necessary for a private civil society to acquire a public voice (Cohen and Arato 1992: 617). Thus, civil society is identified as at once public and private – characteristics it could never have possessed for Marx.

The rejection of orthodox Marxist theory

Two factors seem to have had a particular bearing on the shift in the Latin American left's thinking on democracy and civil society. The first, more theoretical, influence came from developments in European communism and in post-Marxist thinking, particularly in Southern Europe, which many Latin American intellectuals encountered firsthand while in exile in Europe during the mid–late 1970s. Latin American Marxists had also always been influenced by French thinking, within which Marxism had been dominant, and therefore followed closely the post-Marxist turn there. Second, and of more material significance for those leftists who remained behind, was the brutalising experience of military rule. This forced a rethink about the place of violence in effecting social transformation, about what a realistic location for opposition under conditions of such effective and widespread repression might be, and as to whether the state apparatus was an appropriate target for the popular forces. As Francisco Weffort – an influential Brazilian social scientist and former Marxist – put it with regard to Brazil, 'out of these years of confusion and fear arose in the country a new attitude in relation to the state, society, and democracy' (1989: 432).

Turning first to the influence of evolving thinking on the European left: for many Latin American theorists it was this that initially prompted the retreat from Marxist categories, with their exclusive focus on class struggle and the necessity of revolution. The scale of this shift is illustrated, for example, by the transformation in Ernesto Laclau's thought. In 1971 Laclau, an Argentinean social scientist, had attacked André Gunder Frank, a dependency theorist, for his lack of Marxist orthodoxy in emphasising capitalist exchange rather than capitalist production (Chilcote 1990: 5). Yet by 1985 Laclau, by this time resident in Europe, co-authored with Chantel Mouffe one of the most influential post-Marxist works to date, *Hegemony and Socialist Strategy*, which turned away completely from class analysis and the revolutionary agenda in favour of a radically pluralist democratic theory.[2]

The emergence of post-Marxist thinking of this kind owed much to the analysis made by Eurocommunism of the need to build a broader socialist coalition than orthodox Marxism, with its exclusive emphasis upon the workers' movement, would allow.[3] The democratic transitions in Southern Europe during the mid-1970s also suggested for the first time the possibility of a bloodless revolution in overthrowing military dictatorships. This more pragmatic, political perspective – reflected also in the increasing concern with mainstream politics by socialist parties in France and Italy – supported the claim made by Marxist theorists such as Althusser and Gramsci that politics and ideology were relatively autonomous from political economy (Chilcote 1990: 6). Such developments in theory and praxis were of course closely observed by Latin American exiles in Lisbon, Madrid and Paris, who, being orthodox structural-determinists, were surprised by the presence of purely 'political' openings and by the European left's willingness and ability to exploit these (Chilcote 1990: 11). Especially after 1982, with the international debt crisis increasingly undermining the effectiveness and legitimacy of the military regimes in Latin America, the issue of openings for democratisation began to appear directly relevant for the home region as well (Munck 1990: 113–14).

In Latin America during the 1970s, the impetus for the left to re-examine its political theory and practice was, as in Eastern Europe, at once a matter of pragmatism and principle. On a pragmatic level, the success of the military regimes in quelling armed insurrection, and the ferocity with which they destroyed and disbanded traditional left parties and unions, forced a major rethink of tactics. Even more worrying was that the defeat of the left in Chile, Uruguay and Argentina had come at the peak of its influence and power in each of these countries (Barros 1986: 50). In the short run this reversal, particularly in the case of the 1973 overthrow of Allende's socialist government in Chile, merely highlighted the apparent restriction of options for the left to that of violent revolution – especially in a situation where the dominant classes had signalled *their* intention to fight a brutal class war. But the sheer scope of the authoritarian regimes' ability to close down oppositional space signalled that such opposition must prioritise basic survival. Thus political resistance now included, as a *sine qua non*, calls for the recognition of the basic civil and political rights once dismissed as a bourgeois luxury; the imperative of the defence of freedom outside the state had replaced the dream of socialist revolution in seizing the state.

Yet this politics of survival from the state also alerted leftists to new possibilities for action outside of the state:

> The discovery that there was something more to politics than the state began with the simplest facts of life of the persecuted. In the most difficult moments, they had to make use of what they found around them. There were no parties to go to, nor courts in which they could have confidence. At a difficult time, the primary resource was the family, friends, and in some cases fellow workers ... What are we talking about if not civil society, though still at the molecular level of interpersonal relations? ... 'State terror' had reduced all its opponents – generally on the left, but also many liberals – to their common denominator as unprotected and frightened human beings. Civil society was born out of the experience of fear ... In a situation of enormous ideological perplexity, the discovery of civil society was much less a question of theory than of necessity.
>
> (Weffort 1989: 347–8)

Necessity it undoubtedly was that promoted the turn to civil society, yet reasons of principle were paramount also, as the overwhelming, violent presence of the state under military rule encouraged a self-criticism of the left's own statism and militarism.

A further spur to reflection came, as in Europe, from the left's realisation that its traditional tenets struggled to accommodate the idea of a broader, more inclusive, popular movement without which there could be little hope of progress:

> Irrespective of the working class's 'inherent revolutionary potential', repression, the suppression of political society, and changes in social

> stratification, class composition, and values during military rule have dramatically eroded and transformed the former constituencies of the Left. In this situation, a continued reliance on analytical categories, strategies, and styles of political work that implicitly presume already constituted subjects – precisely where their dissolution is the critical issue – can only be detrimental.
>
> (Barros 1986: 64)[4]

The influence of Gramsci

Close observers of the metamorphosis in the Latin American approach to opposition are unanimous in the importance that they attribute to the influence of the work of the Italian Marxist Gramsci in this process (Chilcote 1990: 12; Munck 1990: 118; Castaneda 1994: 199; Pearce 1996: 148, 1997: 63). Although only schematically, Gramsci's thought was appropriated by the left for the timeliness of its central theme: the suggested strategy of constructing popular resistance in a civil society conceptualised as distinct from both state and economy. The institutions of civil society, such as churches, trade unions and neighbourhood associations, offered the state the opportunity to disseminate its ideology and thereby achieve hegemony; yet they also contained the possibility of being turned against the state in the gradual process of the formation of popular counter-hegemony in civil society. For Carlos Villas, an Argentinean social scientist who held various posts in Nicaragua's revolutionary government from 1980:

> If, as Gramsci (1977) argues, people become conscious of structural conflicts through the contest between ideologies, then the more important these kinds of unproletarianized groups and factions are in a society, the more likely are political struggle and ideological practices to be the determining factors in the development of the social formation as a whole. Therefore, in these societies we find that democratic, patriotic, religious, and, in general, ideological considerations have enormous relevance in determining the definition and alignment of the popular masses, and in their constitution as subjects of political action.
>
> (1988: 58)

Villas goes on to say that the failure of the Latin American left to recognise the 'disruptive potential' of these groups – which they had previously dismissed as 'reformist, populist and petty-bourgeois' – has 'insulated them from the popular masses' (1988: 59).

Before the rediscovery of Gramsci's treatment of civil society, those on the left were certainly wedded to the idea that the popular classes lacked the institutions and practices to offer the possibility of a genuinely transformatory politics. This civil society-blind view of political action took different forms but was a shared feature of the left nonetheless. For the Marxist intellectuals of the structuralist dependency school, for example, nothing could change through local action since what really mattered was the linkage between state elites in the periphery and the core. For the armed left, meanwhile, the rejection of strategies built upon a broader social base was a function of the single-minded goal of seizing state power so as to achieve top-down change in the manner of the Leninist vanguard.

However, the failure of state-centric strategies made leftists think again. In an article written in 1983 entitled 'Why Democracy?', Weffort portrays Brazil as akin to Gramsci's description of Oriental societies, where 'The state was everything, and society, inarticulate and gelatinous, was nothing' (Weffort 1989: 347). In other words, state power is the whole of the problem, not part of the solution. From this standpoint, Gramsci's own turn to civil society in the face of ubiquitous state control was directly relevant. It provided the left with hope even in its darkest hour by offering up an arena for transformatory political action from under their very noses, one that they had never noticed before but whose potential was enormous. Of course, the severe limits placed upon any directly confrontational tactics by the state's military apparatus transformed the strategy of the gradual construction of popular hegemony in civil society into just about the only viable option. Yet the recognition of the need for a more democratic and broad-based socialism, one in which the popular classes could actually participate, was important too. A Gramscian strategy would certainly be more inclusive, owing to its emphasis on a widely articulated popular movement made up of alternative forms of culture and organisation in civil society (rather than the military tactics of the vanguard).

Examples abound of this 'Gramscian turn' towards a more inclusive definition of the left. In the words of one Chilean former communist:

> I would say that a lot of [my inspiration] came from Gramsci. I really began to study Gramsci in 1977, and I began to publish articles about Gramsci in 1978. I remember a great feeling of revelation when I took *Prison Notebooks* with me to a conference in Poland and read it in fifteen days, and I returned to Italy transformed. I realised there was an alternative Marxism to the Stalinist one. Gramsci had created political categories that transcended the Marxist–Leninist ones, the concept of hegemony so important for socialists today …
>
> (interview in Hite 1996: 317).

Antonio Leal, a former Chilean Communist Youth leader, also highlights work on Gramsci as instrumental in leading him to propose an alternative political culture to that of the orthodox partisan left, one that would permit 'a kind of linking or bridge' for a multidimensional cultural project in order to 'open socialism to a plurality of needs and issues' (interview with Hite 1996: 317–18). 'Would it not be better', asked Borda in agreement with Leal, 'to move away from Karl Marx and V.I. Lenin, with their theses of social class monopolies over states, and closer to Antonio Gramsci to define the multiclass orientation of new, more generous political hegemonies' (1992: 314).

The logic of arguments like these began to seem obvious to many on the left, and for several reasons. First, small bands of guerrillas could be (and had been) easily destroyed, whereas a plethora of popular organisations from neighbourhood groups to larger social movements would be much less vulnerable. Second, the revolutionary strategy to seize state power had been an all or nothing gamble that had largely failed; building the 'prefigurative practices and institutions of socialism in the here and now' (Munck 1990: 118), in everyday life, held out the promise of a decentralised and gradualist strategy that would prove much more sustainable and tangible. Finally, traditional organisations of the left stood accused of replicating the authoritarian and hierarchical culture of the right; the internally democratic groups of civil society could be ideologically and organisationally counter-hegemonical as well.[5] For Barros:

> the Gramscian themes of 'intellectual and moral reform', the 'critique of common sense', 'hegemony', and the construction of a 'national-popular will' provide the raw material for setting out a radical democratic alternative to limited democracy ... This renaissance of [Gramscian] theoretical work clearly has given rise to a strong commitment to democracy amongst [left] theorists, as well as serious theoretical efforts to articulate democracy with socialism.
>
> (1986: 66–7)

The emergence in Latin America of the Gramscian understanding of the life of civil society was untypical of developments elsewhere on a number of levels. First, there was an acknowledged debt to Gramsci, whereas for the intellectuals of the Eastern European opposition, despite their similar thinking on civil society and counter-hegemonical action, Gramsci was not mentioned explicitly. Second, although many Latin American leftists encountered Gramsci in Europe and came to share Eurocommunism's Gramscian approach to forming a broader socialist movement, in other ways their commitment to separating out civil society from the state ran somewhat counter to intellectual trends on the left in Europe at the time. For, particularly among French intellectuals previously so influential in Latin America, the move was actually to transcend the state–civil society distinction. Marxist-structuralist theorists such as Poulantzas and Althusser, for example, now emphasised that the 'state was everywhere', and that 'thanks to micro powers, linguistic, ideological, and anthropological structures, there was no area of society actually exterior to the state' (Castaneda 1994: 200). In short, as we have seen, there were political reasons for Latin America's 'theoretical untimeliness' (Castaneda 1994: 200).

Although Gramsci can be credited with providing the epiphany that caused the Latin American left to realise the radical potential of organisation in civil society, his approach was not adopted in full. The left's renegotiation of their relationship with Marxism saw to that. First, most Latin American theorists, unlike Gramsci, did not see the counter-hegemonical struggle in civil society's various institutions as involving, in the final analysis, classes alone. For although Gramsci contended that hegemony was applicable only in reference to the 'fundamental classes', this could not capture the realities of 'societies with low levels of inter-sectoral integration, pockets of intensive capitalist production controlled by transnational and local oligopolies, and a relatively small industrial working class which is extremely variegated' (Barros 1986: 76). Thus the church, social movements and women's groups, for example, were generally not seen instrumentally as 'fronts' for a deeper class struggle. Second, the potential autonomy of civil society from the state was not for Gramsci, as implicitly for many Latin American neo-Gramscians, an indication that the state was effectively disassociated from class structure, having a life of its own. Third, few theorists retained Gramsci's exclusive focus on capitalism as the object of counter-hegemonical struggle: 'for the left, the essential point was that it offered a new rationale for a more multi-faceted struggle against dictatorship and militarism rather than capitalism as a whole' (Pearce 1997: 63). Fourth, Gramsci's Marxist teleology led him to expect the withering away of civil society once the popular forces within it had achieved the transition to socialism; Latin American leftists, given the priority now afforded to democratic self-organisation, came to a much less instrumental understanding of action in civil society. Finally, while Gramsci called for a 'latter day Prince' (namely, some form of vanguard party) in order to coordinate the anti-hegemonical struggle in civil society, the Latin American left became generally suspicious of the party form itself for reasons of their wider critique of the state power sought by political parties as well as the vanguardism deployed in the process. (Not to mention that, in Latin American history, political parties had always co-opted and/or demobilised the very associational life that now seemed so important.)

There were, of course, also some more directly critical voices. For Cardoso, Gramscian categories raised as many new questions as answers when he first began to engage with them in the early 1980s. While accepting Gramsci's location of the 'moment of hegemony' in civil society (in the limited sense of the recognition that there is more to class power than exploitation and coercion at the point of production), Cardoso, in an article written in 1983, proclaimed himself concerned that:

> The notions of the moment of hegemony and of the germination of liberty in civil society [should not obscure] that the boundaries of the old natural law distinction and also the Hegelian opposition between producers and the state have been blurred. The state produces, regulates economic relations, and is a key part of manufacturing and service society.
>
> (1989: 319)

At first sight this analysis is the same as that of Marx: the separation of spheres between state and civil society is a mystification of class power. Yet

Cardoso accepts that Marx's notion of civil society's 'dominance' over the state – in the sense of seeing the state as an instrument of class rule for the dominant class located in civil society – must be replaced in a Latin American context, where development is dependent and state-led, by the idea of the state absorbing and shaping civil society. However, although turning the Marxist order of determination between civil society and the state on its head, the outcome is the same in terms of the rejection of the idea that the two spheres can ever be understood separately. Cardoso is thus suspicious of using Gramsci's work, as many around him were doing, to outline a form of resistance located only in civil society:

> As suggested by Gramsci's analysis we must not only stress that hegemony is developed at the level of classes as a struggle *in society* but also show that the state, in becoming a 'producer state,' becomes part of the economic order and *ipso facto* of civil society.
>
> (Cardoso 1989: 308)

In short, Cardoso had not yet broken substantially with the Marxist-structuralist account of civil society as economic society. This is, then, the main difference between his and the Gramscian understanding of civil society as *relatively autonomous* from the economic base, and therefore as a site for resistance outside the state (whether or not the state is defined as intimately linked to productive activities). The lack of substantive autonomy attributed to civil society also explains Cardoso's emphasis on the need for political parties to build 'movable bridges' between the 'society of producers' (as a Marxist conceptualisation of civil society) and the 'society of administrators and collaborators' (the state) (Cardoso 1989: 319). Cardoso argued this because he knew that many of those in Latin America who were proposing civil society as a separate sphere also saw it as desirable to replace political parties with the more 'authentic' 'social movements' that made up civil society (Cardoso 1989: 319). Of this tendency he was one of the first to be critical; but at this stage his criticism was largely motivated by a refusal to see civil society and the state as essentially separate. Nevertheless, the degree of his engagement with Gramsci at this early stage, and his conclusion that Gramscian categories have left 'a living heritage' (1989: 319), once again demonstrates how important and influential they undoubtedly were.

The rediscovery of democracy

> Whatever meaning the word 'revolution' had … the fact remains that between 1968 and 1974 we lived under the sign of violence. How can we explain that we emerged from this phase talking – or at least trying to talk – the language of democracy?
>
> (Weffort 1989: 328)

As a result of the political and theoretical developments outlined above, the 1980s saw democracy replace revolution as the unifying concept for debate among Latin American intellectuals. 'The antagonism between authoritarianism (of all forms) and democracy has largely superseded that posited between capitalism and socialism', as Munck put it (1990: 113). For a leader of the Chilean Socialist Party, Jorge Arrate (writing in 1982), the experience of authoritarianism 'meant the consolidation of antiauthoritarianism in the heart of the left ... The loss of democracy and its denigration in the [dictatorship's] official discourse induce a more profound appreciation of the value, meaning and contents of political democracy ...' (cited in Bermeo 1992: 278). An indication of the degree of change is that there had been little or no debate about the meaning and worth of democracy as recently as the 1960s and 1970s (Barros 1986: 52). Indeed, Weffort claims that it was as late as 1979 before a Brazilian intellectual (Carlos Nelson Coutinho in an essay entitled 'A Democracia Como Valor Universal') first treated democracy seriously 'as a universal value' (Weffort 1989: 332). This rediscovery of the value of democracy was not limited to one or even just a few of the countries in the region. It was a debate in which 'most of the leading thinkers of the Brazilian intellectual left participated', according to Pakenham (1992: 214). Also 'in Peru, as in most of Latin America, almost the entire left has replaced the themes of class struggle, revolution, and socialism with that of democracy' (Silva 1988: 77). In Chile too, 'the central preoccupation among [leaders of the Chilean left] has been with the meaning of democracy and democratic practice' (Hite 1996: 326).

Wherever there was talk of rejecting orthodox revolutionary socialism for 'democratic socialism', then increasingly during the 1980s it involved paying homage to 'civil society'. In El Salvador, Joaquin Villalobos, one of the military commanders of the left-wing guerrillas, stated, 'The classical concept of a vanguard that hegemonizes power is history. What we are pursuing in El Salvador is a revolution of civil society' (interview in Castaneda 1994: 201). On a similar note in Brazil, Weffort asserted in 1983 that 'The discovery of the value of democracy is inseparable, within the opposition, from the discovery of civil society as a political space' (1989: 345). But what did leftists like Villalobos and Weffort mean by civil society and democracy, and why did the two concepts relate so closely for them?

As we have seen, many leftists came round to the Gramscian view of counter-hegemony as constituting a *plurality* of popular subjects, and by the self-evident need to abandon the idea of pre-defined political subjects (the 'revolutionary' working class). For Villas, a member of the Nicaraguan Sandanista government:

> the *a priori* attribution of revolutionary characteristics to the working class of the region ignored the evidence that, in many countries, these characteristics had still to be forged ... It is evident that [this] perspective

> [is an] *essentialist* approach in which any class, group, or faction that occupies a given place in the division of labour is either revolutionary or counter-revolutionary ... This is a mechanistic approach to social structure ... The repeated failures of this essentialism in generating results in terms of a popular project speak for themselves with respect to its limitations.
>
> (1988: 60)

Thus, the Latin American left sought from around the mid-1970s to end its isolation by increasingly allying with popular movements as these were already constituted. During this decade, as a response by the popular classes to their almost total exclusion from the formal political sphere and from state resources, there had been a huge upsurge in the numbers of associations of the (mainly urban) poor and marginalised throughout Latin America. Yet it had taken a real shift in their thinking for many leftists to see these popular struggles as those of natural allies. The key development was that, having rejected any 'ontology of the popular', autonomy and self-constitution remained as the only legitimate values by which the socialist movement could approach questions of agency (Barros 1986: 65). The idea of civil society came increasingly to express these values:

> In terms of the project of democratic socialism, autonomy entails a recognition of the diversity of social interests, the refusal of class reductionism, and, above all, of economism ... It leads to a 'new way of doing politics' which fully accepts the autonomy and validity of this dimension of society .... The pursuit of a socialist and pluralist civil society requires the weakening of all bureaucracies and the establishment and strengthening of spheres of autonomous public life.
>
> (Munck 1990: 118)

As for many of the theorists of the Eastern European democratic opposition, the idea of civil society was, at this early stage, connected to radical socialist notions of democracy (indeed of socialism) as self-management. As Cardoso described this thinking with regard to Brazil in 1983:

> [One] version of why Brazil is breaking with authoritarianism combines a radical vision of autonomy of civil society with a socialist critique of social domination ... *Real* democratization will arrive (and is arriving, according to those who hold this perspective) as it is crystallised in the spontaneous solidarity of the disinherited. It lives as *comunitas*, experiences of common hardship which form a collective *we* based on the same life experience that is transformed only when, through molecular changes, the simultaneous isolation of the state and the exploiters – which will perish at the same time – comes about.
>
> (1989: 313)

Cardoso's characterisation of the Brazilian approach to civil society bears a remarkable resemblance to elements of the model developed by the Polish democratic opposition at around the same time. A self-managing society turns away from state power, which is then undermined through evolutionary, rather than revolutionary, change. Also remarkable is Cardoso's observation – again strikingly similar to those made concerning Solidarity in Poland – that in the most 'radical formulation of this type of democratic theory there is a fusion of lay anarchism and Catholic solidarity thought' (1989: 313).

Pakenham, categorising Brazilian intellectuals, claims that the group who began to emphasise 'civil society' the most were those formerly Marxist scholars who had become 'social democrats' (although he concedes that they also accepted the label 'democratic socialists', which is perhaps more accurate as well as being the self-definition of the original theorists of civil society in Poland). They included Francisco Weffort, Marilena Chaui, Jose Alvaro Moises, Lucio Kowarick and Eder Sader, all of whom began to focus on 'social movements, trade unions and the like' (Pakenham 1992: 216). For Weffort in particular, civil society had become the centre of the 'new politics', almost to the exclusion of any other sphere:

> If the state had formerly been the solution, now it was the problem … Yet if politics were to have a new meaning, a new sphere of freedom for political action had to be developed. For political Brazil, civil society, previously either ignored or seen as an inert mass, began to signify that sphere of freedom.
>
> (1989: 328)

Later in the same essay Weffort concludes strongly that the state is the enemy of civil society, and thus of freedom, 'We want a civil society, we need to defend ourselves from the monstrous state in front of us … In a word, we need to build civil society because we want freedom' (1989: 349).

This view of civil society as playing a defensive role for society against the all-pervasive state was, as we have seen, also a feature of the opposition debate in Eastern Europe. In Poland in particular, the independent trade union Solidarity described itself as a 'self governing republic', expressing the hope that it could win democratic concessions from the state while at the same time providing a sphere of societal autonomy within which 'citizenship' could be practised and protected. Interestingly, in Brazil a similar 'new unionism' was articulated by, among others, Jose Alvaro Moises. In 1982 – only a year after Solidarity had been disbanded in communist Poland – Moises uses the term 'the new syndicalism' to describe how Brazilian unions had moved beyond traditional economic demands in order to seek social and political rights as well:

> The significance of the new syndicalism is not only its character as a broad social movement of the masses which pressures for its own internal

> democratisation, but also the unique penetration of this movement in the process of the struggle for Brazilian democracy. By linking its social demands to the economic struggle, the new union movement collided with the limits imposed by Brazilian authoritarianism on the exercise of citizenship by the workers.
>
> (1982: 67)

This 'new syndicalism', as in Poland, also involved Brazilian unions in a defensive role in which the protection of political space outside the state became more important than traditional demands made to the state:

> Squeezed into a terrain [by the military government] in which their specific functions are not recognised, while pressured by the reality of a mass of workers from whom the rights of citizenship were literally torn, the union is converted into an instrument of protection for the working class and of defence of the condition of citizenship.
>
> (Moises 1982: 69–70)

Thus, as in Eastern Europe, the prioritisation of civil society was not just a function of the battle to democratise the state as has been implied latterly in accounts of democratisation in Latin America. To the extent that he practically calls for the complete resocialisation of state power to civil society, this 'civil society first' radicalism is exemplified by the work of Argentinean leftist, Atilo Boron:

> The control of statism can be guaranteed only by the social expansion of democracy – by the empowerment of the activism and initiative of civil society; its classes, groups, and institutions; and its parties, unions, and social movements ... By doing [this] Latin Americans will be able to place the state more and more under the control of civil society.
>
> (Boron 1995: 164)

As Barros points out, the imperative in accounts such as these of participation from below 'leads to an almost exclusive concern with the organisation of civil society at the expense of consideration of the state and formal democratic institutions' (1986: 68). The deinstitutionalised vision of democracy, with 'civil society' viewed as the location for self-determining praxis by the subaltern classes, arose (as also in Eastern Europe) in part as a critique of *all* politics with an orientation to the state, that is, of liberal democracy also. This can be seen in Weffort's assertion that:

> If before it had been possible to call 'democracy' what were merely juridicio-institutional forms of democracy, it was possible no longer. Out of an ambiguous historical legacy new meanings had to be developed,

> and, slowly and fearfully, democracy began to be seen not as a means to power but as an end in itself.
>
> (1989: 329)

Here is revealed the importance attributed both to the 'self-limitation' of the popular forces in not seeking power in the state, and also to self-managing or council forms of democracy. Lowy's (1986) account of democracy is another example of this approach: 'Democracy is not a problem of "political form" or institutional "superstructure": it is the *very content* of socialism as a social formation in which workers and peasants, young people, women, that is, the people, effectively exercise power ...' (cited in Chinchilla 1992: 43).

Emphasising the democracy of civil society over other, statised, forms was, crucially, part of the attempt to recapture agency. The predominance of structuralist paradigms in the region, which had focused variously upon the vanguard party (Marxism–Leninism); the working class (orthodox Marxism); capitalist development (the modernisation school); and external capital (dependency theory), seemed all to write out the role of the popular forces in making their own history rather than inheriting one already determined for them. 'I remember', writes Weffort (1989: 330), 'that in 1968 ... there were those who said that we were moving towards revolution by imposition of historical necessity. Are the implications of the words "democracy" and "revolution" so devoid of human agency?'

This focus on agency and on self-management led to a relatively deinstitutionalised conception of civil society in which, rather like the Czechoslovakian motif of the 'parallel polis', the imagery is spatial rather than organisational:

> Our habitual equivocations on the meaning of politics has always been a privilege of the few; a history in which, until now, there was barely a public space where political activity, almost always limited to the dominant classes, could be differentiated from the activities of private lives.
>
> (Weffort 1989: 330)

The tendency, as illustrated by Weffort's writings from this period, to see civil society as a pure, unmediated democratic agency did not go entirely unchallenged. Of particular interest is Cardoso's argument at the time that civil society can only ever be a mediating arena rather than the end point of political practice.

Cardoso's approach to the idea of civil society, as we have already seen, took longer to emerge from the orthodox Marxist view of civil society as essentially private, individualistic, competitive and egoistic – in other words as the market sphere in capitalist societies. As he begins to engage with the concept in a new way, this critical perspective leads Cardoso to a more sombre assessment of the possibilities contained within it:

> It is evident that 'possessive individualism' and the idea of citizen–property owner as the basis for democracy is a weak basis for justifying the democratic struggle ... What is at stake is not the 'freedom of the individual' versus the totalitarianism of the state ... [T]he social inequality and the fragility of the individual before business and the bureaucracy calls for the legitimating of a 'collective' historical subject – that is the union, the community, the movement, and even the party – which appear as actors in the making to oppose themselves to arbitrariness and exploitation.
>
> (1989: 322–3)

Yet it is really the classical conception of civil society that Cardoso is critical of here; his call for collective actors in the making has overtones of the idea of popular self-constitution, which is also what the new theory of civil society prioritised. Where there is a difference of emphasis, this is that Cardoso includes 'business' (i.e. the market) as well as 'bureaucracy' (the state) in his list of the threats to civil society. In most instances, only the state is seen as the enemy of civil society. As a consequence of his wider perspective, Cardoso also sees civil society as acting ideally against exploitation (in the market), and not just arbitrariness (in the state). Such socialist concerns led Cardoso to suggest that 'What is happening in Latin America calls for a simultaneous reading of Rousseau and Montesquieu in a post-Marxist light that would not deny the prevalence of class conflict' (1986: 41). Again, though, his critique of the 'classical' theory of delegation and representation for privileging the 'citizen-elector (individual and rational being)' over the 'collective we', 'the only thing that is capable of legitimizing a general will which is becoming concrete' (1989: 323), is in tune with the civil society theory of the time. Cardoso appears to accept this much:

> This radically democratic and collectivist attitude ... demonstrate[s] the emergence of the will to renewal on the part of civil society which rejects the notion that the 'political opening' remains at the level of *re*democratization, based on liberal-individualist principles which in the past safeguarded social injustice, class inequality, and traditional bourgeois domination.
>
> (1989: 323)

Sympathetic as he is to it, however, Cardoso maintains that this vision of civil society does not identify sufficient conditions for the institutionalisation of democracy in Brazil or elsewhere. It is here that his concern with civil society as a sphere of mediation, rather than as the moment of democracy itself, comes into play. First, he believes that prioritising self-management in civil society should not preclude recognition of the need for a democratised state:

> [W]hat we have [in Brazil] is more a meeting between strongly associative, solidarity-based motivations and the state's recognition that the neighbourhood or group has rights as a social category. So, [the] error is to believe that the Latin American democratic spirit can do without the state and without parties. Anarchist and libertarian readings of some social movements' actions and analyses by social movement intellectuals have promoted theories of a 'pure society'.
>
> (Cardoso 1986: 37)

Cardoso's lingering concern is that, taken alone, a radically democratic, self-managing practice leaves civil society still defenceless in the face of unaccountable state and market power – vulnerable to isolation, co-option or coercion 'from above'. Thus Cardoso marries a reform-democratic acceptance of the state to the more radical democracy of civil society, in order to advocate popular control over all spheres (Cohen and Arato 1992: 57):

> If, on the one hand, the *basista* (grass-roots) thrust and the constitution of a collective-popular subject so as to support a new historical subject of democracy breaks the confining bonds of past institutional forms, on the other hand the reform-democratic thrust which accepts the contemporary reality of the pervasiveness of the State breaks the illusions about the possibility of a democracy 'of civil society'.
>
> (Cardoso 1989: 323–4)

For Cardoso, then, the need for popular control in all spheres signals the inadequacy of 'civil society against the state' as a strategy to minimise the state and maximise civil society. Even if such a strategy leaves the state hollowed out it remains outside popular control. Instead, 'the anti-state struggle becomes more a struggle for clear-cut government action and more social (public) control of official policies and state management …' (Cardoso 1986: 38). In circumventing what he sees as anarchism's utopia of a stateless society, Cardoso's strictly limited project for 'resocialising' the state centres around institutionalised mechanisms for its control, rather than its abolition. Furthermore, civil society without the state, even if it is attainable, is viewed as carrying the danger of overpoliticising the social realm, which 'cannot in itself rebuild institutions or ensure the necessary balance between different levels of society. The new democratisation entails rebalancing power among the state, the civil society's movements, and the political parties' (Cardoso 1986: 41).

As a consequence of this analysis, Cardoso, unusually at the time, includes parliaments and political parties in his definition of civil society (1986: 28). He is also critical of those who imagine parties to be genuine only when directly representing, or arising from, movements in civil society (1989: 319). If civil society is the mediating arena between society and the state, and if it is to have sufficient control over both bureaucracy and the market, then what is often elsewhere differentiated as 'political society' (parties and parliaments) must for Cardoso be included in it.

Unlike Cardoso, with his more liberal democratic understanding of the mediating role played by civil society in a democratic polity, most leftists saw the category in the clearer binary terms of 'civil society against the state'. Thus, as Cardoso observed of Brazilian political language in the early 1980s, 'everything which was an organised fragment which escaped the immediate control of the authoritarian order was being designated *civil society*. Not rigorously, but effectively' (1989: 318). This crude sense of civil society as associational life outside of the state was certainly common. As Burbach and Nunez put it, for example, 'By civil society we mean all the groups and organisations that are not part of the dominant order or the ruling class' (1987: 28). And yet, despite theoretical weaknesses, the notion of the existence (let alone usefulness) of political life outside of the state was novel in a Latin American context, where the state had always dominated the thinking of reactionaries and radicals alike. In this connection we might point to Alain Touraine's work *Actores Sociales y Sistemas Politicas en America Latina* (1987) in which, writing about the difference between the European and Latin American experiences of social organisation, he highlights that Latin America had not historically seen a 'clear separation between social actors, representative political forces and the state – the former having lacked an autonomous identity outside their political status' (translated in Pearce 1997: 64). Touraine argues that a democratic political system 'does not presuppose only the representativity of political forces and the freedom of representation; it rests equally on the existence of autonomous social actors, representable, that is, conscious and organised, in a direct manner and not only through political agents' (Pearce 1997: 64). This popular self-organisation, a 'civil society' in the terms used by the leftists included here, was what Latin America had never experienced. Even in countries where political parties had a long history, such as Chile and Argentina, constituencies were still articulated from above rather than below.

From structuralism to voluntarism?

The rejection of the Marxist understanding of class and revolution, and the growing interest in a radical democracy located in civil society, led sections of the Latin American left inexorably away from structuralist analyses towards an agency-centred perspective. The problem with this analytical shift for some commentators is the 'absence of sociological realism' and turn towards political voluntarism involved. As we have seen, Cardoso, in particular, pointed to the ways in which many leftist accounts of civil society and democracy did not properly address structural and institutional questions. Although the idea of the self-constitution of popular action represented a normative position of some power – breaking as it did with the left's previous vanguardism – there was little sense provided of what might constitute constraints to action in civil society: 'We [find] a recovery of Gramsci's emancipatory teleology, but not of his "absolute historicism" '(Barros 1986: 66–7).

As an example of this type of voluntarism, we might take Weffort's assertion that 'if [civil society] does not exist, we need to invent it. If it is small, we need to enlarge it. There is no place for scepticism in this question, because it would only serve to make the weak even weaker' (1989: 349). Barros argues that in these cases, 'despite the rejection of the discourse of the working class as an already constituted subject, the problem of the sources for "radical needs" for a transcendent project is never fully resolved' (Barros 1986: 67). That is, we find here the prioritisation of agency but no readily identifiable agents.

Salutatory as they are, such structuralist critiques miss their mark precisely because it was the intention of leftist theorists of civil society to move beyond the vanguardist 'recruitment' of already constituted popular subjects to already constituted political goals. Given the history of the Latin American left, moving in this direction was important in breaking with failed attempts to make revolution 'from above' and also to the democratisation of these revolutionary projects. The concept of civil society played a crucial part in this shift as it helped to articulate the importance of the self-determination of the popular sectors. As we shall see in the next chapter, to a remarkable degree the label 'civil society' was indeed taken up by the popular sectors in Latin America in this sense.

4 The idea of civil society in the theory–practice of Latin American new social movements

> The thesis that the new social movements prefigure a new type of democracy – whose salient features are the autonomy of civil society and rank-and file participation in decision making at all levels – is as important for the Latin American Left as it is for that of Europe.
>
> (Ellner 1993: 11)

New social movement theory and practice in Latin America during the 1980s represented a high-water mark in terms of hope placed in a democracy located in civil society. This hope arose out of the plethora of grass roots associations and social movements of various kinds that spread throughout the region in the 1970s and 1980s. Particularly through the rise of neighbourhood associations with significant degrees of internal democracy and high levels of participation, an experience of self-management in civil society became everyday reality for many Latin Americans.

Although there were undoubtedly more of these movements than ever before under military rule, to what extent there was anything genuinely 'new' about them is not such a straightforward question. Part of the reason for their sudden appearance within the academic viewfinder was that a new lens was being used by theorists to focus upon properties of civil society previously deemed superfluous to meaningful political change in Latin America. Thus, the increasing attention to social movements constituted a 'search for evidence of a profound transformation of the social logic. What is at stake is a new form of doing politics and a new way of sociability' (Escobar 1992: 80). Indeed, as Calderon *et al.* admitted in their introduction to a collection on Latin American social movements:

> If we had proposed, a quarter of a century ago, to undertake a study of social movements, we would have analyzed national liberation; populist or national popular movements; labor union, peasant, and agrarian reform movements; and student revolutionary movements.
>
> (1992: 19)

Yet the fact that these authors did *not* look at these kinds of movements only partly reflects their undoubted demise in many countries of the region;

it was also that their organisational and ideological features were deemed 'old' compared with the 'new' political logic of what was articulated in terms of the birth of civil society. Therefore, although it is right to be cautious about the extent to which the 'newness' of Latin American social movements was purely in analysts' minds, it would be wrong to dismiss evidence of the emergence of a qualitatively different political theory and practice within some of these social movements themselves. It is to this feature, that is to the discourse on civil society within movement theory and practice itself, which we now turn in this chapter.

Let us return to the objection occasionally levelled here that the Latin American contribution to the new social movement paradigm emerged only through the slavish imitation of developments in the West – developments which, moreover, constituted a procrustean bed for an understanding of Latin American movements on their own terms. The error of this view is revealed once we consider the evidence more carefully. The wider self-transformation of the Latin American left's theory and practice is an instructive example here for, as we saw in Chapter 3, this involved adopting European thinking only in as much as this contributed to understanding developments in Latin America, or overlapped with experiences there. Such syncretism has a long history in Latin America. Latin American Marxist-structuralists were foremost among those who constructed the Dependency model in order to explain what European Marxism could not about underdevelopment; and Latin American theorists such as Cardoso and O'Donnell inverted the European Marxist understanding of the (determined) nature of state power to make it more applicable to the periphery. Thus one fairly critical commentator, though suspicious of the fact that analysts of Latin American new social movements were sometimes foreign to the settings in which movements unfolded, admits that many of their observations were highly sympathetic to the self-understanding of the movement participants themselves (Hellman 1992: 54). Escobar, going further, points to the influence that Latin American developments had on the new social movement paradigm from the very start:

> Does [the application of the new social movement paradigm] reinforce … 'intellectual dependency' on Europe and North America? Such thought arises from a relatively conventional reading of the nature of the social movements research area. Why not admit, on the contrary, that for authors like Touraine, Castells, Laclau, Mouffe, Evers, and Slater – all of whom have had very significant experience in Latin America, usually spanning many years – Latin America has become a 'center' of theories and insights.
>
> (Escobar 1992: 81)

Thus the surge during the early 1980s of the application of new social movement theory to Latin American associational life reflected the sense that something new was emerging in the region. 'Who or what is moving in the so-called new social movements in Latin America?', wrote Evers, 'How? Why, and where? Our doubts have multiplied alongside the multiplication of these new social groupings' (1985: 43). Initially, therefore, it is necessary to provide an explanation for this upsurge in Latin American associational life upon which the movement approach to conceptualising civil society was premised.

Between the mid-1970s and the early 1980s there was, by general consensus, a flourishing of grass roots associations and social movements throughout Latin America. These ranged from neighbourhood associations to human rights organisations, from 'new unions' (Brazil) to women's or feminist groups and from ecclesial base communities (CEBs) of the Catholic Church to urban popular movements. In Brazil the crucial date was 1974, after which, according to Mainwaring (1987: 134), the easing of government repression and gradual political liberalisation (the *abertura*) provided more space for self-organisation. In Brazil, as elsewhere in Latin America, there was also the spur of engagement by elements of the left with the grass roots after the failure of vanguardist strategies in the previous decade. In many other countries in the region, on the other hand (for example in Chile), social movements emerged in the 1970s precisely because of the degree of repression by the state – both in order to play a defensive role in the one area left for political self-organisation and out of practical necessity owing to the retreat of the state from its role as service provider. Across the region, and at root, 'these organisations represented a collective response to the economic, political, social, and cultural exclusion imposed on the popular sectors by the military regime[s]' (Oxhorn 1994: 57). The severe restrictions placed upon political activity of the traditional kind led to the discovery of new forms of political practice and, by extension, to new definitions of the political itself (Chinchilla 1992: 38). At exactly the point when all transformatory projects at the state level seemed unrealisable, simply participating in collective movements, however apparently limited and local they were, became a highly valued activity.

There were also structural factors at work that help explain the explosion of grass roots movements from a longer-term perspective. Foremost of these was the exhaustion of development in the region – such that traditional party systems and populist or corporatist mechanisms of incorporation were breaking down (Alvarez and Escobar 1992: 318). This process created both the space and the need for new forms of collective organisation among the popular classes, even in countries where military repression was less fierce. Yet as Alvarez and Escobar point out, structural factors are insufficient in explaining the emergence of innovative organisational and ideological resources within these movements (1992: 318). Indeed, in order to gain real insight into these innovations we must look at the self-understanding of the movements themselves.

To the grass roots

While a distinction must be drawn between the self-understanding of movement leaders and of grass roots participants generally, what is notable is the degree to which movement leaders saw themselves as part of a wider debate surrounding new social movements and their alternative form of politics located in civil society:

> All of the movements have some leaders who can discuss the global nature and goals of the movements and can articulate a sophisticated vision of society and social transformation, including an awareness of the movement's importance in the contemporary western world.
>
> (Mainwaring and Viola 1984: 31)

As new social movement activists were usually on the left, many of them had been in exile in Europe – which was where they had experienced at first hand the feminist, ecological and other movements with whom they sought to retain contact after returning to Latin America (Mainwaring and Viola 1984: 34). Alvarez gives the example of the return of exiled Brazilian feminists, who 'literally flooded feminist groups in São Paulo' on their return after the Brazilian regime's concession in 1979 to opposition demands for political amnesty:

> [The] *exiladas* [returning exiles] shared their experiences of feminist activities unheard of in Brazil until the late 1970s ... [They] elaborated on the concept of movement autonomy, one that readily caught on among Brazilian feminists struggling to define their relationship to the political opposition as a whole.
>
> (Alvarez 1994: 30).

Yet Latin American activists added something distinctive to the conceptualisation of new social movements as articulated in the West: they described themselves as part of a wider popular movement based in civil society:

> The Zapatistas in Mexico make it clear that they considered themselves a 'civil society organisation'; in Guatemala, the 'Civil Society Assembly' (Asambla de la Sociedad Civil) brought together many organisations trying to influence the peace process in that country. The concept is mentioned in nearly all the literature emanating from these and many other popular organisations and NGOs [non-governmental organisations] working throughout Central and South America in these years.
>
> (Pearce 1997: 66)

A key theme of civil society which movement leaders emphasised was that of autonomy from the formal political sphere – specifically the state, but including political parties as well. Explanations for this shift in thinking and practice cannot be reduced to the fact that links with political society were severed for many popular organisations after the imposition of military rule. If this were all that was at stake then similar approaches would not have been found even in countries like Mexico, where no such coup occurred: 'What we reject', said one leader of the *coordinadora* movement, referring to the main political parties of the left in Mexico, 'are attempts by parties to manipulate the CNPA [National *Plan de Ayala* Coordinating Committee]. They see us as "booty" and want to take advantage of our strength, something we will never allow ... the vanguard of the left is among the masses, not in the parties or in the Chamber of Deputies' (cited in Hellman 1992: 53).

Feminist movements and women's groups in the region were particularly vocal in their calls for autonomy. Alvares points to no less than seven women's groups that had raised the issue of autonomy by 1979 in Brazil (1994: 60). In Chile too, most of the women's groups active in the 1980s 'were cognizant of the tendency of political parties to co-opt women's struggles. For this reason, movement autonomy was one of the most important issues for the Chilean women's movement during the pre-transition period' (Chuchryk 1994: 82). Also, in Peru, the Coordinating Committee of the five feminist groups there circulated a document in the late 1980s in which they argued for feminist autonomy from the political parties (Barrig 1994: 159). Meanwhile, in Nicaragua and Central America generally, there was 'an intense discussion ... about the meaning and importance of autonomy for feminism' (Chinchilla 1994: 191).

The issue of autonomy was not restricted to women's movements, however. In a case study of the 1980 metalworkers' strike in São Paulo, Brazil, Nico Vink recalled the stress placed upon the autonomy of the unions by one of their leaders, Lula: 'The ex-union leader is very proud of the autonomy of the S. Bernardo union. It has no ties with the church, the government, employers, communist Party nor other leftist organisations. The only responsibility is to the working class, which elected it' (Vink 1985: 117). Vink noted the influence of the Catholic church's liberation theology on Lula's approach, and also that the general attitude towards the state was antagonistic, but not clearly elaborated (1985: 120). Perhaps as interesting is the antipathy from a labour movement towards traditional parties and organisations of the left; clearly the priority of the movement over the party form was as important for these Brazilian workers as it was for many other activists elsewhere in Latin America. Indeed, even for those under-resourced organisations of the urban poor for whom total disengagement from political parties (and from their patronage) was a less realistic option, the movements themselves came increasingly to be seen as sovereign. In just one example, Francisco Saucedo, a leader of the Asamblea de barrios in Mexico City, stated that:

> The movement is very important to the party and it is the movement

> that moulds the party which, in turn, serves as the political instrument that the people require. We have to play an active role in the party so that it will be permeated by the movement and so that it will be the people that shape its program.
>
> (cited in Hellman 1992: 59)

However, the importance of autonomy for Latin American social movements during the 1970s and 1980s was not simply a matter of catering for alternative political identities. For workers in particular, autonomy meant the opportunity to develop appropriate political organisation and strategies in alliance with other movements (Keck 1989: 254). The neo-Gramscian concern with the creation of popular hegemony meant that, for many Latin American social movement leaders, asserting a plurality of identities was not an end in itself. These identities were important to *collective* autonomy from the state, which is why there were often heated debates (as in Poland over the umbrella role played by Solidarity) concerning the degree of autonomy that movements should have from each other. For example, a male leader of one of Lima's neighbourhood organisations was highly critical of the demands by women's groups for autonomy from other popular movements such as his own:

> I have seen conflict between neighbourhood organizations and women's organisations ... since the beginning of the 1980s. One thing that bothers me is this business of autonomy ... It's been taken up so strongly that it has become autonomy against the whole world. In my view ... we need to distinguish who we need to be autonomous against, who we need to coordinate with, and how we gain hegemony. They are two distinct things: the autonomy we want is against the state ... But between the organizations in the popular sector, we need coordination.
>
> (cited in Jaquette 1994: 229)

The desire to construct popular hegemony in civil society as an alternative to state power – of great importance to Latin American social movements, but less so to their Western counterparts – reflected a further difference between these two sets of movements. In the West, societal self-organisation has centred on post-industrial or post-material issues of consumption, lifestyle and identity, such as relations between the sexes and ecology. For the bulk of Latin American social movements, however – particularly the base communities and neighbourhood associations – self-organisation also constituted a response to pressing material needs. To the extent that this involved focusing on the realm of consumption rather than production, then there were similarities with Western movements, but deepening democratisation through promoting recognition of a plurality of alternative lifestyles and identities was not sufficient under conditions of state authoritarianism and scarcity.

That the ends of Latin American new social movements cannot be directly compared with those of new social movements in the West again raises the question of what was 'new' at all about the Latin American movements. Self-organisation out of basic economic and political necessity is hardly without precedent in this region or any other, and it was precisely political action that went 'beyond' these imperatives that first led to the suggestion of the newness of certain social movements in the West. Thus it is to the organisational and ideological 'newness' of the Latin American movements that we must return. It is already clear how important autonomy was to the self-understanding of many different kinds of social movements. This was certainly a new emphasis, even if it reflected the reality of the decline or destruction of political society. Yet many of these movements also seem to have been characterised organisationally by a significant degree of internal democracy, including 'participation by the grass roots, open meetings, collectivization and rotation of leadership, and absolute administrative transparency' (Borda 1992: 304–5). For societies traditionally characterised by authoritarianism in every sphere of social life, including oppositional spheres, these ideological and organisational changes were alone sufficient to deserve the title 'new', as we shall see in the course of this chapter.

Brazilian urban social movements and the influence of practice on theory

The political significance of social movements in Latin America first began to be noticed in Brazil during the late 1970s (Assies 1994: 82). At a time when many oppositional theorists and activists were still wedded to orthodox Marxism, the thinking at this point continued to advocate resistance to capitalism as the answer also to the problem of state authoritarianism. Yet in a Latin American context, where the working class formed only a minority of the popular sector, workers had historically been more easily co-opted by the state. Thus the search for agents of transformation always needed to move beyond Western Marxism's focus on the working class, which is exactly what happened when many Brazilian activists and theorists began to take notice of what they termed 'urban social movements' (neighbourhood associations in particular). The recognition of the political nature of these movements – albeit seen mostly in terms of an anticapitalist project – was also made possible by the left's increasing acceptance of the view that the contradictions of peripheral capitalism created a plurality of social subjects (Chinchilla 1992: 44). In particular, these contradictions were seen as manifest in the inability of dependent states to secure the urban services that private capital was disinclined to provide, necessitating provision by the popular urban sectors themselves (Mainwaring 1987: 140). The struggle between urban social movements and the state over basic material conditions came to be understood as the site for a broader class struggle located at the point of consumption (or reproduction) rather than production. Indeed, the capitalist state, and not the employer, came to represent the enemy in this scenario – as it had done already for theorists of dependency and bureaucratic authoritarianism (Assies 1994: 83).

On the basis of this analysis, the view of Brazilian theorists such as Castells, Borja, and Lojkine was that 'the orthodox view of urban struggles as secondary to class struggles should be rejected for its Eurocentrism' (Assies 1994: 83). Somewhat along these lines, Kowarick also argued in 1985 that there was

> a direct and logical link between the struggles of workers in the realm of production and those of neighbourhood groups concerned with consumption issues ... The Brazilian 'miracle' rested on a strategy of exploitation of labor in the factories *and* the limitation of collective consumption goods and services available to the urban poor.
>
> (cited in Hellman 1992: 57)

Indeed, this analysis seemed to Kowarick and others to be justified by the 'new situation of frontal opposition to the state', whereby neighbourhood associations, previously successfully co-opted by the state, now pursued a 'radical anticapitalist, antigovernmentalist and autonomist discourse' (Assies 1994: 84).

The growing awareness in Brazil of the significance of urban social movements reminds us that the Latin American vision of new social movements had its own distinctive provenance and was not simply a spin-off from post-Marxist currents in the West. Here, by contrast, the movements receiving attention were usually organised around post-material issues relating, in particular, to identity. Thus:

> Alongside points of rupture, there appear to be lines of semi-conscious continuity in our ways of thinking [which] ... look more like an opening up of old concepts rather than their suppression. The 'recognized' list of political actors and forms of action organised around the state and the sphere of production receives the important addenda of 'civil society' and of 'social movements' ... With this, *cultural* production as well as the whole sphere of reproduction are accepted as valid political fields.
>
> (Evers 1985: 47)

Yet despite the recognition given to urban social movements in terms of their inclusion within the political, initially Latin American intellectuals took it upon themselves to interpret the significance of this new movement politics in traditional class terms – that is as instrumental to an already defined class struggle. This resistance to the actors' self-interpretation of the meaning of their own struggles, which emphasised movement autonomy as an end in itself, is typified by the Peruvian leftist Guillermo Rochabrum, for whom urban social movements

> are more a continuation of, than a break with, the struggle for 'class political autonomy' of the previous decade. The deepening of the economic crisis made the defence of wages based on the trade unions insufficient or inoperable, while wages themselves dropped below the value of labour power. This made it necessary to extend the efforts of survival to other economic activities (self-employment), and other arenas (in particular, the neighbourhood) in which the struggle to obtain what is necessary takes other forms. Situated outside of the arena of work, in general they face 'circumstances' and not a personalised 'enemy'. This forces them to create solutions that they then carry out themselves, rather than in conflict with the capitalist or the state ...
>
> (cited in Silva 1988: 92)

Such theoretical accounts reduced the forms of autonomous self-organisation characteristic of the new movements to determined outcomes of the changing economic base (to be understood still under the banner of class struggle). Yet the self-managing practice of these movements was, in time, to put the shoe on the other foot – forcing theorists to revisit their exclusively instrumentalist and class-based understanding of political action in civil society. Although the original telos attributed to urban social movements was the overcoming of capitalism through class struggle, the practice of these groups themselves shifted the locus of the political to non-class actors working to carve out spheres of autonomy from the state. Thus, the increasingly doubtful prospect of an orthodox transition to socialism in the late 1970s did not exhaust utopian energies to the degree that might have been expected by leftist observers, since self-constituting social subjects had identified *their* goals as incompatible with power-seeking in the first place. In this way, the urban social movements *themselves* contributed to the decline of exclusively class-based and instrumental analyses of political action, contra Mainwaring's privileging of developments in theory in accounting for this shift:

> While correct in asserting the heterogeneity of the class base of urban social movements, paradoxically the Marxist literature exaggerated this point such that class conflict ceased to be a fundamental concept of analysis. Whereas they saw the labor movement in terms of class struggle, Lojkine (1980), Castells (1974; 1980), Evers *et al.* (1981), Borja (1975), and their Brazilian adherents generally saw the main struggle in urban areas as the 'people' (an undifferentiated category) versus the state ... These authors influenced, and virtually shaped, Latin American thought on ... social movements.
>
> (Mainwaring 1987: 155)

The influence on theory of a new, more broad-based and self-determining practice within urban social movements can be seen widely. Most of the contributors to one influential volume on social movements, for instance, state their continuing commitment to the importance of class analysis but in fact concentrate on the broader, more inclusive, notion of popular hegemony (Slater 1985: 12). Other leftist theorists now see social movements as working in alliance in the formation of 'fronts' (Alves 1989), or as constituting a 'multiclass base' (Garreton 1989: 260). Similarly, Marxist activists Roger Burbach and Orlando Nunez refer to the revolutionary agency of a 'third force' that, 'unlike propertyless wage labourers, is not a new class or even a consolidated class but a category made up of diverse groups and social movements that are more defined by their social and political attributes than by their relationship to the work-place' (1987: 64). This prioritisation of the attributes of movements themselves, rather than their instrumentalisation in some wider definition of the political, leads us to question just what these attributes were understood to be.

New social movements and democratic politics beyond the state

A key component of the novelty of Latin American new social movements was the value they placed on 'basis democracy' and, relatedly, 'the importance given to high levels of participation' (Slater 1985: 7). According to Slater the question of 'basis democracy' – read in terms of the 'quest for autonomy, the deconcentration of power, the construction of a new political morality and the fight against all forms of oppression' – inhered as much in the new social movements at the Latin American 'periphery' as in the European and North American 'centre' (1985: 11).

Many other accounts of the 'newness' of Latin American social movements emphasised their internally democratic and participatory character. For example, Mainwaring and Viola singled out the emergence of groups 'inclined towards affective concerns, expressive relations, group orientation, and horizontal organisation' (1984: 19–20). Their argument here was made on the basis of the consistently democratic, participatory practices of the five different types of movements that they studied, namely ecclesial base communities, neighbourhood associations, the women's movement, ecological associations and human rights organisations (1984: 36–7). The neighbourhood associations that Mainwaring studied in particular were also exercising a greater degree of coordination between groups, and there was evidence of far more grass roots participation within them. Mainwaring concluded, 'neighbourhood associations are not new ... Nevertheless, the character of the post-1974 movement ... has changed in relation to the pre-1964 movement in several important ways' (1989: 189).

The overall tone of the early accounts of new social movements, particularly in social science journals and alternative newspapers within the region (Escobar and Alvarez 1992: 2), was highly optimistic. Latin America's social movements represented nothing less than the discovery of a new politics;

their radically democratic, participatory practice held out the possibility of a 'third way' for a radical transformatory project from below. As already indicated, the most commonly referred to attribute of the Latin American social movements was that of movement autonomy – both from the state and political parties. In one empirical study of a poor Brazilian city near Rio de Janeiro, Mainwaring found that movement autonomy *vis-à-vis* political parties had increased substantially in the post-1974 period compared with the pre-1964 period (1989: 189; cf. Mainwaring and Viola 1984: 28; Evers 1985: 45; Mainwaring 1987: 149). Indeed, the emphasis placed on the autonomy of social movements is one feature that has endured beyond the optimistic analyses of the early 1980s into the later – more sober and reflective – literature on these movements (cf. Calderon *et al.* 1992: 22; Cardoso 1992: 300; Chinchilla 1992: 47; Escobar and Alvarez 1992: 10, 322; Hellman 1992: 54).

Also present in the theory–practice of new social movements, and linked to the privileging of movement autonomy, was a critique of statist politics that is sometimes expressed in ways reminiscent of the Eastern European opposition, that is in the wider terms of antipolitics. Evers in particular saw this feature as constitutive of Latin American new social movements:

> It is my impression that the 'new' element within the new social movements consists precisely in creating bits of social practice in which power is not central ... Social movements are not questioning a specific *form* of political power, but the centrality of the power criterion itself.
>
> (1985: 48, 61)

The rejection of the 'power' criterion by these movements, Evers claimed, could not be reduced to specific political circumstances (such as the military dictatorships), since he found movements to be similarly persuaded in countries like Venezuela, where liberal institutions had survived to some degree. Evers also recognised that movement activists' denunciation of 'power' was, as for the Eastern Europeans who adopted similar terminology, actually acutely political, the 'anti' element really being directed at the state rather than at politics per se:

> Could it be that the historical contribution these [Latin American] movements are about to offer does not consist in enhancing the political potential of a revolutionary left, but on the contrary in rescuing fragments of a meaningful social life from the grip of politics (including that of the left)? In other words: are these movements 'new' insofar as they are aimed at reappropriating society from the state?
>
> (Evers 1985: 49)

Movement antipolitics is thus concerned with a redefinition, rather than a rejection, of the political:

> Even though we talk of *social* movements, we are obviously not interested in new *social* agents emerging from them, but in political ones; we are not paying attention to new ways of 'doing society', but of 'doing politics'. In one word, our agenda continues to be that of *power*. What do these practices represent, converted into the universal currency of power?
>
> (Evers 1985: 47)

Similarly, Mainwaring and Viola view the contrast between 'new' and 'old' Latin American social movements as turning on the latter's demands to the state *vis-à-vis* the former's concentration on social relations, 'sometimes to the point of being relatively apolitical. To the extent that they deal with the state, the demands are frequently symbolic and non-negotiable'. This, for Mainwaring and Viola, is an 'apolitical' way of 'doing politics' (1984: 20). Yet here, again, antipolitics is really antistatism and such actions are only defined as *a*political to the extent that the state is taken to be indispensable to acting politically. This was precisely what many movement activists refused to accept. Thus, Carr makes the observation about Mexican new social movements, for example, that, while they 'clearly form part of the left, ideologically they are very diverse, drawing on anarchist and syndicalist traditions ...' (Carr 1993: 86). Orlando Borda's initial (1986) analysis of 'new' social movements was also that they came close to anarchism. Influenced by their approach, Borda claimed sympathy with it, though not to a 'red' anarchism, which seeks to do away with all government, nor to the Marxist idea of the withering away of the state:

> More than anything, my position involves a different way of conceiving of and understanding power, as is suggested by some movements, albeit still rather timidly ... [F]urther inspiration [may be derived from] ... contemporary critics who tend to rescue from oblivion the function civil society has performed.
>
> (Borda 1992: 312)

Close on the heels of movement suspicion of the state came the warning that the popular forces, so constituted, would do well not to seek power within it. The idea of self-limitation in order to avoid a revolution that 'devours its own children' is present, just as in Eastern Europe. Therefore, the call for the popular seizure of power is defined as a smoke screen that obscures the fundamental incompatibility between the desired popular control at the grass roots and the emasculated 'people power' handed down by revolutionary elites. Democracy has to be built locally, in the here and now, and cannot be expected as a gift from above at some point in the future:

> These movements have learned an important lesson: that the seizure of power in itself is not the whole answer [since] it runs the risk of continuing the violence that preceded it or indefinitely reproducing the warlike

> tendencies that were rife during the process of struggle. The model of the Jacobinic seizure of the Winter Palace in Petrograd as a requisite for successful revolution has been largely dispelled. Hence, there is an insistence on putting democratic forms of authentic participation into practice right away ... There is a need to sow, from this very moment throughout civil society, the ideological seed of respect for life, the environment, and cultural diversity – to obtain life's fruits, in the form of better social bases and more consistent leaders of movements, without waiting for these movements 'to seize power'.
>
> (Borda 1992: 311–13)

Turning away from the state was not just a response to 'totalising' politics but, as in Eastern Europe, stood at once as a redefinition of how and where the political should be enacted. Although it was not just the presence of the state that was the problem for Latin Americans, but also its absence in terms of welfare provision, the end result was the same in terms of it leading to calls for more self-management in society:

> By ... reclaiming politics as a constituent element within social life and not separated from it, the socio-cultural potential of the new social movements may turn out to be not less, but more political than action directly orientated towards existing power structures.
>
> (Evers 1985: 51)

Influenced by new social movement practice, which decentres the state and focuses instead on politics as it is located in other spheres of social life, Corragio states that

> the liberation project of the people cannot be reduced to the idea of 'seizure' of governmental power by a given oppositional social entity; rather it presupposes a permanent *revolution of civil society* and thus a continuous *transformation of the subject*, that is, the people.
>
> (1985: 206)

Similarly for Quijano, another observer of new social movements:

> The identities in gestation begin to develop new forms of understanding and questioning the state, not from the vantage point of the power of the state, but, on the contrary, from that of the construction of a different social power. To this extent their goal is not to replace the state but to construct an alternative society.
>
> (cited in Escobar 1992: 81)

New social movements and the democracy of civil society

What model of civil society are we encountering in the discourse of new social movements in Latin America? A relatively uncontroversial interpretation is that 'social movements ... strengthened a civil society that had always been dominated by the state' (Mainwaring 1987: 132). Yet in the more radical terms outlined by activists themselves, civil society denoted instances of societal self-organisation, or even self-management. The leitmotif of popular space outside the state is also central, as in the following accounts: 'Latin America is witnessing a reappraisal of civil society as an ordinary lebensraum, reflected in the growing importance of the micropolitics of everyday life' (Calderon *et al.* 1992: 30); Social movements are trying 'to recover some of the space lost because of the closing of civil society' (Mainwaring 1987: 33).

This public 'space', however, reflecting the Eastern European sense of civil society, is not to be created through the development of capitalism's market-individualism, as it had been classically in Western political theory and is again in much current democratisation theory (as we shall see). 'Often working at the margins and in the fissures of peripheral capitalism, social actors of various kinds take space away from capitalism', as Escobar (1992: 68) expresses this still socialist sentiment: 'By creating spaces for the experience of more collective social relations, of a less market-orientated consciousness ... these movements represent a constant injection of an alien element within the body of peripheral capitalism'. Indeed, 'for the counter-foundation elements within the new social movements, it is precisely the non-market elements within social relations that are being reappraised; and so is human expression in all aspects *except* that of buying power' (Evers 1985: 51, 64).

Also crucial to the civil society project as articulated by new social movements is the recovery of the local and particular spaces which, taken together, point to a 'field of construction of democracy that ... is important in itself, that of the social relations of daily life' (Jelin, cited in Escobar 1992: 70). The idea of the importance of the politics of daily life is not meant, however, to imply a privatised civil society. On the contrary, 'the most important goal' of the movements of civil society 'is the creation of a *popular collective* capable of constantly redefining itself through action (Quijano, cited in Escobar 1992: 81). It is in this emphasis on the democratic, self-determining moment in civil society, in which individual social movements come together to form a broad coalition of the popular forces, that the Latin American approach is most distinct. Movements in civil society, contra liberal theory, are not understood as representing purely particular interests, but are seen rather as the agents of a counter-hegemonical project that is greater than the sum of its parts. The 'political significance of an ecological struggle or of a regionalist social movement, or of a local community struggle is not pre-given; rather it depends on its hegemonic articulation with other struggles and demands' (Slater 1985: 15).

The notion of the hegemonic coordination of social movements, to reiterate, is a key point of difference from the liberal democratic celebration of difference in civil society for its own sake. Civil society is about popular agency, singular, and not just multiple identities, plural. Thus Slater, representatively of wider movement thinking, uses Gramsci's concept of a 'war of position' as directly relevant to the politics of civil society:

> [With a war of position] we have a close link with many aspects of the new social movements, since in a war of position we are referring to wide-ranging social organization and ideological influence whereby the struggle for popular hegemony on these fronts makes possible or conclusive a frontal war of movements against capitalist state power. In countries like Brazil and Argentina with relatively densely structured civil societies a war of position is indispensable and the radical democratic struggles of the new social movements provide a crucial contribution to just such a 'war'.
>
> (Slater 1985: 18)[1]

Crucially, though, this 'war' fought by movements in civil society, as Slater's terminology indicates, is understood to be 'against' the state rather than 'for' power in it. In this sense it is a defensive struggle for self-management in civil society; and it is this defensive logic that should be seen as characteristic of the movement's neo-Gramscian approach in general. That is, the argument for popular hegemony as 'positively indispensable' (Evers 1985: 47) is made because the alternative is a disarticulated civil society, built solely around separate identities and interests, which plays into the authoritarian state's hands.

Part III

The taming of the idea of civil society since 1989

5 Civil society and theories of democratisation in Eastern Europe

As we have seen in previous chapters, the idea of civil society re-emerged initially in the 1970s and 1980s as a way of articulating a form of political action or self-determination located in society rather than the state. In both Eastern Europe and Latin America this new approach to civil society served two interrelated purposes. First, living under an authoritarian state there was a strategic case for the discovery of autonomous associational life as an alternative to statist politics from which the opposition, and popular forces generally, were excluded. However, as we have also seen, the turn to civil society was not merely tactical or instrumental, informed as it was by the attempt to suggest an alternative to statist political philosophy based on the principles of self-limitation and self-organisation. According to this philosophy, the accepted wisdom of the ruling political ideologies of modernity that the state is sovereign undermines the politics of everyday life and replaces the self-determining actions of free citizens with the dead weight of distant and unresponsive institutions organised in the interests of 'power'. Thus it was from this normative position, and not just out of pragmatism, that flowed the rejection of traditional state-directed oppositional strategies, whether revolutionary or reformist. What was sought after was nothing less than the democracy of civil society.

Yet such a model of civil society is now hardly encountered in academic discourse. The argument that this is because it was intended only as a theory of opposition under authoritarian conditions, to be surpassed on the transition to liberal democracy, will not hold for the following reason: this theory of civil society was seen also as a critique of statist features of liberal democratic politics itself; liberal democracy was certainly not its telos. It follows that there must be deeper reasons for the passing over of this vision of civil society; perhaps it does not even appear as a model of civil society at all if a state-centric understanding of the political is taken as axiomatic.

Indeed, it is my contention in part III that part of the explanation for the apparent 'demise' of the radical model of civil society, with which we have been concerned so far, is the liberal democratic 'taming' of the idea of civil society during the course of the 1990s. By this I do not mean so much that the radical model has been intentionally demobilised, but that the now dominant liberal democratic standpoint is so opposite to it – seeing civil society as instrumental to democratising the state rather than as a democratic end in itself – that the former effectively disappears from view. In this chapter and the next, I seek to demonstrate this largely unconscious process of 'taming' by addressing, in turn, conceptualisations of civil society that dominate the two largest and most influential literatures on the so-called 'third wave' of democratisation: those relating to the democratic transitions in Central–Eastern Europe and Latin America. (Of course, my selection here also enables me to ensure maximum continuity with our discussion so far, which has also focused on these regions.)

Apart from charting the prevailing liberal democratic understanding of civil society from which the alternative voices in this book diverge, the wider picture that emerges in these two chapters is of a near consensus among analysts of democratisation that actually existing liberal democracy is the only form of democracy on offer. While it might come as no surprise that, following the watershed of 1989, the tenets of liberal democracy are in the ascendance within political science, the story of civil society theory reveals that in some fields this ascendancy is more accurately described as hegemony. This spontaneous consent that liberal democratic 'civil society' is all that civil society could or ought to be should give cause for concern to opponents of discursive closure, whether or not they wish to advocate more radical alternatives. For the purposes of these two chapters, and bearing in mind that the central aim of this book is to demonstrate that there *are* alternatives, this means questioning just how axiomatic and value-free the new civil society orthodoxy really is.

Civil society and theories of democratisation in Eastern Europe

As has been shown, during the 1970s and 1980s there emerged an ideal of civil society as societal space, autonomous from the state, wherein a self-managing form of democracy could be worked out. That is, the idea of civil society was a critical one, as for example in a series of lectures given in 1982 under the title *Power and Civil Society* by Leszek Nowak, a philosopher and Solidarity activist, where civil society is defined as 'the sphere of civil autonomy', even though such autonomy was not possible in Poland at the time (1991: 29). Since 1989, by contrast, civil society has been used mostly as a descriptive, rather than critical, term – one used to describe various sets of non-state institutions. In these cases, knowledge of the earlier normative-political idea of civil society, or of the self-definition of movements such as Solidarity as 'civil society', often seems completely absent. The term civil society is also used often as a label for the 'popular upsurge' that took place immediately before the transition to liberal democracy in 1989. Splichal, in just one example, effectively dismisses out of hand the self-understanding of Solidarity that it constituted a civil society when limiting the role of civil society to the events of 1989: 'Civil society was created in East-Central Europe in a very short period of time; almost overnight it succeeded in overthrowing the old regimes and inaugurating parliamentary democracy' (1994: 305). Of course, although 'civil society' is used here as if it were an unproblematic and value-free description of the role of a mobilised society in overthrowing authoritarianism, such 'descriptive' uses, as we shall see, are highly selective regarding the form and duration of citizen self-mobilisation that they allow under the category civil society. What masquerades as mere description is actually deeply normative.

When not used descriptively in relation to the transition processes themselves, the concept of civil society is now viewed as an analytical tool with which to account for democratisation in the region and to explore the likelihood of democratic consolidation. Bibic and Graziano's (1994) introduction to their volume on civil society and democracy is a typical example here. They begin, 'Civil society has played a crucial role ... in the transition from authoritarian regimes to political democracy ... A strong civil society is important in the consolidation of democracy in post-authoritarian regimes as well as in deepening democracy in already established liberal democracies' (Bibic and Graziano 1994: i). In another case of civil society used as an analytical tool for students of democratisation, Szakolczai and Horvath (1992) observe, 'In explaining the revolutionary changes that occurred in Eastern Europe during 1989, one often encounters a discourse centring upon the resurrection of civil society' (1992: 16). Thus, even though the concept of civil society is deployed more reflectively in analytical than in descriptive accounts, here too it is mostly limited to assessing the role of societal self-organisation in the transitions of 1989. As will become clear, this specific application of the idea of civil society to issues concerning liberal democracy closes down more ambitious, critical approaches that posit self-organisation in less instrumental terms.

For even where it is used analytically, rather than merely descriptively, contributors to the debate on civil society and democratisation in the region still do not see themselves as involved in political discourse, but instead deploy 'civil society' as a putatively neutral social-scientific concept. Lewis, for example, is critical that 'with reference to Eastern Europe during the 1980s, "civil society" became more of a slogan than an analytical concept' (1993: 300). Frentzel-Zagorska similarly wants 'to avoid' theoretical approaches to civil society 'since I intend to use the concept ... as an analytical tool for the particular historical developments taking place in Eastern Europe' (1992: 40–41).

But why are such commentators so confident that, even after the supposed death of positivism, they can circumvent the political theory of civil society for an objective social science of civil society? Central to answering this question, the implications of which will be explored now in more detail, is that it is clear to these commentators what a concept of civil society should do. Put simply, they think that it should further understanding of the conditions necessary for the transition to, and consolidation of, liberal democracy. Since these apparently indisputable ends are known, the means of civil society are all that really need to be understood.

Civil society instrumentalised and demobilised

To recap, for the democratic oppositionists that we have considered in communist countries such as Poland and Czechoslovakia, civil society itself was the seat of democratic legitimacy and practice:

> Hope ... lies ... [in] the realization of a social order in which the formalized and functionalized structure of society will be regulated and controlled by this 'newly discovered' spontaneous civic activity, which will be a *permanent and essential* source of social self-awareness.
>
> (Battek 1985: 108)

However, as the following quotation illustrates, civil society is now used to denote a very different kind of activity:

> The [opposition] model of civil society has been superseded. The idea of civil society has by no means been discarded as a consequence, however. On the contrary, it has become a virtual 'buzz-word' in the discourse of post-communist politics. But the tasks assigned to civil society are substantially different: its role is to be constitutive and preservative of the liberal-democratic political systems and free-market economies ...
>
> (Miller 1992: 8)

In keeping with the democratisation genre here, Miller blatantly reifies the category civil society, since he moves from acknowledging its status as a concept to a description of its supposed character 'on the ground'. But the central change to the theory of civil society so understood is that civil society is now seen as external to democracy. This is because democracy itself is viewed exclusively as a political mechanism for representation in the state such that civil society, while it furthers such representation and is therefore indispensable to a democratic polity, is effectively not of it. Only in the light of this approach can we make sense of Skapska's assertion, for example, that, 'as the post-communist experience indicates, the alternative forms of civil society flourishing before the collapse of communism prove to be dysfunctional in democratic society' (1997: 158). Skapska is here referring to the negative impact upon the new institutions of political democracy that has ensued from the 'mistrust and hostility towards official institutions' engendered by the radical, autonomous and antistatist model of civil society. Skapska may well be correct in this analysis, but the underlying and unreflected assumption remains that the self-management in civil society present before transition was not an instance of democracy in the absence of 'official institutions' and 'legal rules of the game' (1997: 158). Here we find the substitution of procedural, statist understanding of democracy for a self-managing and non-statist one, but without any acknowledgement that the latter is even a model of democracy at all.

This reassessment of the value of civil society in accordance with liberal democratic theory has been close to universal within the literature on democracy and civil society after 1989. Essentially, it involves the instrumentalisation of civil society as now merely supportive of statist liberal democracy, rather than as a site for democratic self-determination that it came to signify before 1989. Examples of this shift are numerous. Bibic and Graziano, for instance, write that the 'real or potential role of civil society with regard to democracy and democratization ... refers above all to political democratization and political democracy' (1994: ii). Bernhard likewise begins his analysis of civil society and democratic transition in Central–Eastern Europe with the assertion that modern democracy has

> only existed in conjunction with a civil society. It constitutes the sphere of autonomy from which political forces representing constellations of interests in society have contested state power. Civil society has been a necessary condition for the existence of representative government including democracy.
>
> (Bernhard 1993: 307)

Bernhard also declares that he will question whether civil society 'can be more than this'. Yet it becomes clear that his intention was never to examine the potentialities of civil society as a democratic end in itself, but merely to ponder whether, apart from its role in curtailing 'state autonomy and as a basis for interest representation', civil society might also assist 'the process of democratic consolidation and the transition to a market economy' (1993: 326). Serious questioning of whether civil society can be more than this requires throwing off the assumption that democracy takes place solely in the state – only then can civil society be considered in non-instrumental terms.

Indeed, this is precisely what theorists of democratic opposition before 1989 sought to do. *These* theorists, as we have seen, in addition to their calls for a more liberal politics of constraint on power, saw civil society as indicating a movement beyond statism. For control of power, while not unimportant, would be insufficient for the fundamental re-socialisation of power itself. If this was to be achieved, self-management in civil society was necessary. As Havel expressed it in 1979, 'the classic impotence of traditional democratic organisations' (which he elsewhere identified as parliamentary institutions) 'can only be overcome through the structures which 'naturally rise from *below* as a consequence of authentic self-organisation' (1985: 93). From a Hungarian perspective also, in the words of Konrád from the early 1980s:

> In Eastern Europe today, self-management is society's prime demand ...

> Workplace and local community self-government, based on personal contact, exercised daily, and always subject to correction, have greater attraction in our part of the world than multiparty representative democracy because, if they have their choice, people are not content with voting once every four years ... When there is parliamentary democracy but no self-administration, the political class alone occupies the stage.
>
> (1984: 137)

Konrád's Polish contemporary, Michnik, although he appeared to hark back to a civil society from the past, also emphasised self-management as the core of civil society:

> The essence of the spontaneously growing independent and self-governing Solidarity lay in the restoration of social ties [and] self-organisation ... For the first time in the history of communist rule in Poland 'civil society' was being restored ...
>
> (1985: 124)

Yet returning to the current debate about democratisation and to the starkly contrasting view of civil society that it contains, we look in vain for such possibilities to be considered. Ralf Dahrendorf, an influential commentator on the transitions of 1989 with thorough knowledge of events before transition, defines civil society as merely strategic to liberal democracy. He introduces civil society – which he notes only in passing had been an idea central to opposition thinking – as the key to pulling together 'the divergent time scales and dimensions of political and economic reform ... It is the ground in which both have to be anchored in order not to be blown away' (Dahrendorf 1990a: 93). Elsewhere, Dahrendorf has written similarly instrumentally that 'civil society is the common denominator of a functioning democracy and an effective market economy. It is only if and when civil society has been created that political and economic reform can be said to have credence' (Dahrendorf 1990b: 15).

Since Dahrendorf, Bernhard and others understand democracy as restricted to interest representation in a limited, liberal state, and because they view civil society as simply associational life outside the state, civil society is in a sense 'outside' democracy, it being of little consequence whether its movements are themselves democratic or not. Rather, civil society fulfils its role *vis-à-vis* democracy by representing interests to the state in a functionalist fashion. Examples abound of this functionalist approach. What makes civil society 'civil', writes Miller, 'is the fact that it is the locus where citizens freely organize themselves into ... associations ... in order to pressurize the formal bodies of state authority into adopting policies consonant with their perceived interests' (1992: 8). In another account, the 'basic function of civil society ... is to link the goals of the activity of the state with those of the independently structured population through different mechanisms of mediation' (Frentzel-Zagorska 1992: 41). To reiterate, while civil society is indispensable to the presence of pluralist interest representation to the state, there is no need for it to be at all democratic. This is why many such commentators warn of the dangers of 'uncivil society' and of the non-democratic elements of civil society (see Dahrendorf, 1990a: 96; Lewis 1993: 302; Hirst 1991: 222). From the standpoint of the democracy of civil society, of course, if associations are not democratic (understood in terms of self-management), then they are not part of civil society.

In keeping with seeing civil society as merely instrumental to liberal democracy, democratisation theory seeks to deny that action in civil society (beyond the 'transition' phase) is part of the democratic moment at all. This is in the sense that 'too much' popular participation in civil society is thought to be deleterious for democracy. For example, in apparent agreement with the opposition theorists who originally coined the term 'self-limiting revolution', Bozoki and Sukosd emphasise the importance of the self-limitation of popular movements, which they see as preserving human rights and as necessary because democracy is only possible if self-limitation becomes a '*collective experience* in society' (1993: 228). Yet Bozoki and Sukosd go on to reveal that their enthusiasm for self-limitation is less an endorsement of non-violent and post-statist politics (the realisation that the revolution 'devours its own children'), which was what the oppositionists had in mind, and more like antipathy to a mobilised citizenry per se, which was precisely what the oppositionists called for. 'The role of society in democratic transition', they write, 'is vital, nevertheless it is primarily symbolic ... there is no need for constant mass political mobilization' (1993: 229). Reinforcing the impression of a basically elitist outlook, Bozoki and Sukosd ask, 'How could the masses that through the program of civil society had originally been mobilized ... be demobilized?' Although they concede that the demobilization of civil society and the rise of political society (political parties) has turned out 'only too well', Bozoki and Sukosd's preference for a civil society that encourages high levels of participation only *prior* to regime transition is already clear (1993: 233).

Bozoki and Sukosd are not alone in this regard. Dahrendorf also wants to downplay the participatory aspects of civil society that the earlier oppositionists sought variously to encourage. For Dahrendorf:

> A civil society is civil, even civilized, and this requires men and women who respect others, but more important still, who are able and willing to go and do things themselves ... I do not particularly like notions like 'active citizenship', which seems to place all the emphasis on the obligations associated with membership of society ... civic virtues are indispensable but [so is] self-reliance.
>
> (1990a: 99)

The perennial liberal fear of an 'over-mobilized' society that lurks behind

Dahrendorf's statement here is even more starkly present in Lewis's account of the dangers of an unmediated civil society:

> The apparent victory of civil society over communist dictatorship might be construed as leading less to political democracy than to populism, referring to the direct political dominance of 'the people' with little regard to constitutional arrangements, the institutional mediation of power relations or any protection of minority rights. It is an outcome seen in societies not dissimilar to those of Eastern Europe, where political processes have been, at least initially, relatively unconstrained ... The desires and aspirations of a greater fraction of society might indeed be better satisfied by the arrangements of such a political order – but this is not the same thing as the establishment of political democracy.
>
> (1993: 301–2)

Although differently from the liberal theory that those such as Dahrendorf and Lewis provide, even radical theory has contributed to the widespread rejection of the self-management vision of civil society. Typical here is that influential figure of the New Left, Habermas, who has claimed that 'the public opinion that is worked up via democratic procedures into communicative power cannot "rule" of itself, but can only point the use of administrative power in specific directions ...' (1994: 9). Following Habermas in his hostility to autonomy in civil society, for example, is Miller, who understands 'self-restraint' in civil society as involving the recognition of 'the imperative of specialized expertise for the exercise of governmental policy-formation and regulation' (1992: 8).

Civil society as the property of liberal democracy

Against the model of civil society that sought a new and more participatory way for democracy beyond that of state-socialism and statist liberal democracy, civil society is now seen as the exclusive property of liberal democracy. Curry, for example, concludes her study of the 'realities of civil society in the light of post-communist society' by asking:

> What are the necessary ... conditions making institutions of democracy/pluralism like 'civil society' work a la the Western model? ... How do local groupings build a base for and encourage the development of a national level 'civil society' that also works in the way Western democracies work?
>
> (1994: 247)

That civil society is increasingly viewed as fully present only within liberal democratic societies is revealed also by an increasingly common cluster of assumptions as to why Eastern European countries apparently do not possess civil society after all. One such assumption is that civil society requires a pluralist political culture that is simply not present in the region. This is what Sztompka (1991) argues via the accusation of 'civilizational incompetence' on the part of post-communist countries; which is an analysis similar to the one provided by Tarkowska and Tarkowski (1991) under the rubrics 'amoral familism' and 'privatized society'. And in an edition of the journal *Democratization*, Tempest refers to Hann's report into the 'ingrained apathy and suspicion of all outsiders' in rural Hungary, which Tempest sees as being 'in contradistinction to the pluralist civil society theme' (1997: 137). Questioning the analyses of these commentators – some of whom are anthropologists with wide experience of the societies within which they live and work – is not the point here (and Tempest himself is rightly critical of the implicit projection of 'civilizational competence' onto Western society). However, quite apart from the detail of research findings is the impression given by these analysts that they are investigating whether it is possible for civil society to exist in the culture or not. Clearly, for them, civil society is about the sociology of liberal, pluralist polities, rather than a more or less universal space for democratic action such as the opposition theorists of civil society had in mind. This is apparent when Tempest, for example, talks of the crisis of 'civil society' also in the West: '[T]he middle class is in the process of disintegration and [thus] *the principal social requisite for civil society* is in dissolution' (1997: 139, emphasis added).

Other interlocutors also question whether the label 'civil society' is appropriate to Eastern Europe. Lewis's particular concern is that the earlier equation of civil society in the region with social movements obscures the following problematic:

> These [movements] were often not conducive either to general processes of democratization or to the development of the multi-party systems that are the prime institutional expression of modern representative democracy. They were, to varying degrees, inclusive and relatively undifferentiated forms of organisation ... not so far removed from ... Marxist resistance to pluralism ... These movements were ... not well suited to one of the core processes of modern democracy ... that of interest representation.
>
> (1993: 302–3)

Lewis's problematic is that organisations such as Solidarity did not constitute 'a process of representation in any way related to the articulation and pursuit of interests observed in developed western democracies' (1993: 303). He thereby makes it quite clear that the only relationship between civil society and democracy that he is able to envisage is premised on actually existing liberal democracy in which civil society is limited to promoting interest representation in the state.

Another proposition concerning liberal democratic civil society that sets it apart from its radical alternatives is that it is not understood as a realm of substantive citizen equality (viewed as a primitive form of equality), but only of formal political equality:

> The vision of civil society that the anticommunist opposition in Central and Eastern Europe used in its fight for liberty has lost out as a social program. The moral civil society ... could endure as a viable ideal only so long as it remained unencumbered by the need to make real choices. Actual postcommunist civil society ... is challenging the egalitarian outlook that numerous opinion surveys have shown to be deeply rooted in the minds of Central and East Europeans.
>
> (Smolar 1996: 37)

Going further, Smolar moves on to argue that civil society is the basis of private property and of the market economy itself. Having stated that, 'The major problem facing postcommunist societies is how to relegitimate private property and the open society with all the uncertainty that accompanies them', Smolar looks to civil society to provide 'the moral foundations of private property' since 'the civic principle is not just a principle of equality; it also creates the normative basis for the integration of civil society as well as its integration with the political system' (1996: 37–8; cf. Federowicz 1993: 98).

The argument that civil society is a precondition of a successful market economy is also reversed in many accounts – in other words, it is claimed that marketisation is itself a precondition of a mature civil society. An extreme version of this argument is made by Narojek (1994: 15), who sees the reconstruction of civil society as necessitating the exclusion from the sphere of democratic decision-making of the option of going back on market reform. Morawski, in a more moderate fashion, also sees the 'transformation into a mature civil society' as possible 'only when economic changes make marketization and property changes [towards the consolidation of private property] effective' (1993: 110). Korbonski, too, is persuaded that 'in the absence of a private economic sphere or a competitive market economy, it makes little sense to talk about civil society, whose dependence on the market has been emphasized by many scholars' (1994: 222). The complacent identification of civil society with capitalistic forms of economic organisation, offered largely without justification and as an accomplished fact, once again reveals the lack of critical content to this whole discourse on civil society.

Returning to where we started, the core assumption concerning civil society and democracy is that democracy is a process that occurs at the level of the state, thus effectively emasculating self-organisation in civil society. Such an assumption also makes the legitimacy of the state an unquestioned aspect of the liberal democratic approach to civil society theory, where, by contrast, it constituted the central problematic for the radical model. Bibic, for example, begins his work on democracy and civil society by first outlining Schumpeter and Lipset's proceduralist models of political democracy and, second, by baldly concurring with O'Donnell and Schmitter that political democracy 'is *the* goal of the recent democratic revolutions and debates' (Bibic 1994: 45). Actually, as we have seen, earlier debates about civil society in the region characterized the mechanisms of the state and democracy as in many ways antithetical to one another. Some of the theorists in question, Michnik in particular, conceded that a limited state was necessary because maximal self-management would lead to society becoming over-politicised once again (and also because the notion of the withering away of the state was considered utopian). But they were little able to recommend the state as positive for the democratic ordering of society, which was why civil society became so central to their democratic theory and not just to their oppositional tactics.

Since 1989, however, the positive role of the state *vis-à-vis* civil society is emphasized repeatedly. In some accounts, it is the democratisation of the state that constitutes civil society in the first place: 'Civil society is a society of citizens, and this notion is more or less equivalent to political democracy' (Ehrlich 1994: ix). More generally, the state's legitimacy, contra earlier models and reflecting the influence of liberal contract theory, is simply not open for discussion at all (unlike civil society, which must be legitimised from above). Thus 'Sovereign state power may be considered an indispensable condition for the democratization of civil society', writes Lewis (1993: 302). In agreement, Bernhard states that for societal agents

> to constitute a civil society they need the sanction of the state; the public space must be guaranteed as a realm of freedom from the state by the state itself ... Barring this, a liberated public space would be but an anarchy of competing interests.
>
> (1993: 309)

Bernhard uses this argument to support the notion that the Polish democratic opposition, while establishing 'important landmarks in the self-liberation of civil society ... fell short of a full reconstruction of civil society [itself] ... This was because the Polish party-state had still made no de jure recognition of the opposition, its right to exist, or the boundaries or of the public space it had carved out' (1993: 315). On this highly statist reading, again offered with absolutely no attempt at normative justification, civil society only comes into being once the state legalises its associations and movements. It is the gift of the state to bestow the status of civil society; the legitimating move is the state's and the state's alone. Thus Dahrendorf asks, 'Can one *build* a civil society ... ?' Citizenship certainly can be built, he muses, it is simply a 'matter of legislation and supporting policies' (1990a: 96).

Finally, the liberal democratic vision of civil society appears to have fundamentally influenced even those more radical theorists who, though they no longer stand by their earlier models, are still concerned with civil society's radical potentialities. The evolution of Arato's work is instructive here. In his original analysis of the Polish model of civil society in 1981, Arato was optimistic about the possibilities for greater self-management in all spheres that the strategy of putting 'civil society first' held out. He was also convinced of the need for the Western liberal democracies to be transformed through an encounter with a radical civil society. Yet in a 1994 analysis of *The Rise, Decline and Reconstruction of the Concept of Civil Society and Directions for Future Research*, Arato ends up in a not dissimilar place to the theorists of democratisation examined above. That is, his focus is now limited to the question of what civil society can do for liberal democracy in terms of extending its legitimacy and deepening its democratic practices.

Arato concludes his study by highlighting a number of issues of importance for a theory of civil society. These include, first, the problem of democratic legitimacy: civil society is seen to make a contribution here in terms of extending the legitimacy of parliamentary politics through providing networks for participation. In addition, Arato calls for further exploration of the possible role of civil society in 'constitution making, in the stability of constitutions, and in the development of constitutional patriotism' (1994: 15). He finishes by stating that:

> I certainly do not think that these ... areas of research are the only ones relevant to those who wish to turn the theory of civil society into a more differentiated set of analytical instruments, more intellectually plausible for the decades ahead.
>
> (Arato 1994: 16)

Thus while Arato is more aware than most of the various possibilities presented by civil society for democracy, in the final analysis he too now turns to the concept as an analytical tool with which to explore how existing liberal democracy might be improved. This project is some distance removed from his original enthusiasm for a democracy of civil society that held out the prospect of a new form of politics altogether.[1]

6 Civil society and theories of democratisation in Latin America[1]

The democratic transitions that swept away military regimes throughout much of Latin America in the 1980s caught academic observers by surprise. Previously, these observers had had to explain the *failure* of political democracy in the region, rather than its apparent success (Remmer 1991: 479). Dominating the field, consequently, was a whole range of structuralist models that accounted for Latin America's authoritarian politics as variously due to low levels of modernisation in the region which therefore had a weak middle class; authoritarian values inherited from Iberian colonialism and Catholicism; excessive political demands from the popular forces in the absence of developed institutions; and economic dependency between core and periphery. When democratisation occurred without any of these structural conditions changing to a significant degree, structuralist paradigms were at once robbed of their predictive power and also rendered largely obsolete for the new task of explanation.

Civil society and democratic transition

The most widespread response to the breakdown of the structuralist paradigms in the mid–late 1980s was 'the retreat into voluntarism' (Remmer 1991: 483). Instead of trying to explain democratisation in terms of long-term processes of change, this portion of the literature, particularly O'Donnell and Schmitter's seminal volume *Transitions from Authoritarian Rule* (1986), disavowed determinism in favour of an open-ended account of the role of 'key actors' during the transition period. 'Transition', these authors wrote, 'is that terrain where the unpredictable combination of *virtu* on the part of leaders, and *fortuna* in the combination of circumstances, may make the crucial difference' (1986: 17).

Within this largely voluntaristic early literature on Latin America's democratic transitions, there was little emphasis placed on the role of civil society in democratisation. Of course, the sphere of civil society, however defined, was not of paramount importance to theorists with an elite-centric focus. Non-state actors, on such accounts, merely form the backdrop to transition, as can be seen when O'Donnell and Schmitter begin their chapter entitled 'Resurrecting civil society (and restructuring public space)' by claiming that:

> elite dispositions, calculations, and pacts ... *largely determine* whether or not an opening will occur at all and ... they set important perimeters on the extent of possible liberalization and eventual democratization. Once something has happened [within the elite] ... a generalized mobilization is likely to occur, which we choose to describe as the 'resurrection of civil society'.
>
> (1986: 49, emphasis added)

The understanding of civil society as a generalised mobilisation that only appears once the elites are already travelling along the road to transition subsequently became the dominant one in the literature. Stepan, for example, also writes of 'the civil society that emerged once liberalization began' (1989: vii). As in the literature on Eastern European transitions, this sense of civil society as a 'popular upsurge', or as 'pressure from below', is a largely instrumentalist one – instrumental, that is, to transition in the state to liberal democracy. The associations and movements of civil society are not celebrated as democratic ends in themselves, but only in as much as their 'heroic, exemplary actions' provide the conditions for elites, or rather for reformers within elite circles, to negotiate these transitions. 'The importance of civil society's resurrection cannot be exaggerated', states O'Donnell, since this 'mobilization and the intense demands it places upon all political actors greatly strengthen the position of the democratic opposition' (1989: 67).

The link between democratic theory that sees democracy as occurring only in the state and a similarly state-orientated view of civil society is important here. In an example of this approach, Linz and Stepan claim that:

> Democracy is about an open contest for state power by means of elections and the oversight and control of state power by the representatives of the people ... Therefore, by definition, civil society must consider how it can make a contribution to the democratic control of military, police, and intelligence systems.
>
> (1989: 51)

Understanding civil society's contribution exclusively in terms of a 'popular upsurge' during transition means that, while it is heralded as vital to this particular stage of opposition, there are doubts expressed about its uses after transition. Analysts of transition generally fear that 'excessive' political mobilisation by the popular classes would be damaging to the political stability of the new democracies:

> [H]istorical experience in Latin America underscores the importance of ... demobilization [of mass actors], given that no stable political

> democracy has resulted from regime transitions in which mass actors have gained control, even momentarily, over traditional ruling classes. The double paradox that emerges from this pattern of mobilization is that the political significance of the popular sectors may actually be greater *prior* to the restoration of a democratic regime – and this may actually be good for democracy!
>
> (Oxhorn 1994: 50)

O'Donnell is another analyst who, for the sake of democratic 'consolidation', does not regret the 'demobilization of society' and the re-emergence of parties 'as the main interlocutors of the government' (1989: 72). Since O'Donnell does not see political parties as part of civil society, there is a sense in which civil society itself ceases to have any importance for him after transition. Here he places far more weight on the consolidation of liberal political institutions than popular mobilisation, for the latter is believed, following Huntington and the Political Development school, to have led to earlier breakdowns of parliamentary democracy (Hagopian 1993: 480). According to this model, the only tangible contribution that civil society can make to democratic consolidation is by restraining its demands (Pearce 1997: 60). This is self-limitation in the sense of handing back the political reins to the state, the notion of self-limitation as necessary to ongoing self-management could not be further from it.

A further implication of the statist approach to civil society is that, as in the literature on Eastern European transitions, the character of civil society groups themselves is of little or no interest to theorists of transition, so long as they can provide a 'general upsurge' during transition and acquiescence during consolidation. Paradoxically, because civil society is articulated as logically distinct from democracy in this way, there appears to be no good reason why non-state associational life should be equated with 'civil' society in the first place, as quite uncivil groups can adequately play the role of providing a 'general upsurge' (Pearce 1997: 62).

Given their thesis that civil society only emerges 'once something happens' within the authoritarian elite, elite-centric theorists actually have difficulty accounting for the origins of transitions at all. Why would splits within a regime take on a democratising momentum if there were no pressure from social forces for this to be so? In a somewhat self-contradictory turn, O'Donnell and Schmitter attempt to get round this problem by pointing to the importance of civil society's role in eroding the normative and intellectual basis of authoritarian regimes (O'Donnell and Schmitter 1986: 51). (Interestingly, this is a role identified by civil society activists for themselves in the Gramscian terms of counter-hegemony – though in this instance without the statist teleology informing theories of democratic transition.) In effect, O'Donnell and Schmitter thereby admit the importance of regime legitimacy or, rather, its absence. Ultimately, however, as Przeworski observes, 'the "loss of legitimacy" theory is an "up" theory of regime transition', because it suggests that a regime's crisis of legitimacy occurs initially in civil society, and that it is only when this crisis becomes apparent that the ruling bloc responds (Przeworski 1986: 50). In this case, mass unrest or non-compliance should be observable *before* liberalisation begins. This lack of coherence within elite-centric accounts stems from their failure to allow for instances in which popular pressure itself leads directly to a process of liberalisation. In arguing that civil society only resurrects 'once the government signals that it is lowering the costs for engaging in collective action and is permitting some contestation on issues previously declared off limits', civil society is portrayed as purely reactive. The best that can be said for it is that it 'performs the role of pushing the transition further than it *would otherwise have gone*' (O'Donnell and Schmitter 1986: 47, 56, emphasis added).

Essentially, the problem is one of the narrow focus – that of the transition period alone – that these theorists have. If civil society is primarily experienced as a 'popular upsurge', then it should be unsurprising that we find it taking place when the state begins to liberalise. But this is to ignore the fact that in at least some countries in the region (e.g. Chile), the movements and associations that are recognised as carrying out the 'upsurge' were formed long before transition and, indeed, arose during the period of severest repression. It is the apparent indeterminacy of the transition period that encourages this exclusive focus on the outcomes of upsurges; exploring the conditions necessary for the emergence of groups and movements that actually carry them out would require the reintroduction of structural variables that take more seriously the relationship between civil society and the state.

In the final analysis, the indeterminacy thesis has been dominant in accounts of Latin America's democratic transitions because theory building has been thrown into crisis by these very transitions themselves. A harsh reading would be that the description of events as entirely undetermined is to all practical purposes an admission of theoretical inadequacy: 'We describe events as unpredictable, random, and idiosyncratic when we have no way of explaining them' (Remmer 1991: 485). In keeping with this paradigm crisis, the analysts of transition do not adequately theorise civil society. Their inability to explain where the civil society that they identify came from is obscured by a pervasive elite-centrism that largely overlooks action in civil society in the first place.

Civil society and democratic consolidation

The more recent literature on democratic consolidation in Latin America engages with the concept of civil society to a greater degree than the literature on transition, dominated as the latter is by the elite-centric perspective. However, despite the increasing number of references to civil society, it is just as true of the discourse of consolidation that civil society is seen solely in terms of its function for liberal democracy. Indeed, the very term 'consolidation' should alert us to continuity with the 'transition' approach, since the implication is that the task for democrats is merely to safeguard the establishment of formal liberal democratic institutions in the state. The word consolidation implies that the desired ends have been achieved and that the sustainability of these ends is all that matters for the future.

Diamond and Linz provide a typical example of the way in which civil society is understood as having an important role to play in achieving democratic consolidation:

> Just as democracy requires an effective but limited state, so it needs a pluralistic, autonomously organized civil society to check the power of the state and give expression democratically to popular interests ... there is a strong correlation between the strength and autonomy of associational life and the presence and vitality of democracy.
>
> (1989: 35)

Jelin echoes this view of civil society by arguing that 'the hard task of demanding, persuading, prompting, and policing [the state] falls to the makers of civic society' (1995: 92). Civil society is thus afforded far more significance here than in transition; however, it is nonetheless pictured only in relation to the liberal democratic state. All of the strengths of civil society listed by Diamond, Linz and Jelin connect to its role in either counterbalaning the state or increasing the state's effectiveness in representing interests. In short, these authors are a long way from the self-management agenda of the theorists of civil society from Latin America in the 1980s, who, like their Eastern European counterparts, turned away from politics directed at the state towards the democracy of self-organisation in civil society:

> This radically democratic and collectivist attitude ... demonstrate[s] the emergence of the will to renewal on the part of civil society which rejects the notion that the 'political opening' remains at the level of *re*democratization, based on liberal-individualist principles which in the past safeguarded social injustice, class inequality, and traditional bourgeois domination.
>
> (Cardoso, cited in Stepan 1989: 323)

Cardoso's summary of the earlier radical approach to civil society reminds us that, contrary to the impression given in the democratisation discourse, many activists in civil society did not see civil society in terms of liberal democratic transitions at all. Yet so focused are theorists of democratisation on the transition to, and consolidation of, liberal democracy in the state, that they are quite willing to see civil society's activism sacrificed for a world made safe for such a democracy. Thus, although the literature on consolidation (unlike that on transition) includes the call for civil society to police the state, it is implied strongly that civil society activity should not be system threatening. Valenzuela, for example, although he agrees with O'Donnell and Schmitter that restraint by civil society is useful for transition, does not call, as these authors do, for civil society effectively to be demobilised after transition. On the contrary, he sees pressure from civil society as desirable for democratic consolidation. However, according to Valenzuela, this pressure should fall within the 'demand–processing–settlement' criteria. This includes:

> the establishment, expansion, or recreation of popular and other associations to voice demands and negotiate some resolution to them, with leaders who have the necessary legitimacy and support to be able to call off demonstrations and other collective actions.
>
> (1992: 86)

In other words, Valenzuela is happy to support demands coming from civil society, but only to the extent that these do not cause significant disruption to the status quo or call into question society's wider power settlement. Indeed, Valenzuela continues by arguing that 'these settlements are most adequate to facilitate democratic consolidation when they are perceived by all those concerned to operate with a minimum of politicization' (1992: 86).

Allocating civil society a purely technical (or means directed) rather than political (or ends directed) function is fundamentally tied up here with an elitism that dramatically constrains what it is possible for agents in civil society to question:

> In brief, democratic consolidation is favoured if social conflicts and demands are handled through predictable and broadly accepted procedures that are inclusive of all the relevant groups but are, at the same time, insulated within the narrowest possible boundaries in terms of the specificity of the issues and the state, political and social actors who are involved.
>
> (Valenzuela 1992: 86–7)

This idea that the contribution of civil society is to further interest representation in the state is by far the dominant one in the literature on consolidation. Schmitter (1995), in a recent collection on the consolidation of democracy in Latin America, doubts whether social movements have 'determined either the degree of consolidation or the type of democracy'. What he will allow, though, is that, nevertheless, these movements 'have broadened and complicated the policy agenda of most new democracies'. Schmitter believes that many social movements will decline as their demands are met and also because they will 'have trouble focusing on subsequent issues' (1995: 24). He seems to have missed the non-instrumental character of many new social movements established in the 1970s and 1980s – such as neighbourhood associations in the *favelas* and women's groups – which were not orientated towards the state and which did not seek to make demands on it in the first place. Indeed, the self-understanding of many of these groups was that autonomy from statist politics (including political parties) was their very *raison d'être*. Although the co-option of some social movements by political parties has been a feature of the 1990s, this is hardly the same thing as demand settlement.

A striking feature of the instrumental view of civil society here is that it overlooks the possibility, held up by the radical model, that civil society can provide spaces for political participation and, indeed, itself constitutes the public sphere. As Weffort put it, 'The discovery of the value of democracy is inseparable, within the opposition, from the discovery of civil society as a political space' (1989: 345). The possibility, as outlined by Weffort and others, that political life can take place outside the state escapes most contemporary theorists of consolidation. The editors of one volume, for example, ask whether 'civil society is adequately connected through political parties and other channels of representation to the evolving political debates' (Mainwaring *et al.* 1992: 4). The implication here is that publicity occurs in the state and that civil society, unless otherwise connected with this, the 'true' public space, is relatively apolitical. Even where civil society is seen as a space for politics in the literature on consolidation, it is implied, by Reilly for example, that it constitutes only a school for citizenship. Thus while, in a Toquevillian manner, 'opportunities for negotiation, competition, contained conflict and the search for consensus' (Reilly 1995: 264) are found in civil society, these experiences implicitly count only as a 'dry run' for politics proper at a state level. Here the emphasis is upon the contribution civil society can make to a democratic political culture, not to political participation itself (as with the radical model).

From these perspectives, non-state associations, given their relatively weak institutionalisation and their 'micro' outlook, are simply not very important to an understanding of the political. Such an academic focus systematically masks the many ways in which less institutionalised political movements are often both more effective and more legitimate as far as non-elites are concerned. Within Latin America, a good example here would once again be the many new social movements that arose in the 1980s, especially the neighbourhood groups. In terms of collective provision for basic needs and of providing opportunities for political participation, these movements succeeded where the state in Latin America – whether 'democratised' or not – has almost always failed.

The minimalist approach to democracy

Why then do analysts of Latin American democratisation processes have so little time for civil society in their accounts of transition, and why do they offer a purely instrumental conception of civil society in discussing democratic 'consolidation'? It could be argued that these theorists have been influenced in restricting civil society's role by the theory of moderation, which has grown out of events in Latin America (such as the Chilean coup of 1973), where radical popular action provoked a reactionary backlash. However, Bermeo

(1997) argues that if theorists of the Latin American transitions chose to look further afield, to Portugal and Spain for example, they would see that transitions *can* survive radical pressures from below and even radical provisional governments. In fact, it is actually necessary to look no further than these analysts' theory of democracy in order to explain in large part their conceptualisations of civil society.

For there is a clear relationship between the eclipse of the view that civil society represents the possibility of a sphere for democracy in its own right, and the dominance of the statist approach that sees democracy as present only within liberal democratic institutions. To put this point another way, the one feature that most accounts of transition and consolidation have in common is a minimalist notion of democracy as a form of government constituted by practices extant in Western liberal democracies. Of particular significance here is Dahl's notion of 'polyarchy'. Defined by Dahl as the 'highest feasible attainment of the democratic process in the government of a country', polyarchy expects no more of democracy than that there be a universal spread of citizenship rights – these being identified narrowly as 'the right to oppose and vote out the highest officials in the government' (1989: 220, 222).

The degree of acceptance of Dahl's proceduralist or anti-substantive model of democracy is remarkable. Diamond and Linz, for example, use polyarchy as the benchmark for the democracies studied in their volume on Latin American transitions (1989: xvi). Similarly, Whitehead, claiming that 'Dahl's observations apply with special force to Latin America', describes his 'litmus test' for democracy as being captured by the questions: 'How does a purportedly democratic regime treat those held in its prisons?' and 'Would we describe the regime as sufficiently democratic to qualify as a leading western democracy' (Whitehead 1989: 77). In the same volume of works on Latin America, Huntington – announcing that the ultimate cynic of democratic theory, Schumpeter, 'has won' – celebrates the 'prevailing effort ... to make democracy less of a hurrah word and more of a common sense word. Democracy has a useful meaning only when it is defined in institutional terms ... [t]he key institution [being] the selection of leaders through competitive elections' (Huntington 1989: 15). The highly tautological aspect of these arguments is revealed when we consider that institutions such as Huntington's 'selection of leaders through competitive elections', or Whitehead's humane treatment of prisoners, must be considered democratic for reasons of certain of democracy's characteristics or core values. That is, there must be *reasons* advanced for why certain practices are taken to be democratic in the first place. Yet once these values have been identified, presumably it is possible to imagine their realisation (whether to a greater or lesser degree) in and through institutions *other* than those of liberal democracy.

This critical approach leaves open discursive space for the radical model of a democracy in civil society too, but it is effectively closed off in the democratisation literature where we find, for example, a major collection which acknowledges that, 'The essays in this book attach their conception of democratic consolidation to a minimal and procedural definition of democracy' (Mainwaring *et al.* 1992: 5). Similarly, Valenzuela's work on 'Consolidation in post transition settings', begins with a defence of Dahl's definition of democracy, arguing that, 'the notion of democratic consolidation should ... be linked ... to a minimalist, not a maximalist conception of democracy'. Drawing on Schumpeter's notion of competitive democracy, Valenzuela debunks 'participatory' models as simply 'inadequate' (1992: 60). Mainwaring, in the same volume of works on consolidation, also accepts that Schumpeter's focus on electoral competition amongst political elites and parties has 'prevailed'. Mainwaring adds only universal suffrage to this Schumpeterian framework (which he terms the 'participation' element), arriving thereby back at Dahl's definition of polyarchy (1992: 297).

In fitting with these statist approaches to democracy, more substantive definitions are rejected in the democratisation discourse for applying democracy to spheres where it supposedly does not belong. 'Democratization', claims Stepan, 'refers fundamentally to the relationship between the State and civil society' (1989: ix). For Pastor, democracy 'is impossible if the government exercises complete control over the economy' (1989: 18). Diamond and Linz also see democracy as 'political' in the narrowest sense of the word:

> We use the term 'democracy' ... to signify a political system separate and apart from the economic and social system to which it is joined ... Indeed ... [we] insist that issues of so-called economic and social democracy be separated from the question of governmental structure.
> (1989: xvi)

Accordingly, alternative perspectives on democracy tend to be reduced to a crude caricature of 'totalitarian democracy' premised upon the domination of the 'general will': '[S]ubstantive views of democracy', Lamounier writes, 'often appear associated with more or less utopian conceptions of "participatory" democracy, aiming to replace or subordinate representation to a more "authentic" expression of the people's will' (1989: 15).

At points, this antipathy to participatory or self-managing democracy manifests itself as something approximating hostility to popular sovereignty itself. Mainwaring, for example, is so concerned with protecting 'political expertise' and property, and with warding off the 'tyranny of the majority', that he basically ends up removing majoritarian decision-making altogether from his vision of a democratic polity. Criticising Przeworski's claim that democracy represents 'institutionalized uncertainty', Mainwaring raises the spectre of workers, for example, voting to nationalize the means of production:

> However, even if workers did vote to nationalize the means of production,

> this fact in itself would have no legal effect ... in democratic regimes, because it is not generally workers who make this kind of decision, but rather executives and legislatures functioning in well-defined institutional and legal structures. Workers help elect those who decide, but modern mass democracy is representative democracy, not direct democracy.
>
> (Mainwaring 1992: 313)

More typically, the issue of democracy in spheres other than that of the state is simply deemed unimportant. 'I do not [believe] that associations ... are models of participatory democracy. Nor do I believe that small-group democracy is necessary to maintain democratic politics on the national level', states Levine in one example (1989: 280).

Thus the model of the democracy of civil society that Cardoso described as recently as 1983 seems already to belong to a different epoch:

> [One] version of why Brazil is breaking with authoritarianism combines a radical vision of autonomy of civil society with a socialist critique of social domination ... *Real* democratization will arrive ... as it is crystallised in the spontaneous solidarity of the disinherited. It lives as *comunitas*, experiences of common hardship which form a collective *we* based on the same life experience that is transformed only when, through molecular changes, the simultaneous isolation of the State and the exploiters – which will perish at the same time – comes about.
>
> (translated in Stepan 1989: 313)

Indeed, even those more substantive conceptualisations of civil society that do surface in the literature on democratisation in Latin America seem to have lost touch with earlier radical approaches. Przeworski, for example, adheres to the Gramscian notion that loss of legitimacy for the powers in the state only comes about through the organization of counter-hegemony ('collective projects for an alternative future') (1992: 107). Nevertheless, Przeworski still talks exclusively of civil society in terms of the 'transition game', never mentioning the model of civil society that looks to practice democratic self-organisation outside the state. In this sense, Przeworski retains an essentially statist perspective that also involves forgetting the importance of self-limitation; namely, he focuses on how civil society can transform existing power in the state, risking, in the process, the revolution 'that devours its own children'.

Huber is similar to Przeworski in adopting, by her own admission, a Gramscian definition of civil society as, 'the totality of social institutions and associations, both formal and informal, that are not strictly production-related nor governmental or familial in character' (Huber 1995: 172). Yet despite viewing the density of civil society as reflecting the extent and degree of autonomy of the subordinate classes (any other form of civil society, for Huber, is just a 'conduit for the dominant ideology'), Huber too defines civil society only in relation to the state – that is, as deciding the extent to which these subordinate classes have power *vis-à-vis* the state. Thus both Huber and Przeworski do not conceive of civil society as substantially autonomous; they take a Gramscian approach, but not in the sense of using Gramsci's political method (counter-hegemony in civil society) to move beyond Gramsci's more Marxist concern with achieving power in the state.

The taming of the idea of civil society

Part III has demonstrated that, though hidden behind a smokescreen of scientific objectivity, the normative setting of models of civil society in the academic discourse on democratisation is a liberal democratic one. There is thus a pervasive sense that civil society both cannot and should not reach beyond its role as a support structure for actually existing democracy at the state level. This largely uncritical attachment to the democracy that is over the democracy that might be reflects either an implicit acceptance of the thesis that liberal democracy represents the 'end of history' or, to put it bluntly, an elitist fear of 'too much' democracy.

The democratisation literature is obfuscatory about the other values and institutions, apart from those of democracy, with which it is also very much concerned. In analysing conceptualisations of civil society within this literature, these values are revealed more clearly. They include, first, a pervasive 'hierarchism', defined by Blaug as the belief that effective political action requires 'a hierarchy of command, centralized control and the institutionalization of roles of expertise and leadership' (2000: 387). This is seen in the exclusive focus upon the formal institutions of the state as the sphere of politics and democracy 'proper' and the instrumentalisation of organisation in civil society to this end (both of which contrast with our radical's emphasis on localism and horizontal organisational forms). Second, there is close to universal acceptance of the neoliberal case that economic liberalisation and democratisation are inseparable processes and an attendant concern with the role of civil society in the entrenchment of private property and free markets. Contra our radical model, little or no consideration is given to the ways in which the distribution of economic power might undermine or threaten civil society, even if state power has been formally democratised. Third, we find a widespread belief in the necessity of 'limiting' politics, which results in calls for the demobilisation of participatory civil society after 'transition' and for the routinisation of politics in the state. This concern with the domestication of politics is echoed in the notion that civil society is made up exclusively of pluralist interests and allegiances that cross-cut one another, civil society thereby being presented, against the position defined by our radical theorists, as antithetical to the articulation of (counter)-hegemonical popular action.

Above all, it is the transformatory ethos of the radical models of civil society from the 1970s and 1980s that has led to them being overshadowed. For, indisputably, the realism on offer from liberal democratic theorists of civil society does a good job of telling us what democratisation currently means in practice, although this is conflated with what democratisation *ought* to mean. The normative content of the liberal democratic model thus obscured, alternatives to the status quo are scarcely considered; civil society is something that we already possess, not an ideal to which we should aspire. It is the apparent loss of this critical edge to the theory of civil society in particular which should cause disquiet.

However, before we rush to consign radical visions of civil society to the dustbin of history, we should turn our attention to more recent disruptions to the liberal democratic hegemony in this area. Liberal democratic theory may have 'tamed' accounts of civil society and democracy within the nation-state, but, increasingly, theorists and activists are asking what role civil society might play in *global* democratisation. It is to these new alternatives to the domesticated civil society of liberal democracy that we turn next.

Part IV

New alternatives?

7 Models of global civil society

> There are at least three major types of institutions which comprise the emergent global civil society: formal organisations linking national institutions (organisations of parties, churches, unions, professions, educational bodies, media *etc.*); linkages of informal networks and movements (*e.g.*, of women's, gay and peace groups and movements); and globalist organisations (*e.g.*, Amnesty, Greenpeace, Médecins sans Frontiéres) which are established with a specifically global orientation, global membership and activity of global scope.
>
> (Shaw 1994a: 650)

Against the thoroughly domesticated reading of civil society in democratisation theory, in the field of international relations theory civil society has recently become the focus of a more ambitiously transformatory, and also less nation-state-orientated, political vision. Thus for some theorists, global civil society represents nothing less than the outline of a future world political order within which states will no longer constitute the seat of sovereignty, a status first bestowed on them in Europe by the Treaty of Westphalia (1648) and subsequently exported around the globe. Richard Falk, for example, suggests that global civil society 'recasts our understanding of sovereignty' as 'the modernist stress on territorial sovereignty as the exclusive basis for political community and identity [is] displaced both by more local and distinct groupings and by association with the reality of a global civil society without boundaries' (Falk 1995: 100). Lipschutz also sees the transnational political networks put in place by actors in civil society as 'challenging, from below, the nation-state system'. Indeed, 'the growth of global civil society represents an ongoing project of civil society to reconstruct, re-imagine, or re-map world politics' (Lipschutz 1992: 391). The factors enabling such a role for global civil society are identified by Lipschutz as the 'fading away' of anarchy among states in an increasingly norm-governed global system; the functional inability of states to address certain welfare problems; and the growth of new forms of non-statist social and political identity such as are provided by human rights and environmental groups, for example (1992: 392).

Few projections of such a post-Westphalian order assume that the state will cease to be an important actor in global politics, however. More nuanced accounts see the emergence of global civil society as in part a response to the transformation of state power, rather than simply its erosion. Along these lines Shaw argues that the appearance of global civil society is at once a reaction to *and* a source of pressure for the globalisation of state power, which exists *de facto* in the 'complex of global state institutions [that] is coming into existence through the fusion of Western state power and the legitimation framework of the United Nations' (Shaw 1994a: 650). Köhler also suggests that 'the transnationalization of civil society activities is intrinsically related to the state's increasing commitment to intergovernmental cooperation' (1998: 233). Yet this very process also undermines the Westphalian order of state sovereignty in that 'once legitimacy and recognition are granted to transnational coalitions, interest aggregation and policy formulation ... cease to be *national* affairs, subject to the indivisible loyalty requested by the state' (Köhler 1998: 246). Extant global civil society is then, it seems, both an outcome of and a stimulus for the transformation of the states' system. The question is: Can it be more than this? In particular: Can it serve as a constituent part of, even a means to, a democratised world order?

This chapter assesses answers to this question that are in the affirmative. In order to do so it proceeds, first, by categorising different models of global civil society before, and, second, exploring some theoretical problems involved in positing global civil society as connected to the democratisation of the world order as these models variously do. The core argument, presented third, is that there is a continuing, if largely unreflected, statist bias involved in most instances where global civil society is invoked. This narrowness of vision, it is argued, results in part from the idea that to embed global civil society requires a framework of rights, which is to miss the movement character of transnational action in civil society and to risk domesticating such action. The turn towards a rights discourse is problematic also, it is suggested, for requiring some fixed points of sovereignty from which to bestow such rights (institutions of global government), which constitutes a return to statism at precisely the point where an alternative enaction of the political is being suggested, struggled for even.

Models of global civil society

The growing interest in the prospects for a global civil society should be seen against the backdrop of a number of developments. First, the conviction of many analysts that democracy cannot be maintained while tied exclusively to the nation-state. This is because the nation-state is understood to be increasingly losing its capacity to facilitate self-determination in a world of growing economic and cultural globalisation. Allied to this is the argument that the connection between the nation-state and democracy is anyway only historically contingent, rather than a necessary one. These observations, in turn, have helped focus attention on the emergence of transnationally active social movements that appear better equipped to organise around global policy issues such as ecology and human rights and, according to the very nature of their political practice, to transgress the spatial boundaries that have confined politics to the sphere of the domestic state. Thus, for Richard Falk, while we cannot yet

> testify to the emergence of a global civil society inclined towards cosmopolitan democracy ... such a potentiality exists at least to the extent that the statist, territorial character of international society is being decisively superseded by a large variety of technical, economic and cultural trends.
>
> (1998: 328)

Whether or not the state is increasingly redundant as globalisation theorists claim (and this remains a contentious thesis), it is important to note the normative aspect of much of the talk about global civil society, which is motivated as much by the conviction that global power *should* be democratised as by the empirical claim that power *is* increasingly globalised. Yet just what part is civil society understood to play here?

One response to this question is provided within the model of cosmopolitan democracy. In perhaps the most well known of such models from David Held (1995), civil society provides for the public spheres which, taken together, operate as a basis for dispersed sovereignty in a system of global governance; generate critical resources directed towards the institutional power required by such governance;[1] and provide opportunities for voluntary association at the 'local' level. Nevertheless, civil society is by no means self-governing in Held's model, being constrained within a wider framework of cosmopolitan democratic law that 'delimits the form and scope of individual and collective action within the organisations of state *and* civil society. Certain standards are specified ... which no political regime or civil association can legitimately violate' (Held 1993: 43). Of course, for this cosmopolitan democratic law to have any legitimacy and authority, global-level sovereign institutions are required, although Held imagines these also being constrained by such a law, particularly by the principle of subsidiarity (which disperses sovereignty), but also through ensuring that these are representative global institutions.

Held summarises his model as involving the call for a double-sided process of democratisation in both political and civil society. Thus although Held sees civil society as one of the agents of democratic global governance, it is as much acted upon as actor, object as well as subject of his cosmopolitan democracy. This feature is replicated in the theory of other cosmopolitan democrats. Archibugi, for instance, wants global civil society to participate 'in political decision-making through new permanent institutions', but then states that such institutions 'would supplement but not replace existing intergovernmental organisations. Their function would be essentially advisory and not executive' (Archibugi 1998: 219).

Yet although cosmopolitan democrats may not identify global civil society as particularly active within the post-Westphalian order that they desire, it remains implicitly necessary to such an order in as much as 'post-Westphalian communities would promote a transnational citizenry with multiple political allegiances and without the need for submission to a central sovereign power' (Linklater 1998: 181). Indeed, Linklater himself positively identifies these post-Westphalian communities as including 'non-governmental associations, social movements and national minorities [that] can enjoy membership of an international society which is not just a society of states ...' (Linklater 1998: 209).

The second key approach to global civil society, although similarly cosmopolitan in intent, is focused far more directly on nascent global civil society itself – on the potential for world democratisation 'from below', via the moral advocacy of transnationally operational social movements focused on human rights and the environment, for example. The global civil society approach is thus chiefly concerned with forms of political action and organisation operating *outside* of the state and international law, where these forms are, by contrast, very much in the background for cosmopolitans:

> The predominant way of thinking about NGOs in world affairs is as transnational interest groups. They are politically relevant insofar as they affect state policies and interstate behaviour ... I argue ... that [they] have political relevance beyond this. They work to shape the way vast numbers of people throughout the world act ... using modes of governance that are part of global civil society ... [T]he best way to think about these activities is through the category of 'world civic politics'... clarifying how the forms of governance in civil society are distinct from the instrumentalities of state rule.
>
> (Wapner 1995: 336–7)

Starting from the standpoint of global civil society leads to questioning of the impression given by cosmopolitan democrats like Held that democratic global governance can be instituted almost in spite of action in civil society, through the neo-Kantian 'appeal to some supposedly already existing world politics or universal ethics, as if the grungy skin of modern statist politics can be cast off to reveal some essential or potential humanity beneath' (Walker 1994: 673). Walker in particular criticises the cosmopolitical attempt to 'read off' social movements 'as agents of this revelation':

> More interestingly, perhaps, it is possible to appeal to a rather less abstract and apparently more politically engaged account of an emerging global civil society. Indeed, much of the recent literature attempting to make sense of social movements/world politics has begun to draw quite heavily on the notion of a global civil society, not least so as to avoid falling back on some pre-political or even anti-political claim about an already existing ethics or world politics through which social movements

> can act without confronting the limits of modern politics in the modern state.
>
> (1994: 674)

Walker's critique here is interesting because it is true that Held, typically of cosmopolitical theorists, says very little about global civil society as such, focusing instead upon the role in global governance of more or less local or domesticated civil societies. From the global civil society perspective, Held and other cosmopolitan democrats thereby face the problem of accounting for agency in the transition to democratic global governance. This problem can be seen with Linklater, for example, who, having set out a fulsome normative defence of a cosmopolitan ethic, then makes only the following very general comments about its realisation:

> Cosmopolitan citizenship requires international joint action to ameliorate the condition of the most vulnerable groups in world society and to ensure that they can defend their legitimate interests by participating in effective universal communicative frameworks ... Cosmopolitan citizenship acquires its most profound praxeological significance when it is regarded as a guide to the moral principles which should be observed in these circumstances.
>
> (1998: 206–7)

From the standpoint of global civil society theorists, more problematic is that such voluntarism involves wholesale retreat from questions at the global level about the political itself. This retreat is evident from Linklater's summary of recent work on cosmopolitan citizenship as seeking nothing more ambitious than to 'defend the normative project of uncoupling citizenship from the sovereign state so that a strong sense of moral obligation is felt to all members of the species' (1998: 204). The problem here for critics is that to stop at a normative critique of the conjunction between citizenship and the state is to fall short of an assessment of political possibility in terms of identifying potential new forms of citizenship.

Ironically, although Linklater and Held want to move 'beyond' Westphalia (state sovereignty), states appear to be the only actors likely to be in a position to initiate their proposals. Linklater actually concedes this, arguing that 'a post-Westphalian configuration of states committed to the ... transformation of political community is the most involved system of joint rule which can be realised in the present era' (1998: 207). For Walker, this tendency to shy away from a non-statist definition of the political is actually one reason why claims for a global civil society are currently burgeoning, 'as a partial response to the dearth of ways of speaking coherently about forms of political life that transgress the bounds of the sovereign state' (1994: 696).

Falk illustrates this hope in the agency of global civil society with his call for 'globalisation from below' through the activities of transnational social movements. 'Globalisation from below' is seen as an alternative to the hegemonic 'globalisation from above' imposed by elites through a worldwide normative network premised not on human needs but on the needs of capital (neoliberalism). For Falk, echoing cosmopolitans like Held, there *can* be a democratic global normative framework, a 'law of humanity'. Yet unlike Held, with his weak notion of agency, Falk sees global civil society as the only means to this humane law – 'as the hopeful source of political agency need[ed] to free the minds of persons from an acceptance of state/sovereignty identity ...' (1995: 101). Furthermore, such global governance, contra Held, who seeks to achieve it 'from above' (his cosmopolitan law), must be built 'from the ground up' and continue to be anchored in global civil society itself. This universalism 'from below' is also sought by Paul Ghils, who wonders whether the 'universality of action in association' – a phrase reminiscent of Melucci's 'planetarization of action' (1989: 74) – makes 'civil society and its transnational networks of associations ... the *universum* which competing nations have never succeeded in creating' (1992: 429). It is present also in the work of Yoshikazu Sakamoto, who believes that democracy needs to be globalised from below, via 'the creation of a global perspective and values in the depths of people's hearts and minds, establishing the idea of a global civil society' (1991: 122).

The core global civil societarian objection to the cosmopolitan perspective, then, is that the latter's emphasis upon juridical power – cosmopolitan law no less – would lead to a plethora of (top-down, statist) legal regulations and institutions, which could be read as anathema to political agency in civil society (Hutchings 1999: 168). It might be noted at this point that, despite objecting to the statist implications of cosmopolitical theory, global civil society theorists at least share the cosmopolitan concern for the emergence of a global democratic politics. Crucially, however, understanding of the political differs significantly with each approach. Cosmopolitans, despite a dramatic shift in the level of analysis, remain true to the liberal democratic emphasis on mechanisms of law as the framework for a global polity. Global civil society theorists, meanwhile, look instead to the agency of 'bottom up', 'solidarist' transnational social movements – to the struggle for a global ethic more than the construction of a global polity.

What is meant by a 'global ethic' here? Simply that the growth of an increasingly norm-governed world system appears central to claims for an expanding role for global civil society. Writing on transnational civil society and human rights, Risse, for example, claims that the growing influence of the former on the latter stems from the power of global civil society's 'moral authority and accepted claim to authoritative knowledge' (2000: 186). Such moral authority and disinterestedness on the part of civil society is presumed also by Archibugi, who, although recognising that one state's interference in the domestic affairs of another may be instrumental, believes that civil society can and should so interfere (1998: 218).

Finally, it would be helpful to look briefly at one other conceptualisation of global civil society that does not fall within the two categories outlined above – this being the neo-Gramscian approach. Prominent here is the work of Robert Cox. Cox internationalises Gramsci in the sense of seeing civil society *itself* as a field of global power relations – involved, that is, in the reproduction of global capitalist hegemony – but also as containing the potential to organise *counter*-hegemonically at this level. Thus, in the first instance, states (as agencies of the global economy) and corporate interests seek to use civil society in order to stabilise the social and political status quo that is globalised capital, for example through state subsidies to NGOs which orientate them towards operations in conformity with neoliberalism (1999: 11). Yet in the second dimension, and Cox is another to use the phrase 'bottom up' to describe this:

> civil society is the realm in which those who are disadvantaged by globalization of the world economy can mount their protests and seek alternatives. This can happen through local community groups that reflect diversity of cultures and evolving social practices world wide … More ambitious still is the vision of a 'global civil society' in which these social movements together constitute a basis for an alternative world order.
>
> (Cox 1999: 10–11)

Cox sees 'something moving' in this direction across the globe as a counterweight to hegemonic power (global capital) and ideology (neoliberalism), but is also quick to admit that such movement is still relatively weak and uncoordinated: 'It may contain some of the elements but has certainly not attained the status of a counter-hegemonic alliance of forces on the world scale' (Cox 1999: 13).[2] Such elements as are found occur when, following the resurgence of civil society, there is transnational coordination of popular movements.[3] Crucially for Cox, the forces of a transformatory civil society *must* operate globally since this is the level at which hegemony prevails (1983: 171). In resisting this hegemony, however, the goal of civil society-based global action – and here Cox again follows Gramsci – is to effectively challenge and replace political authority in the system of states (1999: 16, 27–8).

Whether or not global civil society can transform the class character of state power, as Gramscians such as Cox anticipate, must remain, for now, a moot point. No less difficult questions remain, however, when returning to our original focus on the relationship between global civil society and worldwide democratisation. It is to more sceptical analyses of the putative connection between these two processes that we now turn.

Critical perspectives

Advocates of global civil society are keen to highlight the lack of formal accountability of the interstate system to nascent global society. Theorists such as Archibugi suggest that global civil society is therefore the only vehicle for representing individuals on global issues, as national political parties are irredeemably tied to national questions. Global civil society, on the other hand, *can* represent global citizens' demands by holding governments to account through campaigning and media pressure (Archibugi 2000: 146). In the words of former UN Secretary-General Boutros Ghali, civil society organisations are 'a basic form of popular representation in the present-day world. Their participation in international relations is, in a way, a guarantee of the political legitimacy of those international organisations' (cited in Köhler 1998: 232).

However, the 'cosmopolitan citizens' supposedly represented by global civil society actually gain no new powers of democratic accountability, since the organisations of transnational civil society are themselves in no way formally accountable to any citizen body. Arguing this case, David Chandler (2001) makes a number of important observations, including, first, that it is hard to see how civil society can constitute a new mechanism of 'accountability' when there is actually little agreement in the first place on the extent to which civil society groups *can* influence government policy-making. Shaw, in agreement here, notes that it is difficult for movement leaders 'to ensure that the peak of a mobilising cycle coincides with the greatest opportunity for influence on the state. Leverage is often a somewhat hit-and-miss affair' (1994a: 656). On the global level, of course, it is even less clear what the influence of transnational civil society is on policy-making – not least because global civil society has no equivalent of the domestic state with which to represent itself to. To the extent that there is an emerging *de facto* global state, this, as we have seen, is arguably the Western state writ large, with all the problems that this poses for the representativeness of the transnational civil society organisations that hope to influence it:

> From the viewpoint of many groups in non-Western society … being involved in global civil society is in fact a way of connecting to Western civil society and hence of securing some leverage with the Western state which is at the core of global power … The question that arises is whose voices are heard and how? If Western civil society is the core of global civil society, just as the Western state is the core of the global state, how do non-Western voices become heard? … How far can non-Western voices makes themselves heard directly? In what ways are they filtered by Western civil society, and how is their representation affected by the specific characteristics of Western civil institutions?
>
> (Shaw 1999: 223)

Second, and here our target shifts specifically to the cosmopolitan approach, because civil society organisations (such as pressure groups, NGOs, grass roots campaigns, single issue groups, etc.) operate almost by definition outside of formal political structures, it is not clear how they could be incorporated into some cosmopolitan democratic framework without either demobilising them as genuine civil society institutions *or* violating the principles of democratic accountability and equality. For as Chandler points out with regard to the latter objection, 'we are not all equally involved in civil society, we do not vote for civil society policies and we cannot hold civil society to account' (2001: 7). Thus to formalise global civil society's input into international policy-making may only further entrench opaque global governance in a situation in which structures of authority and accountability simply do not exist at a transnational level. Falk, for example, wants 'to make the activities of [the UN's] principle organs more accessible to qualified representatives of global civil society', (1998: 319) but says nothing about how, or by whom, such 'qualified' representatives might be selected.

As Canovan remarks, there just is 'no uniform global legal order from which human beings ... can claim uniform rights' (2001: 212). For this very reason, in the absence of some global political framework it is arguably simply mistaken to conceive of the transnational public sphere as an extension of the national one (Köhler 1998: 233). Only once organised around international deliberative institutions could 'a public sphere of democratically organized international associations ... shift the location of sovereignty in the international sphere from nations back to citizens' (Bohman 1997: 196). To put the point another way, only with the onset of global democratic institutions can national citizens become true world citizens. It is therefore difficult to see what official role global civil society could have in providing for world citizenship, given that most of its organisations are not structured democratically.

For Chandler (2000), the post-1945 framework of formal sovereign equality between states, while imperfect, at least upheld the principle of political equality on the international stage. Yet the 'global society' perspective is implacably opposed to state sovereignty, seeking to trump it with the ethical demands of global civil society (for example on behalf of human rights and the environment). Shaw, for example, argues that it is necessary

> to face up to the necessity which enforcing these [ethical] principles would impose to breach systematically the principles of sovereignty and non-intervention ... The global society perspective, therefore, has an ideological significance which is ultimately opposed to that of international society.
>
> (1994b: 134–5)

However, when ethical demands from global civil society are identified as the driving force of an emerging world civic politics, questions about accountability surface again. In an account of transnational civil society from Risse (2000), its growing influence is put down to 'the power of moral authority' and 'the accepted claim to authoritative knowledge'. The example used is that of the human rights area, where it is enthusiastically proclaimed that, 'today, Amnesty International, Human Rights Watch and the Lawyers

Committee for Human Rights *define* what constitutes a human rights violation' (Risse 2000: 186). This is a clear example, as Risse readily admits, of transnational civil society creating international norms, which must also mean, if true, that the norm-setting agenda for global politics is in no real sense under popular control (although Risse nowhere comments on *this* worrying, if unsurprising, feature). Taking a wider perspective, it is worth questioning how institutions that assert moral authority can ever be held to account democratically, particularly when this is tied up, as it must be, with claims to special knowledge. Anyway, as Walker observes, who exactly 'has the authority to act in the name of rainforests and dolphins' is difficult to specify (1994: 675). More certain is that meaningful control by 'global citizens' of institutions that would have their legitimacy defined in these highly moralised terms is unlikely.

In particular, it appears disingenuous for cosmopolitans, Archibugi in this instance, to posit that 'one state's intervention in the domestic affairs of another has no legal foundation and may be instrumental', only then to state baldly that 'the cosmopolitan model entrusts civil society as opposed to national governments with the task of "interfering" in the domestic affairs of another state' (1998: 218). Why global civil society can interfere in other states without legal foundation when this is forbidden to states themselves is not clear, nor is it apparent why Archibugi is so confident that civil society organisations, unlike states, will never act for their own narrow ends:

> The transnational activity of [civil society organisations] is interpreted as evidence that an all-inclusive ethical base of world politics exists from which it is possible to appeal to governments as a supplementary element in the world community. In such a vision, the question of what exactly constitutes the political in the international system becomes unclear. Accountability is replaced by shared responsibility towards common ethical imperatives. The requirements of loyalty and conflict limitation are thus set a priori; they do not, that is, result from political discourse. Conflicting interests seem to disappear together with the political dimension of any transnational public sphere.
>
> (Köhler 1998: 241–2)

Besides, the overruling of sovereignty in the face of the ethical demands of global civil society may in practice be more tied up with interstate politics than advocates of global society would like to admit. One enthusiast for a globally interventionist civil society unintentionally divulges as much when claiming that, 'given the right circumstances', including, tellingly, 'a specific interest on the part of a major power capable of using force', 'civil society might be able to play a role in getting rid of nasty dictatorships' (Kumar 2000: 136). Generally speaking, we can observe that states and global civil society are mutually implicated in each other's affairs:

> [A] state may seek the support of its civil society in implementing its foreign policies *vis-à-vis* another state ... [A] state may appeal to CSOs [civil society organisations] abroad or support them indirectly in their efforts to influence the policies of their state ... CSO's may seek the assistance of their own state in furthering activities in others states.
>
> (Köhler 1998: 245)

What stands out here is that even if global civil society is taken to be the 'ethical' driver behind the overriding of the principle of state sovereignty, in practice it is only states that are likely to have the capacity to enact these 'ethical' demands *vis-à-vis* other states. Shaw, as one advocate of 'global society', lets this slip when stating that 'it is unavoidable that global state action will be undertaken largely by states, ad hoc coalitions of states and more permanent regional groupings of states' (1994b: 186). But which states have such a capability? For Chandler, 'in practice, the prosecution of international justice turns out to be the prerogative of the West' (2000: 61).

Proponents of a role for civil society in global governance seem therefore to have a blind spot in their analyses, which is that in celebrating the ability of global civil society to make ethical demands on individual states, they miss the potentially deleterious effects of this on the right of equal sovereignty *between* states (which has also been crucial in upholding the principle of self-determination). This ought to be of particular concern given that, on the basis of the uneven spread of power and resources, most 'global' civil society organisations are actually thoroughly Western (many based in, even resourced by, Western states) and the majority of the world's 'citizens' are more adequately conceptualised as objects rather than subjects of such organisations. Shaw unintentionally acknowledges this when he writes that 'the activities of globalist organisations, such as human rights, humanitarian and development agencies, make a reality of global civil society by bringing the most exposed victims among the world's population into contact with more resourceful groups in the West' (1994a: 655).

Such obliviousness to the implications for equal sovereignty – and by extension to the principle of self-determination – of providing *carte blanche* to global civil society is widespread in the literature. It figures also in Linklater's work, for example, when he remarks approvingly on the 'powerful developmental pressures in international society' that are shaping the dialogue between states, before commenting, on the same page, that the 'grounds for denying non-Western societies the right of equal membership of the society of states have been eroded in the twentieth century' (1998: 208). Absent here is any reflection on how the growing influence of a Western-dominated 'global' civil society might actually undermine the principles upholding the right of equal membership of the society of states. Falk, meanwhile, advocates the 'emancipation' of the UN from the control of states in order to make it 'more responsive ... to pressure from transnational social forces expressive of global civil society' (Falk 1998: 327). What Falk does not consider is that his proposal could well lead to even further concentration of political influence in the Western societies once the principle of control of the UN by (all) states is supplanted by the principle of lobbying by (mainly Western) civil society organisations.

Visions of global civil society: still statist?

> Claims about an emerging global civil society ... usually reveal the reproductive powers of statist discourse more than they do the capacity of social movements to challenge that discourse.
>
> (Walker 1994: 674)

Regardless of the priority given to the activities of global civil society in the construction of the hoped for 'world civic politics', it is remarkable that, across the range of theoretical debate, commentators conceive of such activity as in pursuit of – requiring even – a framework of rights. Thereby implicitly affirmed, it can be argued, is the principle of state sovereignty over all other claims to political possibility – precisely when global civil society represents such a possibility (Walker 1994: 670). The implications of this turn to rights will be explored here, focusing on how attempts to fit a theory of global civil society into a discourse about rights may well constitute a procrustean bed apropos the self-determining, *movement* character of action in global civil society. The danger, for Walker, is of positing 'already constituted ethical traditions rather than [asking] how emerging political practices challenge and reconstruct such claims' (1994: 695):

> If social movements are to be taken seriously in relation to claims about world politics, at least some attention will have to be paid to ways in which they do, or do not, challenge the constitutive practices of modern politics. It is futile to gauge the importance of social movements without considering the possibility that it is precisely the criteria of significance by which they are to be judged that may be in contention ... This is not least because whatever they are ... social movements are usually designated precisely as *movements*, as phenomena that are explicitly at odds with the spatial framing of all ontological possibilities ... that have made it so difficult to envisage any form of politics other than that associated with the modern state ...
>
> (Walker 1994: 672–3)

The form which statist modes of thinking about global civil society most often take, as already indicated, is to imagine that a settled structure of rights is required for such a civil society to be embedded. For cosmopolitan democrats, a truly global civil society would not only be dependent on such a rights framework but actually be partially constituted by it. The paradigmatic example here is Held's model, where all 'groups and associations are attributed rights of self-determination specified by a commitment to individual autonomy and a specific cluster of rights ... Together, these rights constitute the basis of an empowering legal order – a democratic international law' (Held 1993: 43). In another example of the cosmopolitan approach, Bohman (1997: 180–1) argues that 'cosmopolitan right', emerging from a federation of nations, creates 'the institutional conditions necessary for a cosmopolitan public sphere and an international civil society'. While this 'cosmopolitan right' does not have the character of 'the supreme coercive power of public right in the state', it is a formal principle of publicity that would 'ultimately reorganize existing republican institutions and political identities' by formalising such a right within new, sovereign, international institutions.

It might be expected that cosmopolitan democrats would take a rights approach to global civil society. Yet it is also present for theorists of global civil society because these theorists see democratisation in terms of ethical advocacy (regarding the environment and human rights, for example). Although by a different route, this aspiration to entrench a particular global ethic via the agency of global civil society also leads to demands for rights. Risse, for example, contends that

> transnational civil society needs the cooperation of states and national governments. To create robust and specific human rights standards [international nongovernmental organisations] must convince enough states that international law needs to be strengthened ... Transnational civil society also needs states for the effective improvement of human rights conditions on the ground.
>
> (2000: 205)

Falk similarly calls for 'the transnational social forces that constitute global civil society' to work towards 'individual and group rights' within the 'structure of the states system of world order' (1995: 114, 183). Kaldor too sees 'the concept of global civil society' as 'equated with the notion of a human rights culture' and even writes that civil society 'issues such as peace, gender equality and the environment ... can easily, and in some cases rather usefully, be reconceptualised as human rights issues'. Kaldor states it quite explicitly – global civil society is an adjunct to human rights; in her own words again, 'the language of civil society ... adds to the human rights discourse the notion of individual responsibility for respect of human rights through public action' (1999: 210–11).

Yet there is a real predicament involved in reducing the role of global civil society to the pursuit of a rights agenda: namely that arguments for legal rights produce arguments for the state, not civil society, because structures of rights are compromises secured through contract, and valid contracts presuppose a sovereign state, except this time presumably on a global scale (Schecter 2000: 134). Also, once rights become the measure of all things politically, then, in addition to the monopoly of the use of force required for their enforcement, it is even more fundamentally the case that, if 'my conception of rights clashes with yours, we need the state to adjudicate between our claims'; we are now 'in need of protection from one another by the state' (Schecter 2000: 130). Thus (global) rights necessitate but also *stimulate* the growth of the (global) state. Yet it is interesting that few, if any, theorists of cosmopolitan democracy or global civil society actually want a world state or think that such an institution would ever be desirable (given seemingly insurmountable problems of popular control and accountability at such a level of remove from individual citizens). This raises the question of whether advocates of the various rights-based approaches to global civil society have thought through fully the implications of their attachment to rights as the means to global democratisation.

There is also an important sense in which the valorisation of rights implicitly legitimates, takes as given even, a statist reading of the political. This is ironic since it is precisely the reduction of the political to actions associated with the state that many of the same theorists claim is being challenged by nascent global civil society. International civil society, especially in its new social movement aspect, works to remind us of the transient nature of political legitimacy, so it seems disingenuous to argue that the way to consolidate such an emerging world public sphere is through the bestowing of rights by statist forms, as if the legitimacy of these forms was a given feature of the world political landscape that nobody would want to question. Blaug (1999: 120–1) in particular draws our attention to the ways in which civil society (and this is as true of global civil society) has to operate from a position in which state power is extant. Thus action in civil society has, of necessity, historically involved the struggle to 'win back' power *vis-à-vis* states – struggles which, when successful, come to be expressed in the form of rights that guarantee freedoms and set out the limits of state power. Yet these rights are merely the outcomes of a struggle that started with the *questioning* of the state's legitimacy, so in a sense they represent the 'siphoning off' or displacement of suspicions of illegitimacy away from their intended target (the state). That is, rights are 'bestowed' by states as if the state itself operates above the struggles that these suspicions of illegitimacy generate, when in fact it is their original object. Rights offload the burden of proof regarding legitimacy in the wrong direction, from state to civil society rather than from civil society to state:

> [T]he state, being a construct of merely strategic and functional origin, need only address the issue of legitimacy in terms of *ex post* rationalizations and the management of appearances. When the moral outrage of [oppressed] individuals and minority groups expose the legitimation deficit, the state is only too happy to engage in a legalistic argument

> over rights. States thus functionally encourage the process of displacement of questions regarding their legitimacy into arguments over rights. The resulting displacement serves to occlude their legitimation deficit, and to channel the utopian energies of the lifeworld away from the search for institutional structures that ... might more genuinely treat the legitimacy of the state as an inherently entropic affair. Rights are, therefore, *just the place* a state would wish to fight its (now highly distorted) battle for legitimacy.
>
> (Blaug 1999: 121)

By extension, for as long as the actions of *global* civil society are channelled, both in theory and in practice, into struggles for rights, global civil society will be effectively engaged in seeking recognition from the system of states. This is hardly the sort of activity that calls into question, or offers alternatives to, politics as it is practised by states. It is hardly the sort of activity that constitutes global civil society as an end in itself, which is exactly how many of the very same advocates for global civil society want it to be seen. Thus although from the global civil society perspective there is justified scepticism of the statist implications of the cosmopolitan attempt to structure democratic global governance from the 'top down', the attempt to 'say global civil society with rights' implies pretty much the same structure of law and overarching sovereignty as in the cosmopolitan model. Whether from the standpoint of cosmopolitan democracy or global civil society theory, then, transnational civic action loses its self-determining character and, with this, its ability to reshape our understanding of the political. This is a particularly regrettable failure in theory since it is precisely this re-enacting of the political that many groups in global civil society self-identify as their practice.

So, in our search for 'alternative voices' it seems that visions of a global civil society, while offering some resistance to the dominant discourse, ultimately work with the same statist preconception of the political that characterises the liberal democratic model. Are there, then, any remaining voices that continue to call instead for a democracy of civil society? As we shall see in the next chapter, some such voices do survive, although we will have to travel to the remotest region in Mexico to hear them.

8 'An echo that turns itself into many voices'

Zapatismo and civil society as revolutionary practice

Taking our cue from Chapter 7, we might conclude that, although alternative visions of civil society do continue to be articulated, this is so now only in the realms of theory rather than practice. Yet since the mid-1990s, those in search of political alternatives the world over have been absorbed by events in the isolated interior of impoverished southern Mexico, where, remarkably, claims for civil society as radical democratic *practice* continue to be advanced. Such claims, moreover, come from the practitioners of this 'democracy of civil society' themselves, and not just from academic commentators seeking to 'capture' this practice for their own purposes.

Much has been made of the use of the concept of civil society by the Zapatistas, particularly by their figurehead, Subcomandante Marcos, since their uprising began in 1994 in Chiapas, southern Mexico. 'The term civil society', writes Esteva, 'is a substantial part of the political conception of the Zapatistas' (1999: 159). This chapter will explore just how the Zapatistas conceive of civil society as theory and practice, looking in the process at common ground with previous radical discourses as well as new points of departure. Prior to this discussion, it will be necessary to recount briefly the background to the Zapatista uprising.

The region of Chiapas constitutes nothing less than the 'periphery of the periphery' (Hellman 2000: 1). Although always marginalised – Chiapas has been essentially an agricultural export-producing internal colony of Mexico since independence – economic shocks to the region in the last few decades have been profound. After the Mexican debt crisis of 1982 and the imposition of a neoliberal economic adjustment programme under President Salinas (1988–94), Chiapanecos endured both a slump in coffee prices and the elimination of price supports to corn and basic grain producers (Hellman 2000: 3). When to these hardships was added the withdrawal of the land distribution programme, which had previously ensured that land was held as collective property (in 1992 in preparation for NAFTA, a free-trade agreement establishing a trade block comprising the US, Canada and Mexico), the very basis of indigenous communal life came under threat from corporations eager to exploit the new free market in land ownership.

The army of the revolutionary EZLN (Zapatista Army of National

Liberation) had been based in the jungles of Chiapas since the early 1980s, slowly building up a support base with the indigenous communities in the region. As crisis loomed, the EZLN were supported by many in these communities in signalling a dramatic refusal of NAFTA and of the Federal government's imposed policies for their region: they declared war on 1 January 1994, the day of NAFTA's implementation. Three thousand EZLN troops occupied six large towns in the Chiapas region and were met with fierce counter-attacks by the Mexican Federal army, including the bombing of Zapatista villages. After a massive popular demonstration in Mexico City calling for an end to the military's onslaught against the Zapatistas, a government cease-fire was declared on 12 January. The Zapatista communities rejected the government's subsequent terms (on the basis that these offered concessions only in relation to the state of Chiapas, whereas the Zapatistas saw their struggle as a national one) and, although the EZLN has not gone back to war, their communities have still been subjected to violence, often perpetrated by right-wing paramilitaries. In the face of this ongoing 'low-intensity warfare', the EZLN continues to defend its 'autonomous indigenous municipalities' (originally numbering thirty-eight) with varying degrees of success, although there has been significant success in generating global awareness of its struggle – particularly via the World Wide Web and through establishing links with 'civil society' worldwide. The Zapatista communities remain surrounded by 50,000 troops of the Federal army.

The idea of civil society is indisputably central to Zapatismo. Zapatista declarations are replete with calls for civil society to organise itself in Mexico, and the Zapatista leadership see themselves as under the command of a sovereign civil society, or as enacting the sovereignty that they believe resides in civil society (see Marcos 2001: 44). In the *Second Declaration of the Lacandon Jungle* (1994), for example, we read that:

> Another force, a force superior to any political or military power, imposed its will on the parties involved in the conflict [the Zapatistas and the Mexican government]. Civil society assumed the duty of preserving our country. It ... obliged us to hold a dialogue with the government.
>
> (in Marcos 2001: 44)

Also in the EZLN's opening words to the National Democratic Convention (1994):

> It has been said mistakenly that the Zapatistas have placed a time limit on the resumption of war ... They lie. Nobody, not even the EZLN, can impose time limits or give ultimatums to the people of Mexico. For the EZLN there are no time limits other than what the civil and peaceful mobilizations determine. We are subordinate to them, to the point of disappearing as an alternative ... There are no Zapatista ultimatums for civil society.
>
> (in Marcos 2001: 58)

Then, in a paean to 'Civil Society that so Perturbs' (1996):

> Two national projects, two countries, two Mexicos confronting each other. On the one hand, there is their nation, their country, their Mexico. A plan for the nation that Power holds up with bloody hands ... On the other hand, there is the nation of the community organizations, the country of Civil Society, the Mexico of the Mexicans ... Today, we are criticized because we don't seek the support of political organisations – armed and unarmed – but reiterate our belief in Civil Society ... They tell us you don't speak to or listen to Civil Society; rather, you command it.
>
> (1996 EZLN communiqué, *Civil Society that so Perturbs*, in Marcos 2001: 130)

Let us now unpack in some more detail the Zapatistas' theory of civil society and its implications for their political practice.

Against power and vanguardism

Most treatments of the Zapatista discourse on civil society have emphasised its originality. While, as we shall see below, there are certainly unique elements – particularly the more internationalist conception of civil society – it is remarkable how little comment has passed on similarities with earlier radical discourses in Latin America during the 1980s and in Central–Eastern Europe too. Yet remarkably in tune with these earlier voices, Zapatismo, as articulated by its public representatives, involves the rejection both of traditional left revolutionary vanguardism and, more generally, of the aim of achieving power in the state as such, '[T]his revolution will not end in a new class, faction of a class, or group in power. It will end in a free and democratic space for political struggle born above the fetid cadaver of the state-party system' (*Second Declaration of the Lacandon Jungle*, in Marcos 2001: 46).

The motif of political 'space' as not only free from but also fundamentally indifferent to the party-state is redolent of previous pronouncements on civil society as a democratic end in itself. The statement given to the Zapatistas' National Democratic Convention that 'we are subordinate to [civil society], to the point of disappearing as an alternative', indicates the degree to which conventional political power is not the intended goal here (in Marcos 2001: 58), as does the more explicit declaration from Marcos in 1994 that 'we are an armed movement which does not want to take power, as in the old revolutionary schemes' (cited in Lorenzano 1998: 141). Putting theory into practice, the EZLN has declined links with another revolutionary movement in Mexico, the EPR (Popular Revolutionary Front), owing to its stated designs on state power. In an EZLN communiqué to the EPR, this point of difference is stated thus, '[W]hat we want ... [is] not to seize power but to exercise it' (cited in De Angelis 2000: 32). Indeed, during its founding congress the EZLN decreed that it would not take part in elections or even allow its members to join political parties; further, the rejection of all ambition to hold state office became a condition of membership (Cuninghame and Corona 1998: 16; Holloway 1998: 175):[1]

> The 'centre' asks us, demands of us, that we should sign a peace agreement quickly and convert ourselves into an 'institutional' political force, that is to say, convert ourselves into yet another part of the machinery of power. To them we answer 'NO' and they do not understand it ... They do not understand that we do not want offices or posts in government. They do not understand that we are struggling not for the stairs to be swept clean from the top to the bottom, but for there to be no stairs, for there to be no kingdom at all.
> (1997 communiqué of the EZLN, cited in Holloway and Peláez 1998: 4)

Allied to the abandonment of the aspiration to achieve power in the state, Zapatismo – here echoing the wider debate on the Latin American left since the 1980s – also involves turning away from the vanguardist methods of traditional revolutionary movements. In the narrative given by the EZLN, this transformation appears to have resulted from the exposure of the original Marxist–Leninist members of the group (from 1983 onwards, while seeking to make revolution from their hideout in the Lacandon jungle) to the more democratised, decentralised practices of communal organisation employed by the indigenous people of Chiapas. By 1988, in the EZLN's account, it had ceded to these organised communities – 'we surrendered, [admitting] that it would be better to do what they say' (cited in Lorenzano 1998: 143). As Subcomandante Marcos recounted it in 1994, at the beginning of the uprising:

> [T]he EZLN of eleven years ago ... was established to take power through armed force, We were a military organisation in the classic sense of the word. For that reason, the primary contribution of what is known today as neo-Zapatismo came from the clash between that rigid conception and the reality of the indigenous communities. The insertion of a democratic structure into an authoritarian one; decision-making in indigenous communities versus decision-making in a completely vertical political–military organisation.
> (cited in Lorenzano 1998: 141)

And again in an interview in 1995:

> This is the great lesson that the indigenous communities teach to the original EZLN. The original EZLN, the one that is formed in 1983, is a political organisation in the sense that it speaks and what it says has to be done. The indigenous communities teach it to listen, and that is what we learn. The principle lesson that we learn from the indigenous people is that we have to learn to hear, to listen.
> (cited in Holloway 1998: 163)

The upshot of this protracted lesson in listening, in the EZLN revolutionary committee's words, is that the 'indigenous communities have taught us that to resolve a problem, no matter how great it may be, it is always good to consult all the people we are' (in Marcos 2001: 126). Whether or not this new thinking was influenced also by parallel political developments on the left elsewhere in Latin America is hard to say, but examples abound of the ways in which Zapatismo reflects the wider sea change with regard to vanguardism as charted in Chapter 3. In the *Second Declaration of the Lacandon Jungle*, for instance:

> The EZLN has its idea of what system and proposal are best for the country. The political maturity of the EZLN as a representative of a sector of the nation is shown by the fact that it doesn't want to impose its proposal on the country ... [Instead] the EZLN, in a democratic exercise without precedent in an armed organization, consulted its component bases about whether or not to sign the peace accords presented by the federal government.
>
> (in Marcos 2001: 47)

Further, during the National Democratic Convention of 1994 (convened by the Zapatistas and from which groups that supported an armed overthrow of the government were banned), the EZLN explicitly avoided the self-appointed leadership role that might have been expected from most traditional revolutionary movements:

> We have also rejected all possibilities of participating in the presidency of the CND [National Democratic Convention]; this is the convention for the peaceful search for change, and should in no way be presided over by armed people. We are thankful that you give us a place, one more among the many of you, to say our words.
>
> (opening words to the National Democratic Convention, in Marcos 2001: 55)

What, then, did the Zapatista leadership want to achieve through the CND apart from 'to organise the voice of civil society'?

> [N]ot a soapbox for political calculations, for groups or subgroups in search of power; not the doubtful honor of being the historical vanguard of multiple vanguards that we are subject to ... not a springboard to reach a desk, an office, some department, in a government, in a country ... The moment has come to tell everyone that we do not want and cannot take the place that some want us to take, the place from which emanates all opinions, all routes, all answers, all truths; we will not do it.
>
> (opening words to the National Democratic Convention, in Marcos 2001: 56)

For the Zapatista general command, more modestly, 'we are the *possibility* that can defeat [Power] and make it disappear' (*Second Declaration of La Realidad for Humanity and against Neoliberalism*, in Marcos 2001: 126, emphasis added). Such possibility is not understood to be the Zapatistas' sole possession in any sense, in the way that conventional political or military forces might be. Here, then, we can see the influence of radical pluralism on Zapatismo, a feature of their thought that exists in a symbiotic relationship with their abandonment of vanguardism. Yet pluralism appears to be a new, or at least much more prominent, feature than emphasised previously in radical civil society theory. Zapatismo, as defined at the First Intercontinental *Encuentro* [Gathering] for Humanity and against Neoliberalism (hosted by the Zapatistas in 1996), is 'an echo that recognizes the existence of the other and does not attempt to overpower or silence it' (in Marcos 2001: 122); a world in which 'all are equals because they are different' (Major Ana Maria, cited in De Angelis 2000: 22). Analysts have seized eagerly on this radical pluralist ethic in Zapatismo, seeing it as heralding the first postmodern revolutionary movement, one that, uniquely, resists the 'tyranny of globalizing discourses' (Esteva 1999: 171). The Zapatistas' revolutionary theory–practice, from this analytical perspective, is a series of questions rather than an answer. '"*Preguntando caminamos* – asking we walk" becomes a central principle ... The revolution advances by asking, not by telling; or perhaps even, revolution *is* asking instead of telling, the dissolution of power relations' (Holloway 1998: 164). In another similar account:

> The old revolutionary practice started from the condition of exploitation, poverty and misery and indicated the answer: revolution. Here revolution was conceived as *realising* the hopes of the masses understood in terms of party plans ... The Zapatistas' practice starts from the same poverty, exploitation and misery, and from the fact that, despite this ... people are dignified human subjects, able to hope and self-govern themselves and ask: what to do in order to deal with our needs?
>
> (De Angelis 2000: 31)

Zapatismo involves not only appeals for pluralism internal to the revolution, but also an emphasis on the multiplicity of revolutionary movements and forms themselves. Marcos asserts that what is being pursued is a revolution, not a Revolution – 'with small letters, to avoid polemics with the many vanguards and safeguards of THE REVOLUTION' (cited in Holloway 1998: 168). In the closing address to the First International *Encuentro*, this sentiment is reiterated in answer to the question, 'what next'? 'A new number in the useless enumeration of the numerous international orders? A new scheme for calming and easing the anguish of having no solution? A global program for world revolution?' Resolutely answering these questions in the negative, the declaration goes on to call instead for '[a]n echo of this rebel voice transforming itself and renewing itself in other voices ... know[ing] itself to be one and many, acknowledging itself to be equal in its desire to listen and be listened to, recognizing itself as diverse in the tones and levels of the voices forming it' (in Marcos 2001: 121–2). As Holloway sees it, this radical pluralism has surfaced in Zapatista political action, particularly in their constant appeals to, and attempts to build bridges with, not some homogeneous entity such as the 'working class', but instead 'civil society' in all its diversity (1998: 180).

The paradoxical role of armed struggle

Despite all their talk of the errors of power-seeking and vanguardist politics, a striking paradox is that the EZLN is a revolutionary armed movement that makes no attempt to distance itself from the violent uprising of 1994 (despite continuing to observe a subsequent suspension of military offensives). Although the Zapatistas have never viewed armed struggle in the classic Guevarist sense – 'we do not see [it] as a single path, as one almighty truth around which everything else spins' (Marcos, cited in Johnston 2000: 47) – the question remains: what meaningful relationship can there be between *civil* society and the force of arms? This question is particularly pressing because, despite the undoubted similarities between the Zapatistas' discourse on civil society and that of their radical forerunners, at this point the Zapatistas are in entirely new territory. For reasons of principle, although usually out of necessity also, the theory-philosophy of civil society as opposition has always previously been wedded to the principle of non-violence.

The EZLN's line on their bearing arms is as follows:

> We want to say that if anyone doubts it, we have no misgivings of having taken up arms against the supreme government; we repeat that they left us no alternative, we do not regret taking up arms nor covering our faces, we do not lament our dead, we are proud of them and we're ready to offer more blood and more death if that is the price to achieve a democratic change in Mexico.
>
> (opening words to the National Democratic Convention, in Marcos 2001: 55)

> It seems clear to me that there is a consensus among ... civil society that the world has to be shown that military alternatives are not a viable option. I don't know why. The January offensive demonstrated that it's possible to carry out a sizable military operation ... I don't think anyone wants to deal with that.
>
> (Marcos, cited in Johnston 2000: 471)

Prima facie, the Zapatistas' justification for the use of force is an entirely conventional one, expressed in their terms as entailing the search for 'the word of peace, but not the word that surrenders the struggle for freedom;

the word of peace, but not the word of the pacifist complicity with injustice' (opening words to the National Democratic Convention, in Marcos 2001: 57). Yet this justification does not in itself account for the confidence with which the Zapatistas identify themselves with the side of peace over war, and with non-violence over militarism:

> Two countries struggling between themselves to find a place in the future. One, belonging to Power, that uses force. The other, Civil Society's, that uses reason and feeling. The one, belonging to Power, that looks for war. The other, Civil Society's, that looks for peace ... Civil society insists on holding back war and turning back the militarization of the nation.
> (1996 EZLN communiqué, *Civil Society that so Perturbs*, in Marcos 2001: 131)

Although it is true that the Zapatistas do not see themselves as synonymous with civil society – for example, in their insistence that they should not, as an armed movement, provide leadership of the National Democratic Convention – they undoubtedly see themselves as on the *side* of civil society and its values (including, as they themselves identify, non-violence). Thus in their original declaration of war, the EZLN called for 'international organisations [to] watch over and regulate our battles' (*First Declaration of the Lacandon Jungle*, in Marcos 2001: 13). Yet the Zapatistas themselves acknowledge the tension between the path of 'civil society' and armed struggle, with Marcos stating more recently that 'we are an armed movement ... that calls[s] upon civil society to join us in peaceful action, to prevent war. That is the paradox of the EZLN' (cited in Lorenzano 1998: 141).

How, then, did the EZLN move from asking civil society to regulate its battles to joining it in peaceful struggle 'to prevent war'? The turning point appears to have been the National Democratic Convention of August 1994, where, in consultation with unarmed groups, it was concluded that it was necessary to afford priority to the struggle of civil society over armed struggle and also that, if successful, this strategy would lead to the dissolution of the EZLN itself. This stance was demonstrated powerfully during the Convention when the Zapatistas tied white ribbons round the ends of their weapons. Marcos explained, 'Those ribbons signify the purpose of our weapons; they are not arms to be used in confrontation with civil society. Those ribbons on the guns represent, like everything else here, a paradox: weapons that aspire to uselessness' (cited in Johnston 2000: 464).

Comfortable as Marcos is with paradox, the civil society/armed struggle dichotomy at the heart of Zapatismo is seen by some commentators to contain a certain inescapable logic in the harsh context of Chiapas. This is that, far from promoting the 'armed way', the Zapatistas, given their weakness in the face of the authoritarian might of the Mexican state, simply had little option but to create an army (Esteva 1999: 172). This is the 'armed uprising of desperation', as Marcos put it (cited in Johnston 2000: 493), an uprising pursued only 'after we found all other paths were closed' (Marcos 2001: 38). Certainly, aspirations to autonomous political space mean little if that space cannot be carved out in some way, and, given the vulnerability of local communities *vis-à-vis* land owners and corporations eager to exploit Chiapas' natural resources in the wake of NAFTA, other means to this end must have seemed severely limited. Moreover, in such a poor and remote region of southern Mexico there was little chance of gaining the attention of Mexican 'civil society', let alone any wider exposure, short of such an armed uprising. This is certainly how the Zapatistas read their situation, with Marcos stating that 'we didn't go to war on January 1st to kill or be killed. We went to war to make ourselves heard'. Moreover, in an early communiqué, the EZLN stated that the 'primary objective' of their uprising was to inform

> the Mexican people and the rest of the world about the miserable conditions in which millions of Mexicans, especially us, the indigenous people, live and die ... [W]ith these actions we also let the world know of our decision to fight for our most elementary rights in the only way that the governmental authorities have left us: armed struggle.
>
> (cited in Johnston 2000: 467)

Yet having once garnered both the attention *and* the support of 'civil society', the EZLN appear to have found the strength to continue their struggle by other means, stating in 1995 that they intended now to 'open up this space and confront people with ideas, not with weapons' (cited in Esteva 1999: 172). Although the EZLN have not yet given up their weapons, this is no doubt because they remain surrounded by 50,000 troops and face ongoing harassment from paramilitary groups. In such circumstances self-defence seems to require an armed dimension and, according to Johnston, theoretical analysts must also be aware of this, of 'how the lines between democracy and violence are blurred in the context of ... low intensity warfare' (2000: 565). Yet there is every indication from both their words and their deeds that what the Zapatistas seek to achieve through force of arms is self-defence and self-defence alone.

Autonomy and self-determination: Zapatismo as democratic theory

> We are not struggling against the PRI [ruling party]. We are struggling against the system of the Party-State ...
>
> (Marcos, cited in Johnston 2000: 479)

In addition to other characteristics that it shares with previous radical discourses on civil society, Zapatismo is also strongly antistatist, identifying democracy with self-determining practice in the sphere of civil society rather than representation in the state. Scepticism concerning the state's legitimacy was manifest in the very earliest Zapatista declarations, including the response given to the federal government's offer to pardon EZLN troops only eighteen days after the uprising began:

> Why do we need to be pardoned? What are they going to pardon us for? ... Who should ask for pardon, and who can grant it? ... Should we ask for pardon from those who deny us the right and capacity to govern ourselves? From those who don't respect our customs or our culture and who ask us for identification papers and obedience to a law whose existence and moral basis we don't accept?
>
> (Marcos 2001: 38–9)

Zapatismo rejects the state's claim that ultimately only it can act collectively for society, resisting also its assertion, as caricatured by the Zapatistas, that 'the convocation between a group of transgressors of the law [the EZLN] and a mass that is amorphous, disorganized, and fragmented down to its familial microcosm – the so called civil society – would have no resonance nor common cause' (opening words to the National Democratic Convention, in Marcos 2001: 53). Pointing as proof to the experience of civic self-organisation in Mexico City following the earthquake of 1985, the Zapatistas claim that 'you can participate without aspiring to public office ... you can organize politically without being a political party'. Indeed, this is seen as the only alternative to the 'militarization' of Mexican life 'through a state takeover that, although slow, is still authoritarian' (1996 EZLN communiqué, *Civil Society that so Perturbs*, in Marcos 2001: 129):

> The Hydra of the State-Party system tries to completely fill the small boxing ring at the table of San Andres [the location for talks with the government on indigenous rights and culture] – not only to capture center stage and display all its trappings, but to keep any rival from stealing the show or winning. In this way, Power forces the 'others' into the fight, but they are admitted only as losers.
>
> (Marcos 2001: 148)

For the Zapatistas, resistance must therefore operate not on the state's but on its own terms – 'underground' or 'subterranean' in their words, 'because it takes place among those below and underneath institutional movements' (Marcos 2001: 162). Yet it is not only resistance that should take place 'beneath' the institutional monolith of the state (including the political parties that seek control of it), democracy itself should be a matter of autonomy or self-organisation at the 'base': 'The struggle for democracy in Mexico is not only a struggle for fair, free, and just elections; multi-party participation; or a change in power. It is, above all, the struggle for politics to be "citizenized" if you will' (1998 EZLN communiqué, cited in Johnston 2000: 488).

Self-organisation is also closely related to the Zapatistas' central concept of dignity, which is contrasted with dependence and servitude. Zapatismo itself is defined as originating with the sense of having had 'Enough! We no longer have the time or the will to wait for others to solve our problems. We have organized ourselves ...' (Zapatista editorial, cited in De Angelis 2000: 30). This connection between self-organisation and dignity is a constant of Zapatista discourse: 'Let no one receive anything from those who rule. Ask them to reject the handouts from the powerful. Let all the good people in this land organize with dignity ... We will not take anything from the government' (*Second Declaration of the Lacandon Jungle*, in Marcos 2001: 50).[2] Turning again to the example of the Mexican earthquake, the Zapatistas observe that

> while the government vacillated between false promises and stealing humanitarian aid, Civil society organized itself, by itself, to revive and rebuild ... Amid the debris, destruction, and death, these Mexicans rescued self-discovery and dignity ... They discovered that you can take a direct part in solving problems the government leaders ignore.
> (1996 EZLN communiqué, *Civil Society that so Perturbs*, in Marcos 2001: 128)[3]

There are, however, some fairly utopian interpretations of Zapatista anti-statism by theorists sympathetic to the movement. King and Villanueva (1998: 106), for example, see Zapatismo as playing out the elemental struggle 'between the revolutionary community and the statist community', a struggle which, once the revolutionaries succeed in subverting the atomisation wrought by statism, will see 'the days of the statist community ... numbered'. For Esteva also, the Zapatistas' regime of local autonomy 'is not a counterweight against state power, but makes the latter superfluous (1999: 163). Holloway too argues that, 'fully developed', Zapatismo would lead to the separation between state and society being 'overcome' and the state 'effectively abolished' (1998: 175–6).

Yet it is not at all clear that the Zapatistas believe that the state will 'wither away' in the face of civil society's self-organisation anymore than the left opposition in Eastern Europe thought the communist state would (indeed it was because they did not think that the authoritarian state was on the way out that these oppositionists developed their theory of civil society). Less ambitiously and more pluralistically, the Zapatistas' appear to aspire to create alternative *counter*-publics, as if in recognition that there will always be a dominant (statist) public that practices various forms of exclusion: 'The great lesson ... is that we can speak and listen, that without anyone's sponsorship or permission we can develop the mechanisms for dialogue' (Zapatista communiqué, cited in Lorenzano 1998: 156). So although autonomy is a principle that the Zapatistas believe 'could be applied equally to the townships, to the unions, to social groupings, to campesino groups ...' (Autonomedia 1995: 299), the details of self-organisation are understood to be the prerogative of local actors themselves. As one Yaqui leader within the EZLN autonomous region put it, 'Autonomy is not something that we need to ask someone for or that someone can give to us. We occupy a territory, in which we exert government and justice in our own way, and we practice self-defence ...' (cited in Esteva 1999: 163). This is in keeping with the Zapatistas' wider revolutionary principle of *preguntando caminamos* ('asking we walk'), which characterises revolution as a process of self-creative praxis rather than an already constituted 'solution' to be implemented regardless of context.

If democracy must take community form, being located in civil society rather than the state, then what does this mean in practice? *Mandar obediciendo* ('commanding by obeying' or 'leading by following') is the central organisational principle here, stemming as it does from indigenous practice, whereby those who lead should be effectively subjected to the rule of their communal bases. *Mandar obediciendo* comes close to council democracy in its operationalisation, which, in some more detail, involves the indigenous base communities, representing the major ethnic groups, democratically electing the top council of the EZLN, the Clandestine Revolutionary Indigenous Committee – General Command (CCRI-CG). Crucially, however, the base communities reserve the right of instant recall over the members of this committee, as of their own local committees, which are also democratically chosen in assembly. The military is organised in the conventional hierarchical way, but the EZLN leadership are keen to emphasise that strategic political and organisational decisions are taken by the base communities first. Indeed, the original decision to take up arms took this form, as did the decision not to sign the government's peace accords – these decisions then being sent upwards to the leadership via a 'pyramid of delegates' structure:

> There's a discussion of the pros and cons until the community itself decides that it's time to vote. They record results, showing how many were in favour, how many against, how many said they didn't know, with no distinction between men, women and children. Then ... the local representatives pass the results to the regional representatives, from there they go to the area coordination, from there to the Committees, and finally to the High Command.
>
> (interview with Marcos, cited in King and Villanueva 1998: 119)

Zapatismo and internationalist civil society

Much of the Zapatista discourse on civil society, as we have seen, echoes that of earlier radical discourses in both Latin America and Central–Eastern Europe. Far from emerging out of the ether of the Lacandon jungle, as is often implied, this discourse plugs in to a wider tradition of theory and practice that seeks to construct democracy primarily in civil society in the face of an authoritarian state. Yet there are also features of the Zapatista understanding of action in civil society that are distinct, reflecting the particular context within which they find themselves. The place of armed struggle in their political theory is one such unique feature, but perhaps more significant still is the increasingly international account of the agency of civil society that the Zapatistas provide.

As De Angelis observes, the Zapatista conception of internationalism and the value that they place on it arises from their understanding of themselves as 'one oppression among many, as one voice among many, as one struggle among many, as one assertion of dignity among many' (De Angelis 2000: 24). Internationalism has also been an important way of 'breaking out' of the isolation imposed by the virtual military siege of Chiapas, through establishing communication with as wide a set of sympathetic movements as possible. In this there is also an aspect of self-defence, since the more widely that news of events in Chiapas is disseminated, the harder authoritarian 'solutions' become for the Mexican state. Hence the cry, *no nos dejen solos* ('do not leave us alone'), which was made repeatedly in the first months of the ceasefire (Holloway 1998: 176), followed by messages of thanks to 'the national and international civil society for the support they have given us toward a dignified peace and against war' (Marcos 2001: 107):

> [W]e are not alone. With us, as well, are international organisations, such as Amnesty International, Americas Watch, Global Exchange, Mexico Solidarity Network, the National Commission for Democracy in Mexico – USA, Pastors for Peace, Humanitarian Law Project, Doctors of the World, Bread for the World, Doctors without Borders, and many others whose names escape me now, but not their histories or their commitment to peace.
>
> (Marcos 2001: 197)[4]

Yet perhaps the most pressing reason for allying Zapatismo with international civil society (see Marcos 2001: 107) is, according to the Zapatista spokespeople, that their struggle is itself an international one with nothing less than a transnational enemy – neoliberalism. Indeed, as noted above, the launch of the armed struggle was deliberately timed to coincide with the implementation of NAFTA, a free-trade agreement in accordance with neoliberal economic principles. The point has been made repeatedly since the uprising that it is against the backdrop of this hegemonic 'world doctrine' that Zapatismo must be envisaged, as in the following example from the inaugural ceremony of the American Planning of the Intercontinental Meeting for Humanity and Against Neoliberalism:

> Neoliberalism against Zapatismo. Why do they fear us? Why so much hate for so few and so small a group? Because we have defied them, and the worst part about that defiance is that it establishes a precedent? ... The powerful of the world are bothered by our existence and honor us with their threats. They are right. The Zapatista defiance is a global defiance ... A world system makes it possible to transform crime into government in Mexico. A national system makes it possible for crime to

> rule in Chiapas. In the mountains of the Mexican Southeast, we struggle for our country, for humanity, and against neoliberalism.
>
> (in Marcos 2001: 98)

The 'First Intercontinental *Encuentro* for Humanity and against Neoliberalism' was hosted by the Zapatistas in 1996, with 4,000 activists from five continents in attendance. Neoliberalism is seen as a cloak for 'a very powerful enemy' whose crimes 'recognize no national borders'. Putting flesh on the bones of this enemy, it is clear that the Zapatistas identify it as globalised or transnational capital, although the term 'Power' is used frequently as shorthand for such capital and its protectors in the state. 'Power globalizes to overcome the obstacles to its war of conquest. National governments are turned into the military underlings of a new war against humanity' (closing remarks at the First Intercontinental *Encuentro*, in Marcos 2001: 117):

> Neoliberalism is the most dehumanising socio-economic model, it is a factory for misery and exclusion for the benefit of the great transnational capital and their local allies, it sets in place the immunity of the market over the needs and aspirations of the people ...
>
> (FZLN communiqué, cited in Johnston 2000: 504).

Widening the analysis of the perceived source of oppression from the state, singular, to global capital *and* states, entails the transnationalisation of the Zapatistas' understanding of action in civil society also. Since 'the fence [of neoliberalism] is reproduced globally', 'the rebels search each other out ... they find each other and together break [the] fences ... Rebels from the five continents ... set off walking' (closing remarks at the First Intercontinental *Encuentro*, in Marcos 2001: 120–1). Elsewhere, the metaphor for global civil society shifts from one of tearing down fences to building bridges: '[W]e have also, together with others, extended bridges to the entire world and we have contributed to the creation (alongside men and women of the 5 continents) of a great network which struggles through peaceful means against neoliberalism ...' (from the *Fifth Declaration of the Lacandon Jungle*, cited in Johnston 2000: 491).

Yet in the Zapatistas' understanding, the 'echo that turns itself into many voices' (Marcos 2001: 122) is not simply some happy but unintended byproduct of essentially domestic resistance in the south of Mexico, nor does it merely represent worldwide demonstrations of solidarity for the Zapatistas' *particular* struggle. Instead, as stated in the *Second Declaration of La Realidad for Humanity and against Neoliberalism* (1996), the attempt to stimulate a worldwide movement in civil society is a purposeful *and* non-instrumental goal of Zapatismo: 'We declare', states this declaration with deliberate intent, that 'we will make a collective network of all our particular struggles and resistances, an intercontinental network of resistance against neoliberalism, an intercontinental network of resistance for humanity'. The Intercontinental

Consulta 'is part of the resistance we are organizing and one way of making contacts and encounters with other resistances. Part of a new way of doing political work in the world – that is what the Intercontinental *Consulta* wants to be' (in Marcos 2001: 125–6).

A question mark remains over the Zapatistas' putative internationalism, however. To what extent does it conflict with their frequent reference to the 'Nation'? Following De Angelis (2000: 20–1), we can make a number of observations that resolve this apparent tension in favour of a coherent internationalism. First, many such references can be read as shorthand for some notion of the whole or the ideal in political terms. In other words, the Zapatistas' appeal to the Nation functions as a metaphor for that self-determining political space from which they, and many other subaltern groups, are systematically excluded. The real Mexican 'nation' falls short of this ideal of Nation precisely because it is exclusionary and thereby expresses a false unity. Relatedly, this loftier idea of Nation involves putting the general interest before that of particular interests, whereas real nations (Mexico in particular) use appeals to nationalism in order to mask the rule of elites in their own interests. Second, the Nation is not defined racially or even geographically, but according to a 'subversive affinity': 'An imagery that is continually repeated is the one that regards everybody in the world sharing their struggles and visions as carrying a "bit of Mexico" in their hearts' (De Angelis 2000: 21). Cuninghame and Corona (1998: 16) affirm this, writing that the EZLN's concept of nationhood, although they make it sound more like anarchism than nationalism, is 'based on a network of autonomous communities rather than the historically centralised, hierarchical, nation-state'. Such a view concurs also with Holloway's observation (1998: 167) that Nation is used in the Zapatista communiqués 'in the less clearly defined sense of "homeland" (*patria*): the place where we happen to live, a space defined not just against imperialists but also (and more directly) against the state ... "Nation" in this sense refers to the idea of struggling wherever one happens to live, fighting against oppression, fighting for dignity'.

This denationalised, or internationalised, conception of action in civil society is perhaps the Zapatistas' most original contribution to radical discourse on the subject. Unlike most theoretical perspectives on global civil society, Zapatismo, for all that it does not have the character of systematic political philosophy, has a clear account of agency and an obvious target. State authoritarianism – the most immediate obstacle to democratic self-determination for most of the world's population – is to be understood within the wider context of neoliberalism as both global ideology and international political economy. It is to be variously resisted by those who are oppressed by it in a global network of opposition. Thus, with Zapatismo, the struggle of 'civil society against the state' takes on a whole new, this time global, meaning.

Part V

The democracy of civil society

Theory and practice

9 Theorising the democracy of civil society

The alternative models of civil society that we have considered so far clearly differ in many respects, not least in their orientation to questions of global politics. Yet what unites them all is the hope that we might build a democracy, or dramatically extend democratic space, within civil society itself. Thus it is to reflections on this hope that we must now turn if we are to draw any wider conclusions about alternatives to liberal democratic civil society, where it is a matter rather of what civil society can do for the state. In particular, we need to consider carefully what we can expect from the democracy of civil society by offering a theoretical articulation of the ideal prefigured in these various radical discourses. By then interrogating this ideal-type we should arrive at a fuller understanding of the potentialities and problems of such an approach to democratic theory. This ideal-type should be seen as a *reconstruction* of key features of the radical approaches reviewed thus far because the intention is not to offer a new model, but rather to ask some questions about the theory of a democracy of civil society.

In this chapter we shall pursue this objective as follows: first there will be a reconstruction of an ideal-type model of a democracy of civil society through an analysis of Hannah Arendt and Vaclav Havel's theories of political action in the public sphere, theories which in their different ways have done much to refocus attention away from statist democracy towards a less centralised and institutionalised form of democracy that prioritises autonomy. Then, under 'Appraising republican civil society theory', some hard questions will be asked of this more republican model of civil society, speculating in some detail on whether it constitutes a comprehensive and coherent alternative for democratic theory.

Havel and Arendt on politics in the public sphere

Civil society, as we have seen, is now often viewed in instrumental terms. Pluralists emphasise its role in helping to ensure that the democratic state has the information it needs to meet citizen as consumer demands. Liberals point up its function in counterbalancing the state in order to prevent an over-concentration of power in society. Gellner (1995: 142), for example, states that 'civil society is that set of diverse non-governmental institutions which is strong enough to counterbalance the state [and which] can prevent the state from dominating and atomising the rest of society'. What all such approaches have in common, however, is that they see civil society itself (if not its wider effects) as essentially apolitical and also view its importance solely in relation to the state.

Yet as we have also seen, there is a more republican body of thought on civil society that views this sphere as a democratic end in itself, as a space for the realisation of that elusive promise of democracy – self-government. This approach to civil society is now most closely associated with theorists of the democratic opposition in East-Central Europe during the 1970s and 1980s. Subsequently, it is seen by some commentators as applicable only to authoritarian contexts, where the independent life of society has to be defended against the incursions of the 'totalising' state. Apart from performing this – essentially transitional – function, it is assumed by these critics that self-management in civil society is both impracticable and undesirable.

However, two of the most influential theorists of republican self-organisation – Hannah Arendt and Václav Havel – appear to suggest that public space outside the state represents the future of politics (if it is to have a future at all), and not just some transitional phase on the journey towards liberal democracy. By pointing to common ground between these theorists, the intention here is to reconstruct a model of republican civil society that can then be analysed further in the section 'Appraising republican civil society theory'. Against the accusation that this involves constructing a 'straw man', it is important to emphasise the heuristic value of working with an ideal-type model of republican civil society that makes explicit (by making maximal) the implications of valorising the democracy of civil society.

The public and the private

Let us remind ourselves first of the content of Havel's republican theory of civil society:

> What is this independent life of society? ... It includes ... the most varied free, civic attitudes, including instances of independent self-organisation. In short, it is an area in which living within the truth becomes articulate and materialises in a visible way.
>
> (Havel 1985: 65)

Havel's characterisation of civil society as private as well as public, a characterisation that was clearest when he talked of political opposition in terms of the apparently individualistic imperative to 'live in truth', has led to accusations that his *oeuvre* is 'antipolitical'. Yet, for reasons already set out in Chapter 2, Havel will be read here as a distinctively republican thinker who was in fact passionate about the affairs of the polis. So what should we make of this apparent contradiction? Keane puts it well when he observes that, for Havel, the move towards meaningful social cooperation depends in the first instance on developing mechanisms of self-protection and individuation (1988b: 124). With Havel, then, the public and the private are intimately related, it is just a matter of how that relationship should be constructed such that the public is not allowed to destroy the private (totalitarianism), nor the private allowed to destroy the public (atomising liberal-individualism):

> Anti-political politics ... is possible and can be effective, even though by its very nature it cannot calculate its effect beforehand. That effect, to be sure, is of a wholly different nature from what the West considers political success. It is hidden, indirect, long term and hard to measure. Often it exists only in the invisible realm of social consciousness ...
>
> (Havel 1988: 397)

Havel's emphasis upon the private sphere of moral–ethical individuation, Mische suggests, 'paves the way for a type of civic participation in which human subjectivity is not sacrificed to politics' (1993: 245). Crucially, though, *civic participation* is the telos of Havel's account: the individual, 'living in truth', is not an end in his/herself but becomes 'the very basis for civic responsibility and public action in concert with others'. We have here what Mische, comparing Havel to Arendt, terms a 'conciliatory' conception of public and private. Mische goes on to argue that, with Havel, we return to Arendt's 'lost treasure', that all too uncommon synthesis of private concern with public action (1993: 245).[1] However, the importance of *this* synthesis (contra Marxist theory) is that a sense of the *antithesis* between public and private is retained in order to safeguard subjectivity 'against the encroachments of totalitarianism'. Nevertheless:

> the aim is not to maintain two mutually opposed realms, but rather to understand the one as a 'holding area' of the self, from which the self must necessarily emerge to act publicly within the other. In Havel's view, it is the recovery of the 'hidden sphere' of subjectivity that provides the basis for the 'independent life of society'.
>
> (Mische 1993: 245)

For Havel, then, defence of the private sphere is crucial *not* because this is understood to be the only authentically human sphere. Instead, its importance lies in the very political resistance that it offers to the hegemony of the institutionalised 'lie' (state-socialism in this instance), which threatens to undermine the autonomous human subject who forms the basis of authentic public life. The antidote to this, for Havel, is the reconstruction of moral and civic life outside of government control. This holds out the hope of both personal and political autonomy, in short, of self-rule.

It is not surprising that commentators sometimes wonder whether Havel is paraphrasing Arendt (Jorgensen 1992: 39). For, like Havel, Arendt posits a link between the private and political spheres in the sense that the former is a necessary condition for true individuality in the *public* sphere. Writing approvingly of the Greek city-states, Arendt recalls a public realm 'reserved for individuality; it [being] the only place where men could show who they really and inexchangeably were' (1958b: 41). As to the purely 'privative trait of privacy', Arendt again agrees with the ancients that this is a 'state of being deprived of something' and also notes that 'nothing proved easier to destroy than the privacy and private morality of people who thought of nothing but safeguarding their private lives' (1958b: 38).

Agency in civil society

It has been a criticism of both Arendt and Havel that identifying civil society with this form of republican agency is elitist, reserving this, the 'true' public sphere, only for the enlightened few. Yet for Havel, citizens or activists within the 'parallel polis' are not a pre-defined class of people, but identify themselves in context as those who seek publicly to resist the 'normalising' techniques and disciplines of 'totalitarian' regimes (and indeed of mass politics in *all* its forms). It is worth recalling here Havel's assertion that the division between the independent citizen and the 'automated' one is a line of conflict that 'runs de facto through *each person*, for everyone in his or her way is both a victim and a supporter of the system' (Havel 1985: 39; emphasis added). In other words, this is an existential rather than a psychological model of agency (there are none of Pareto's 'lions' and 'foxes' for Havel) and although it has often been attacked for its apparent elitism, it is clear that Havel is not *ex ante* excluding anyone from it. The 'islands' of civic engagement and solidarity', while they will always be small in relation to the sea of apathy and quietism, are open to all who see the need to alight on them (Isaac 1998: 117). Any exclusion from this republican agency is, at least in principle, entirely self-chosen.

The same defence might be used in order to dispel the whiff of elitism surrounding Arendt's conception of citizenship within her 'elementary republics'. While Arendt clearly sees these republics as being fenced off from 'the mass', this is not an aristocratic elite (as can be seen in her celebration of workers councils in revolutionary Russia and, later, in Hungary) but an action-orientated one. The only criterion for what must always be *voluntary* membership of an elementary republic is the possession of a 'public spirit':

> [O]nly those who as voluntary members of an 'elementary republic' have demonstrated that they care about the state of the world would have the right to be heard in the conduct of the business of the republic. However ... th[is] exclusion ... would not depend upon an outside body; if those who belong are self-chosen, those who do not belong are self-excluded.
>
> (Arendt 1963: 285)

Besides, it might be said that the acceptance by Arendt and Havel of the fact that not everybody will be a 'civic engager' is probably a more realistic assessment of the human condition than that of other neo-republicans. Advocates of participatory democracy, for example, return in a more or less explicit way to Aristotle's *zoon politikon*, implying that all citizens would be activists if only access to the public sphere (or spheres) were more readily available. Yet:

> Arendt's emphasis on the formal qualities of citizenship made her position rather distant from those advocates of participation during the 1960s who saw it in terms of recapturing a sense of intimacy, of community, of warmth and of authenticity. For Arendt, political participation was important because it permitted the establishment of relations of civility and solidarity among citizens.
>
> (Passerin d'Entreves 1992: 150)

The republican citizenship of Havel and Arendt is also preferable to the politically even more romantic appeal to local self-organisation based on a return to so called 'organic' communities. Paul Piccone, for example, although starting from a similar point to Havel and Arendt in terms of pointing up depoliticisation and growing technocracy in modern society, ends up with a wholesale rejection of modernity itself:

> The concrete existence of organic communities in remote corners of the Mid-West or in the mountains of the Swiss cantons only means that in these places it is probably much easier to lead a satisfying life within a viable political organisation free of the pathologies of modernity.
>
> (1996: 165)

This conflation of self-management with 'organic communities' is likely to be far more exclusionary and chauvinist than Havel and Arendt's self-constituting republics, which, as purely *political* communities, have no such imagined roots in history.

Civil society and modernity

Havel and Arendt are undeniably critics of modernity. Havel's pejorative identification of the 'essential trait of all modern civilisation' as its 'mass characteristics and its consumer orientation' (1988: 387) is close to Arendt's critique of the 'rise of the social' under modernity. Taking Arendt first, the accusation of a utopian ambition to retreat from modernity back to pre-modern forms of community has often been made on the basis that the classical polis constitutes her frame of reference. One response to this accusation is to reiterate that Arendt by no means rejects out of hand the separation of spheres characteristic of modernity. Her concern lies with the rise of mass society and the closure of public space and not with the recognition of individuality and of the private sphere per se. Indeed, Arendt is approving of the possibility of individuals' self-exclusion from public life, even if this is not a route she herself advocates: '[S]uch self-exclusion ... give[s] substance and reality to one of the most important negative liberties we have enjoyed since the ancient world, namely, freedom from politics, which was unknown to Rome or Athens' (Arendt 1963: 284).

Second, Arendt's republicanism avoids being backward looking in the sense that it is not premised upon pre-political community. This much is clear from her discussion of the American Revolution, when she writes that the revolutionaries were wrong for thinking that they were merely retrieving ancient rights and liberties, but, 'politically speaking, had been right in deriving the stability and authority of any given body politic from its beginnings' (1963: 199). For Arendt, the very fact that these revolutionaries thought of themselves as 'founders'

> indicates the extent to which they must have known that it would be the act of foundation itself, rather than an Immortal Legislator or self-evident truth or any other transcendent, transmundane source, which eventually would become the foundation of authority in the new body politic.
> (1963: 205)

Elsewhere, Arendt reiterates her sense that politics is always an artefact when she states that 'the political realm rises directly out of acting together, the "sharing of words and deeds". Thus action ... is the one activity which constitutes it' (Arendt 1958b: 198). So for Arendt, as Passerin d'Entreves sees it, there is no appealing to 'natural rights' or to the Volk as a basis for political community, since

> [t]he search for intimacy is characteristic of those groups *excluded* from the public realm ... [B]ut such intimacy is brought at the price of worldlessness, which 'is always a form of barbarism', since it represents 'psychological substitutes ... for the loss of the common, visible world'... The true ties of intimacy and warmth can never become political; the only true political ties are those of civic friendship and solidarity, since they 'make political demands and preserve reference to the world'.
> (1992: 151)

Canovan concurs with this reading of Arendt:

> Arendt's conception of the public realm is opposed not only to society but also to community: to *Gemeinschaft* as well as to *Gesellschaft*. While greatly valuing warmth, intimacy and naturalness in private life, she insisted on the importance of a formal, artificial public realm in which what mattered was the people's actions rather than their sentiments; in which the natural ties of kinship and intimacy were set aside in favour of

> a deliberate, impartial solidarity with other citizens; in which there was enough space between people for them to stand back and judge one another coolly and objectively.
>
> (1985: 632)

Havel's attitude to modernity is perhaps more ambiguous than Arendt's. For Havel theorises totalitarianism not only as a function of ideology gone wrong, but as stemming from modernity itself. This is only hinted at in the earlier *The Power of the Powerless* (1979), where Havel is critical merely of a politics that thinks it 'knows best what the people need' and which secures by violence 'a better future' (1985: 69, 71). These criticisms, while they could be construed as being directed at the Enlightenment project in general, must surely be understood as attacking Marxist–Leninist vanguardism and its outworkings under state-socialism. Yet, in a later piece, Havel writes like a much more convinced critic of modernity as such:

> States grow ever more machine-like; people are transformed into casts of extras, as voters, producers, consumers ... In politics, good and evil, categories of the natural world [lifeworld] – and therefore obsolete remnants of the past – lose all absolute meaning; the sole method of politics is quantifiable success ... This impersonal power has achieved its most complete expression in the totalitarian systems ... [However] in the relation of Western Europe to the totalitarian systems, I think that no error could be greater than the one looming largest – that of a failure to understand the totalitarian systems for what they are: a convex mirror of all modern civilisation. They are, most of all, a convex mirror of the inevitable consequences of rationalism, a grotesquely magnified image of its own deep tendencies, an extreme outcropping of its own development and an ominous product of its own expansion.
>
> (1988: 388–9)

This antimodernism appears to set the 'later' Havel apart from his earlier, more specifically republican concern with the public sphere. For Havel, the 'lifeworld' is not now but one of a number of 'differentiated' spheres, it is the *only* sphere of true human existence – the sphere from which Enlightenment reason broke away in a first step towards the modern state and its impersonal, totalising and dehumanising power:

> Both the [child] and the [medieval] peasant are rooted far more intensely in what some philosophers call 'the natural world', or 'life-world' than most modern adults. They have not yet grown alienated from the world of their actual personal experience ...
>
> (1988: 382)

Yet, despite his reservations concerning modernity, Havel does not follow Piccone and the conservative-right in terms of wanting to return, ahistorically, to some mythical organic community of 'the people'. Indeed, there is no sense that Havel thinks that modernity can be undone and so he arguably remains committed to a form of modern politics, or at least to a form of politics located *within* modernity. Like Arendt, he is more concerned with survival strategies necessitated by mass society – particularly with the survival of politics itself within authentic public spaces. For, ultimately, Arendt's 'elementary republics' are still 'oases *in* the desert' of modern mass politics, while Havel's democratic opposition constitutes 'small islands *in* a sea of [modern] apathy'. (Isaac 1998: 115–17, emphasis added.)

Reconstructing republican civil society

Reconstructing a model of republican civil society from the theory of Havel and Arendt, then, involves highlighting the following features. Republican civil society includes, first, a concern with the preservation of private autonomy for the sake of a larger sphere of freedom in those public spaces in which individuals come together non-instrumentally (which is to say politically, in this republican reading of the term). Thus, although the boundaries of the political are extended beyond those of the state, there remains a strong commitment to some form of separation of spheres between public and private. This two-track approach establishes republican civil society as something of a 'third way' between liberal and collectivist understandings of politics. The individual's private sphere matters, but its preservation is not the sole end of politics, as in liberalism. Yet neither is the collective reified, as in more communitarian visions, since the public sphere is understood not as a thing in itself, but as that artificially constructed (though crucial nonetheless) space in which *individuals* come together.

Second, republican civil society requires active citizenship, but not in the sense of explicit calls for high levels of participation, but in the more existential terms of calling individuals out of the desert of depoliticised mass society to pursue self-rule. This agency is therefore voluntary; there are no historically privileged or biologically privileged actors and there is no inevitability. Civil society, rather, depends on those who actively attempt to shape their own world instead of having it shaped for them. It is not about recapturing or artificially constructing intimate communities, but about political action as an end in itself:

> The republican idea ... puts critical inquiry in the heart of community membership; citizens belong to the republic through the active concern with values promoted or neglected by their polity ... If assignment to nationhood is unconditional and making it conditional is an act of treason, the republic is judged and evaluated by the degree of freedom it offers and secures for its citizens in setting the conditions of membership.
> (Bauman 1999: 168)

Third, republican civil society looks away from the modern state as the focus of political action and towards a more decentralised model of self-government (Arendt's 'elementary republics'). There is much scepticism about modernity in as much as this epoch is seen as coinciding with an alarming growth in the technologies and ideologies of rule and manipulation associated with the state. Yet calls for modernity to be replaced by some pre- or postmodern form of society are absent. Unless democratic autonomy in civil society can be carved out from within modernity, it will be nothing at all.

Having reconstructed in broad outline an ideal-type model of republican civil society, the question for the remainder of the chapter is: Can it really work as a means to greater self-government as its proponents suggest? In order to address this question, we need to bring the theory-philosophy of the republican public sphere closer to the ground and to analyse it as a political project in relation to questions of agency and other spheres of social life.

Appraising republican civil society theory

Where will it come from?

One problem with emphasising self-management in civil society (as opposed to more instrumental instances of self-organisation, for example pressure groups) is that there appears to be precious little of it in contemporary liberal democracy. This unwelcome fact appears to have prompted some defenders of republican civil society towards a less ambitious position in which civil society takes on a more communitarian role. In Havel's more recent comments on civil society, for example, he speaks of a sphere that has little to do with defending autonomy and subjectivity as the basis for a politics of 'truth', but which can function as a means to other ends, such as community spirit and civic pride. Although civil society is still defined as a 'society with a large measure of self-government where citizens assume their role in public affairs', Havel goes on to say that:

> a social space that fosters the feeling of solidarity between people and love for one's community ... Civil society encourages ordinary people to participate in government, thereby strengthening relations between citizens and their state ... Collective activism not only improves citizen pride; it also nurtures such positive traits as 'love thy neighbour'.
>
> (interview with Havel 1996: 18–19)

This more 'community building' or 'communitarian' model of civil society, which is currently very popular, is prima facie simply another version of a republican civil society that emphasises political participation. Yet on a number of counts it is actually more problematic than the more ambitious, non-instrumental model outlined by Arendt and the 'early' Havel outlined above. First, it has been a powerful argument of Piccone and other contributors to the journal *Telos* in recent years that 'the fashionable calls for the "reconstitution of [communitarian] civil society" are futile', because 'before it can constitute itself as such, "civil" society needs a communitarian structure which no longer exists, and whose reconstitution cannot be formulated as a bureaucratic project – no matter how well funded' (Frankel 1997: 64). Second, and quite apart from their likely failure, there is an obvious paradox in projects to rebuild self-government from the top down! In addition, as Chandler points out, the desire to extend and deepen political participation is often related chiefly to the level of individual 'inclusion' and there is relative silence on the wider story of the accountability of power holders. The danger here is of a 'shift from a political understanding of democracy, as a collective decision-making process, to a therapeutic one, concerned with an individual's subjective perception' of being involved (Chandler 2000: 7). Making a similar point, Saward notes that:

> The [democratic] requirement of effective inputs holds that inputs must determine outcomes; they must not merely add to a sense of efficacy or belonging via political participation. Inputs must make a difference, must be more than symbolic or tokenistic. This condition follows from the principle of political equality because any shift towards symbolic politics is a shift to a system in which the few decide for the many.
>
> (1998: 50–1)

In sum, the problem of agency for a republican civil society cannot be addressed solely in theory, where it becomes a matter of reconstructing self-organisation from the top down, which is contradictory. Yet the weakness of such agency in the West, which is what has driven theorists to make these mistakes, should not of course obscure what has already been demonstrated: that self-management in civil society *has* been practised in various places and at various times, and continues, against the odds, to be so. In these instances, self-determining actors in civil society have identified themselves, and this, following Arendt and the 'early' Havel, is all that we can hope for.

Is it fully modern?

A further problem with the republican reading of civil society flows from its ambiguities towards some of the chief characteristics of modernity. Notwithstanding Havel and Arendt's awareness that modernity cannot be undone, they can still be accused of not facing up to the complexity of modern social forms in that they focus only on republican publics to the exclusion of the many other moments and spheres of life. For most commentators, by contrast, the modern separation of spheres between state, civil society and economy is central to any coherent account of civil society (see Habermas and his followers, for example). Such *differentia* coincide with the rise of the nation-state and capitalist economy and cannot be wished away.

Yet from a republican perspective, and Havel is particularly strong on this, the rise of the modern state has actually been the most significant threat to the space of civic association. So republican theorists are not, a priori, hostile to 'non-modern', undifferentiated forms of free political association. Nor are they quite so sanguine concerning 'the harsh logic of differentiation', as one republican theorist describes it, which means that '*demokratia* is seen as the antithesis of civic entitlement and of civilisation itself' (Anderson 1996: 114). Certainly, Habermas seems a long way from Havel and Arendt when he claims that

> the public opinion that is worked up via democratic procedures into communicative power cannot 'rule' of itself, but can only point the use of administrative power in specific directions ... Read in procedural terms, the idea of popular sovereignty refers to a context that, while enabling the self-organisation of a legal community, is not at the disposal of the citizens' will in any way.
>
> (1994: 9–10)

This 'harsh logic of differentiation' also informs Cohen and Arato's idea of civil society, which is neatly summarised by Ely as implying that the 'pure republican' formation of political will by elements of the public sphere, 'are only *catalysts* and not the end results of political action'. Ely goes as far as to claim that, for New Left theorists such as Habermas, Cohen and Arato, this hostility to the republican self-management agenda actually motivated their turn to the concept of civil society in the first place. 'At a time when "socialism" and the critique of capitalism had suddenly come into disrepute ... [t]his move was not merely "tactical". The concept of "civil society" systematically turned *libertarian* into *liberal* ideas' (Ely 1992: 177–8).

However, a central weakness of the republican model of civil society, it can be argued, is precisely this libertarian aspect. For the tendency to valorise self-organisation in civil society means that there is little sense provided of how such self-organisation might relate to the modern state. Yet this institution appears to be a more or less permanent feature of modern politics (although it is always changing, it will certainly not just disappear); its potentially destructive effects upon free association will not be overcome merely by seeking to enlarge the realm of civil society itself. On this account, political projects have to be worked out that can deal with the state directly, not by effectively ignoring it. Indeed, the general hostility to the state means that much republican civil society theory, if only by default, is in danger of endowing 'civil society with a deceptive aura of moral purity and disinterestedness' (Mische 1993: 246). Ironically, this is actually quite antipolitical, since it implies that action in civil society is always positive-sum.

Important as these criticisms are, however, returning to actual instances of self-management in civil society, there seems something misguided and unfair about asking practitioners to deliver an account of how better to democratise the state when there is a lack of ideas on this front *wherever* one looks. Turning instead to the more localised democracy of civil society, however imperfect and partial, seems a highly reasonable response in the face of this crisis of radical theory and practice at the macro level, where, repeatedly, the revolution has 'devoured its own children'.

The charge of voluntarism

Returning to the *theory* of republican civil society, there is a perceived failure here to build upon normative foundations by providing practical advice to institution builders. There has undoubtedly been a tendency to describe civil society as pure, unmediated agency. This contrasts unfavourably with liberal democratic approaches to civil society, which, whatever else they miss, are alive to the concrete institutional nexus outside the state, to the instantiation of civil society. Gellner, for example, preferred the idea of civil society to the idea of democracy for precisely this reason. Democracy misleadingly implies an 'underlying model of society which is a fruit of the will of its participants and members ... Civil society is greatly preferable, [since it does not] ignore the fact that institutions and cultures *precede* decisions rather than *follow* them' (Gellner 1994: 184–5). In sum, the critique by Blaug of Habermasian conceptualisations of the public sphere could reasonably be applied to the republican model of civil society as well:

> Talk of the public sphere never quite comes down to earth ... [This] alert[s] us to just how little actual crossing over from normative theory to empirical institutional design is attempted ... There seems, therefore, to be a kind of missing tier of theory – this being an account of what normatively grounded institutions might be like and how they might actually function.
>
> (1997: 112)

The rather prosaic requirement to construct real-world institutions when building republican public spheres is not the only constraint to action overlooked by republican theorists of civil society, however. Agnes Heller (1991) has made a persuasive argument that, given their often relentless privileging of 'the political', radical political models *tout court* tend to exclude too many issues of importance for a nuanced understanding of modern politics. Heller is interesting for our discussion because she analyses the work of Havel and Arendt in this regard. With Arendt, Heller notes, everyday issues seem to be written out of the realm of the political. Arendt's critique – and desired exclusion from political life – of the 'rise of the social' (that instrumental, technical aspect of modern society) is well known. Yet Havel also shows dismay towards an increasingly technical politics in both East and West and talks esoterically of political action as being concerned with self-presentation and with the substantive goals of life and polity.

So republican civil society theory emerges, paradoxically, as being relatively uninterested in the everyday concerns of the very citizens who are being called to discover the wonders of self-government. As Heller observes, although radical conceptualisations of the political come to the rescue of political philosophy with its usual excesses of science and realism, they are often themselves overly narrow precisely for not including 'mere daily practices'. Therefore, while theorists such as Arendt and Havel manifestly do not intend to exclude groups or opinions from their theory, they do exclude issues (Heller 1991: 336). However, we might question whether the exclusion of issues does not also imply the exclusion of groups of people themselves. For so long as republican civil society is concerned only with goal-orientated debate that is 'world disclosing', to what extent can ordinary citizens (constrained by lack of time and expertise, as always) hope to influence the political agenda? In addition, what space is left in republican civil society for the more everyday decisions that will always need to be taken, the outcomes of which might actually concern citizens far more than the philosophical discourse anticipated by Havel and Arendt? It is at this point that a republican theory of civil society just does not seem prepared to make the necessary trade-off with the requirement for some level of efficiency.

Republicans' undoubtedly powerful rejection of utilitarian politics, then, leads to the prioritisation of political action or agency. This much appears reasonable. But it is not enough just to celebrate agency without signalling where it might be thwarted by bureaucratisation, market-capitalism and patriarchy, to name but a few possible obstacles to a revival of 'the political'. In a potentially even more serious omission, neither do republican models of civil society provide an account of how deliberation in the public sphere is potentially distorted, not only by external constraints, but also by power *within* the polis itself. That is, unequal resources and patriarchy, for example, are problems that affect fair deliberation in the first place. The inequalities within civil society, therefore, cannot be bracketed out of the 'parallel polis' simply because it lies outside formal power structures; power is too ubiquitous for this to be possible, and any definition of the political that fails to recognise this is ultimately too narrow.

Whatever happened to the market?

Continuing along this line of argument, a major problem with the republican model of civil society stems from the identification of civil society with a society of free citizens, rather than a society of economically 'free' property owners in the market sphere as in the classical theory. One consequence of this de-economised version of civil society is that the relationship between civil society and the market – so important in the classical theory and for orthodox Marxism – is little deliberated by radical civil societarians, just as it is passed over by the New Left in their overly conceptual tripartite separation of state, market and civil society. Neither properly account for the structural–historical relationship of civil society to the market, a lacuna attested to by the absence of any detailed consideration by radical civil society theorists of the role of the market in the life of civil society and by the claim, in the case of the New Left, that the market and civil society simply have different rationalities. Both approaches have therefore failed to identify how the market sphere of capitalism might in practice be resisted by the 'public sphere' of civil society when the former encroaches on the latter, and who the agents are that could do this. In abandoning the Marxist idea of overcoming the market sphere, these theorists go to the opposite extreme and arguably leave civil society relatively defenceless against market forces.[2] Although he is in many ways close to the Habermasian approach to civil society, this is what Keane argues when he criticises the artificial separation of civil society from the economy:

> First, civil society, because it is defined so narrowly, is left economically passive, and deprived of any property resources which would enable it to defend or enhance its power. Second, civil society, the realm of (potential) freedom, is viewed positively, while the economy is implicitly viewed negatively, as a realm of necessity in which only money speaks (cf. the neo-conservative view). The material conditions of life in civil society are degraded to a mere instrument for the ends desired by civil society – just as the classical concept of civil society rested upon the salience and unfreedom of the *oikos*.
>
> (1988b: 86)

From a more Marxist perspective, the exoneration of civil society from its status as a site of economic oppression, and its transformation into a realm of putative democratic autonomy, obfuscates capitalism – 'as the sphere exerting a systematic compulsion over all other spheres':

> Here the danger lies in the fact that the totalising logic and the coercive power of capitalism become invisible … [The] effect is to conceptualise away the problem of capitalism by disaggregating society into fragments, with no overarching power structure, no totalising unity, no systemic coercions – in other words, no capitalist system, with its expansionary drive and its capacity to penetrate every aspect of social life.
>
> (Wood 1995: 245)

Continuing this attack in the face of the commonplace response that other spheres, apart from the economic or structural, self-evidently exist, Wood writes:

> This argument is circular and question begging. To deny the totalising logic of capitalism, it is not enough merely to indicate the plurality of

> social identities and relations ... But 'civil society' arguments ... do not typically take the form of historically and empirically refuting the determinative effects of capitalist relations. Instead ... they tend to proceed as abstract philosophical arguments ... or, most commonly, as moral prescriptions about the dangers of devaluing 'other' spheres of human experience.
>
> (1995: 246–7)

The problem of power

It is clear that the ambition of republican civil society theory to construct spheres of unsullied self-government is also open to the charge of utopianism. Indeed, from the perspective of Foucault and his followers, the terms 'self-determination' or 'self-government' are effectively oxymorons, certainly when understood collectively. Power is essentially productive rather than merely coercive, so liberty cannot be conceived of as involving the limitation or controlling of power, since there is nothing independent of power to liberate. Crucially, power is constitutive of identity itself, there is no 'true' self (one thinks of Havel's individual 'living in truth' here) ready to step from the shadows once power has been restrained.

More specific applications of this Foucauldian approach to the study of political power are even more unsettling for defenders of a republican civil society. The spectre for Havel and Arendt is one of the state and 'the social' impinging on the public sphere. But recent studies in 'governmentalism' seek to demonstrate that it is neither the 'total' state nor the 'social' state that defenders of self-government have to fear today. Instead, the trend appears to be towards persons and activities being governed by technologies of government through community (Rose 1993). 'Community' becomes 'not simply the territory of government, but a means of government: its ties, bonds, forces, and affiliations are to be celebrated, encouraged, nurtured, shaped, and instrumentalized'. It is this instrumentalising of 'the self-governing properties of the subjects of government themselves' (in enterprises, associations, neighbourhoods, interest groups and communities) that makes some of the categories of republican thought appear so problematic (Rose 1996: 335):

> The political vocabulary structured by oppositions between state and civil society, public and private ... coercion and consent, sovereignty and autonomy, and the like, does not adequately characterise the way in which rule is exercised in modern liberal democracies. Political power is exercised today through a profusion of shifting alliances between diverse authorities ... Power is not so much a matter of imposing constraints upon citizens as of 'making up' citizens capable of bearing a kind of regulated freedom ... individuals are not merely subjects of power but play a part in its operations.
>
> (Rose and Miller 1992: 174)

Thus, while Havel accepts that the line between the free citizen and the automated one runs through each individual, the governmentalists argue effectively that the individual is *all* automaton. Subsequently, that aspect of the individual which Havel identifies with personal autonomy, and thus with the potential for self-government in civil society, is excised completely. Agency itself appears to have been deconstructed beyond the point of no return. What hope for self-rule is there left? For theorists such as Rose, any such hope was only ever mere romanticism. Echoing earlier elitist critics such as Michels, they argue that even if republicans could point to authentically free citizens, they are simply failing to recognise that *organisations and associations* 'cannot be reduced to the equivalence of self-determining individuals. Hence, all theories of further democratisation must dispel illusions of citizen-based communities and come to terms with the complex role of organisations' (Frankel 1997: 87).

We are left, therefore, with the concern that the aspiration for self-rule in 'oases in the desert' contains an unsustainable account of the human subject and of human organisation. Do any of us really know, or can we even imagine, what it is to 'live in truth', to know that all our desires are authentically our own? That is, could we really rule ourselves perfectly even if none of the daunting *external* constraints on autonomy existed? Also, imagining for a moment that we, as individuals, could 'live in truth', how then would we translate this into a *collective* experience of self-rule? Many of our experiences of collective action convince us rather that this is not a positive-sum experience, but a messy business requiring perpetual compromise (though it may well be no less valuable for all that).

In the final analysis, of course, practitioners of political action in civil society must work out the implications of these observations, particularly with regard to the complexity of organisation, for themselves. Here, though, the point that needs to be made is that they will get little guidance in doing so from the theory of republican civil society, which has a tendency to deny the intricacies of power, agency and organisation.

Is it gender exclusive?

The last, but by no means the least, problem with the republican model of civil society to be highlighted here is its potential reproduction of gender exclusions. For feminists, the problem in general with models of civil society is that the line drawn between public and private does not take gender into account. This has been well documented with regard to liberal theory. However, much the same concern applies also to the republican model.

Where then does the line of gender exclusion fall for the republican model of civil society? As with the liberal model, the problem begins with the invisibility of the domestic sphere within it. The republican model of civil society, while not excluding women explicitly from citizenship, is consistent in giving little or no consideration to the means necessary for the high levels of participation desired within the self-managing sphere of civil society. The supposedly universal republican citizen is revealed, therefore, as an artificially unencumbered male. Consequently, the application of this model in practice would mean that women located primarily within relationships characterised by interdependence would be effectively marginalised – both in terms of their ability to participate in the life of civil society and in terms of the types of issues raised within it. Thus republicans appear to be just as guilty as liberal philosophers of assuming that the individual is constituted prior to relationships of dependence. Indeed, given their ethical individualism, collective responsibility for Havel and Arendt begins only in the 'public sphere' of civil society; the domestic sphere, as for the ancients, appears as a realm of mere necessity far from the 'transcendent' political concerns of civil society.

A further problem with republican civil society from a feminist perspective is that, in seeking to overcome the totalitarian implications of the obliteration of the public–private distinction, women's problematic position within liberal society is reintroduced by the back door. As we have seen, this renewed commitment to a separation of public and private spheres has often been symbolic for republicans (Havel wants to protect a realm of privacy in order to reconstitute civic action and publicity – i.e. public and private are linked for him). Yet the problem remains of a wider failure to attempt a redefinition of the private sphere that avoids unthinkingly conflating it with the domestic. For in including the family in the private sphere, domestic relations are at once *excluded* from civil society and male domination within this sphere is labelled as an essentially private matter (with all the implications that this has for reproducing patriarchy with the tacit consent of the political public sphere). Indeed, it is not immediately apparent how republican theorists can move legitimately from a conception of privacy as attached to individuals, to one that identifies the sphere of non-intervention with the family. As Pateman has noted, 'unlike republican critics who seek only to reinstate the political in public life, feminist critics insist that an alternative to the liberal conception must also encompass the relationship between public and domestic life' (1987: 120).

The democracy of civil society: problems in theory

The ambition of theorists articulating a vision of a democracy located in civil society is easy to identify with. They are motivated by the desire to maximise self-government and see in statist forms of democracy the antithesis of such government – one that an orientation towards civil society may help ameliorate. The problems begin to arise, however, as we have seen, with republican civil society as a fully developed democratic theory. First, civil society read as societal self-management runs up against the utopia of the withering away of the state. Besides, Havel, Arendt and other republican theorists of civil society would condemn any such state-free 'utopia' as threatening the over-politicisation of society all over again, except this time, contra totalitarianism, 'from below'. In other words, the desire for maximal self-government in civil society must at some level contradict the call, made by the same theorists, for a separation of spheres between public and private in order to ward off 'totalising' politics. Exactly how much self-government should there be in civil society, then? And how would the state need to be reconfigured in order to take account of these changes? The simple answer is: we do not know; radical theorists do not tell us.

Second, it is not at all clear how republican civil society relates to the market sphere, even though market power is clearly a major, perhaps *the* major, obstacle to meaningful self-government today. In a world of increasingly globalised market power, public spaces presumably also need to go global. Global civil society is much talked about, as we have seen, but appears weak and patchy in practice. The hard truth seems to be that although economic power is global, the communities necessary for self-government in civil society, if they are to be accessible, must be largely local. Thus there is presently a poor fit between the institutions republicans think capable of socialising power and that power itself; the abiding image is of David and Goliath. In addition, even if civil society institutions with the necessary weight to reform market practices existed (and states have fared badly here, so this aspiration appears quite unrealistic), how would they do it? As we have seen, radical civil societarians are almost completely silent on the forms of social ownership necessary to the extension of self-government into the economic sphere.

Third, despite success elsewhere, where are the republican public spheres of civil society to come from in Western liberal democracies? Where is the account of agency that could explain how the gap between the ideal and the real might be bridged in *these* societies? And even having arrived at this ideal, how then would it be preserved from harm and decay? That is, what institutional structures are needed for ongoing self-government in civil society? Because republican theorists of civil society are largely silent on these issues in relation to liberal democracy, they are open to the charge from within these societies that their models are voluntaristic, utopian even.

Finally, taking on board the Zapatistas' insights and following Zygmunt Bauman in his *In Search of Politics*, it can also be argued that a commitment to republican self-organisation today requires a macro framework of analysis in addition to the micro one. For, crucially, the ongoing emphasis on the state as the chief threat to autonomy and self-government seems increasingly partial, inadequate even. Of course, the modern state *did* represent the chief obstacle to freedom for both Arendt and Havel, writing as they did in the shadow of totalitarianism. But, following the promptings of Zapatismo with its new emphasis on global neoliberal economics in addition to the state: Is this analysis comprehensive enough under present conditions? Bauman makes the following observation:

> One often hears alarms about the invasion or surreptitious colonization of daily life by public powers. As a rule the argument used to justify the

> alarm is an updated, rehashed version of once well-grounded fears of the state usurping undivided rule over the *agora*. Under present conditions, however, such an argument ... seems less to derive from the diagnosis of the current dangers than from historical memories ... With eyes fixed on [this] frontier ... less thought was given to the other borderline ... which connected/separated the *agora* and the 'private'... [Yet] the *agora* is, as before, an invaded territory, but this time the roles have been reversed and the invading troops are gathering on the fault-line with the private. No one is there to stop the advance; the regular armies of the 'public' retreated and withdrew, having lost their combat force, their interest in continuing occupation, or both.
>
> (Bauman 1999: 96–7)

Bauman's argument is that today republicans should be less concerned with the possibility of the formal public sphere penetrating and colonising the lifeworld and more concerned with the impact of the abrogation of public responsibility by private – global market – power (which increasingly fixes the set of choices available in that lifeworld). If the threat from the state is taken as paramount, as traditionally, then of course it makes sense for republicans to foster informal publics (civil society) as both an alternative to the 'institutionalised lies' of the formal public sphere and also as a buffer zone to protect the private sphere. Yet what can isolated republican spaces in civil society do about privatised power that, far from needing to be kept *without*, requires bringing *within* the scope of political control and popular decision-making? And the question has to be asked: What sort of autonomy is it that involves civil society wresting some sovereignty from a state that is no longer trying to control events in the first place? For political elites appear to have resigned themselves to the 'political economy of uncertainty', as Bauman terms the global neoliberal order. Deregulation, or 'the set of rules to end all rules', is imposed upon local political authorities by extraterritorial financial, capital and trade powers in such a way as to disarm any institutions and associations that might offer some defence against capital *sans* frontiers. The result of such measures, epitomised by the Multilateral Agreement on Investment, is a 'state of permanent and ubiquitous uncertainty, which is to replace the rule of coercive law and legitimating formulae as the ground for obedience ... to the new, this time supra-state and global, powers' (Bauman 1999: 173–4). Political elites now preach to their citizens not as the vanguard, but as resigned spokespeople of the loftier message by which they themselves are constrained: 'there is no alternative'.

In other words, footloose global capital seems to be increasingly controlling events not by using political power in order to impose its rule directly, but by escaping the clutches of 'stubbornly local' political institutions and operating above all regulation and control, indeed 'beyond' politics. One problem with power that reaches beyond extant politics is that, in its very untameablity, it takes on the appearance of a natural phenomenon and therefore poses a much more invidious threat to republican autonomy. Practitioners of 'scientific' state-socialism sought to convey their rule as historically inevitable and so, in a sense, as part of the natural, unquestionable, order of things. But there always were alternatives, however hidden and distant, waiting to undermine such claims. Where, though, are the alternatives now? Can autonomous republican spaces in civil society really stand alone as a viable alternative to liberalised global market power when they are so small scale? If we follow Bauman, even nation-states are no longer sufficient frameworks for republican politics, so what chance the individual spheres of civil society taken alone?

> Having lost much of their past sovereignty and no longer able to balance the books on their own or to lend authority to the type of social order of their choice, contemporary states fail to meet the other necessary condition of a viable republic: the ability of the citizens to negotiate and jointly decide 'the public good', and so to shape a society which they would be prepared to call their own ...
>
> (Bauman 1999: 169)

Thus republican spaces in civil society, in themselves, offer only the hope of some form of escape, a small measure of autonomy in a world in which the big events are uncontrollable as far as citizens – politicians even – are concerned. Indeed, maybe this is all we can hope for, and cynicism about any hard-won autonomy, however local, should be avoided, as we shall see. Yet 'shelter from the storm' of the political economy of insecurity should not be seen as the final word on republican autonomy, since this is to risk abandoning the very guiding principle that animates republicanism, which is citizens aspiring to shape their own destinies (even if this must remain only an aspiration, given the perennial limitations of human agency). Autonomy involves holding onto a sense that extant institutions and practices, including those of global society, do not represent the final word in human organisation; for pre-political decisions must always lack legitimacy for republicans.

Following Zapatismo, the need therefore appears to be for a more ambitious, wide-ranging imagery of republican politics in a global network of civil society, even if only as an animating ideal, rather than as a putatively practical goal. Subsequently, it is not enough for republicans to look only to particular spaces in civil society in order to win a space of (negative) freedom *from* the local state; the need to expand the range of autonomy beyond that offered by limited market choice requires at least *thinking* about republicanism at the macro level, no matter how taxing this is. Of course, the call for republican civil society with macro-political scope faces an even more acute problem of agency than the model of republican civil society at the local level. Yet it is arguably impossible today even to *imagine* a meaningful degree of republican autonomy without such a macro approach, as the Zapatistas, Bauman and others seek to show.

Yet even once inclusive of Zapatismo's insights, and thereby alerting us to new challenges to the project of autonomy and self-determination, republican civil society theory still seems too underdeveloped to answer our detailed questions about possibilities for self-organisation outside the state. We have developed an even more powerful and comprehensive argument of what stands in the way of such organisation, but retain a still very limited sense of how generally to proceed. Problems for a theory of democracy based in civil society therefore remain as keen as ever.

However, in anticipation of the concluding argument: Are we not changing the very nature of the concept of civil society when we use it in this highly theoretical way *vis-à-vis* the more contextualised models that have been the focus of this book? While it might not be able to answer all our questions in *theory* concerning political practice, what if the idea of civil society is understood less as a set of answers and more as a viewfinder that has helped practitioners to look in a different way at the nature and significance of their *own* practice? It is to this, potentially more positive, assessment that we now turn in conclusion. The theory of the democracy of civil society may not be able to give detailed guidance for practice in the abstract, but is this a job for political theory in the first place? Maybe, instead, we should see the idea of civil society as animating practice that then guides itself.

Conclusion

The democracy of civil society as practice

The previous chapter appears to end our discussion on a negative note. Maybe the promises of a democracy of civil society, intoxicating as they have been in various political struggles worldwide, are ultimately utopian visions which, while they animate opposition in the face of authoritarian states, provide precious few answers to the compound questions facing democratic theory. Certainly, as we saw in the course of Chapter 9, the theory of the democracy of civil society hardly begins to tackle questions of institutional complexity apropos its own organisation, never mind that of states and (global) markets.

Yet the 'alternative voices' that we have heard, if we really listen to them, nonetheless pose striking and relevant challenges to our democratic theory. First, we are reminded that, no matter how successful we have been in our attempts to democratise the state (and this itself remains open to serious doubt), we are left still with precious little in the way of self-determination, with hardly a semblance of being the authors of the laws under which we live. Thus we are forced to question whether, regardless of how sophisticated our efforts to place the state under popular control, democracy located only at the level of the state can *ever* deliver the experience of democratic autonomy that we desire. It is at this point, then, and not only under the shadow of totalitarianism, that action in civil society becomes central to democratic theory and practice. For attempts to legitimate the state must always proceed after the fact of the state power and dominance – about which there is no more choice in liberal democracies than any other regime – while action in civil society can in principle be constituted by citizens themselves for their own purposes. In short, if democracy is to continue to have any relation to self-determination, then we cannot afford *not* to include civil society in our democratic theory, since this aspect of a democratic way of life will not be meaningfully provided for by states. Relatedly, the focus on civil society reminds us that self-determination will always need to be local and particular in some way, sensitive to context in the ways in which only actors themselves 'on the ground' can be. Self-organisation (i.e. action *outside* the state) and self-determination therefore go hand in hand, and, arguably, neither can be conceived adequately 'above' the level of civil society, where layers of representation progressively dilute them. From this perspective, it is not self-organisation in civil society that should have to justify its existence in democratic theory, but rather states that have, *still*, to offer a satisfactory theoretical account of their legitimacy (given that they are, in large part, pre-given and fixed obstacles to genuinely self-determining practice).

Yet we have seen that, in opposition to our alternative voices, recent academic discourse on civil society replaces this critical approach to legitimacy with a realist account, such that it is the state that is taken to be unquestionably legitimate and action in civil society that becomes secondary. Theorising civil society through the lens of statist discourse in this way, as shown in part III, leads to an understanding of the relationship between civil society and democracy framed entirely in terms of civil society furthering interest representation in the state. This means that civil society itself need not be democratic, which restricts the meaning and scope of democracy itself while also marginalising struggles for more democracy in civil society.

Then, in Chapter 7, it became apparent that this statist bias is present also in the propensity to see the success of civil society for democracy in terms of the spread of rights. Illustrative of this increasingly popular Habermasian approach, Cohen and Arato, in one of the most influential recent works on the theory of civil society, define their concept of civil society as 'the institutional framework of a modern lifeworld *stabilized by fundamental rights*'. They argue that, 'A civil society in formation ... (as in Eastern Europe recently) may for a time have to do without a settled structure of rights. We would argue, though, that the index of their success in institutionalising civil society is the establishment of rights ...' (1992: 440). The significance of this move, detailed in Chapter 7, deserves repeating here: reducing the role of civil society to its pursuit of rights constrains civil society within statist discourse, because arguments for legal rights produce arguments for the state, not civil society. That is, political struggle conceived solely in terms of winning rights masks the state's own legitimacy deficit while at the same time placing the onus on actors in civil society to make their case for recognition. Cohen and Arato's defence of their discourse of rights – 'While the state is the agency of the legalization of rights, it is neither their source nor the basis of their validity' (1992: 441) – therefore misses the point. Although the state is undoubtedly not the source of rights or of their legitimacy, it remains, as Cohen and Arato admit, the agent without which rights cannot be instantiated. The state is therefore *functionally* indispensable to a rights agenda and so escapes, as a result of this function rather than through making an adequate case for its legitimacy, effective critique from a rights-centric perspective.

We here return to our previous point – that civil society must operate from a position in which state power is extant. Historically, civil society has therefore had to 'win back' power from states – a struggle which, when successful, has been expressed in the form of rights that guarantee freedoms and delimit state power. Such rights, however, are merely the end point of a struggle that began by *questioning* the state's legitimacy, which means effectively that rights represent the 'siphoning off' or displacement of suspicions of illegitimacy away from their intended target (the state). Rights are 'bestowed' by states as if the state itself operates above the struggles that these suspicions of illegitimacy generate, when in fact it is their original object. They thereby offload the burden of proof concerning legitimacy in the wrong direction, from state to civil society rather than from civil society to state (Blaug 1999: 121).

However, the 'civil society first' actions considered in this book (though not hostile to rights in themselves) encourage us to be attentive to this conundrum, which appears opaque to liberal democratic theory. For across otherwise very different contexts, these actions have rarely involved seeking 'concessions' from the state. In the words of Marcos, 'Let no one receive anything from those who rule. Ask them to reject the handouts from the powerful'. And on the Zapatistas' own experience of negotiating for rights, 'Power forces the "others" into the fight, but they are admitted only as losers' (2001: 51, 148). Also from Michnik, half a world away, 'what sets today's opposition apart ... is the belief that a program for evolution ought to be addressed to an independent public, not to ... power' (1985: 144).

The 'alternative voices' on civil society that we have heard also alert us to problems with the very role of democratic theory itself. For there is a crucial sense in which we can misinterpret the 'alternative voices' on civil society considered here if we expect of them the sort of theoretical complexity and explanatory power of liberal democratic variants, which, after all, have the distinct advantage of being effectively *descriptions* of the status quo of civil society. While it might not be able to answer all our questions in *theory* concerning political practice (particularly *vis-à-vis* states), what if the idea of civil society is understood less as a set of answers and more as a way of framing questions about the political that has helped practitioners to look in a different way at the nature and significance of their *own* political practice? After all, participants themselves, logically, must work out self-determination; and there seems something paradoxical about democratic theory worked out in full from 'above', which then writes off forms of self-organisation that do not conform. In part III we saw this approach taken in the theoretical literature on democratisation, which is sceptical of the lasting relevance of ideas of civil society developed as a rejection of the state, seeing civil society entirely in terms of its relationship to the (liberal democratic) state. Yet the case of the Zapatistas' theory–practice shows us that 'civil society first' is still relevant for actors even under liberal democracy. In response to the objection that the Mexican state's governance in Chiapas is far from democratic, it might be argued: Is this not just an example, albeit extreme, of how states, even liberal democratic ones, *do* respond to radical instances of self-organisation within their territories?

The point, returning to our theme, is surely that the idea of a democracy located in civil society is precisely part of the attempt to conceptualise democracy from the actors' perspective in the face of an otherwise hegemonic statist discourse on democracy and democratisation. The concept of democracy in civil society might be short on detail, but is this not because such an image is more about re-directing our attention and energies away from the state and finding space within which to act anew? In this sense it is an animating ideal, a field of possibility, and we ought not, perhaps, expect more from it. Indeed, to expect more (more theory, detail, guidance) may also be to close down such a field, effectively denying the possibility of democratic self-organisation taking any forms other than those theorised for it in advance. This looks more like paternalism than democratic theory. Besides, why should an idea of democracy worked out in civil society *for* civil society provide a theory of the democratic state? This is ambitious at the best of times, but when the state's legitimacy is seen as framing the question rather than providing the answer, it seems particularly inappropriate to write off such an approach for failing to deliver a target that it never set for itself in the first place (and which, for the most part, it sees as unobtainable anyway).

Finally, the civil society-directed visions of democracy that we have considered here offer crucially the possibility of difference in our deliberations about democracy. In the face of the exhaustion of utopian energies and the apparent historical triumph of liberal democracy, we see the aspirations of democrats reduced, for the most part, to little more than the hope that the state might be made more accountable to its citizens and that it might provide greater opportunities for involvement in decision-making. Laudable as these goals are, considered alone they involve a significant restriction of our horizon of possibility, which must surely continue to include the desire to rule ourselves more completely than states can ever allow for. For democrats *are* often tempted to believe that their only option is to continue to expend their energies taking on the state, efforts which leave them for the most part exhausted, disillusioned and, given the sheer scale of their undertaking, open to temptation to vanguardist 'solutions'. Yet the idea of democracy worked out in civil society, sometimes falling into disrepair only to be revived in other times and places, resists just this narrowing move. At the moment when cynicism threatens to take over, the vision of 'civil society first' is a salutary reminder that democracy does not have to be conceived as taking place somewhere above and beyond our everyday lives. For this reason, and also because from time to time the vision takes concrete form even in the most inhospitable of circumstances, we should continue to give it our consideration.

Notes

Introduction

1 There is more to the concept of civil society than its links to democratic theory, including its role in debates about civility, nature, ethics and virtue. The focus of this work, however, remains on civil society and democracy, an increasingly important area within the wider field of democratic theory.
2 I use the term 'radical' in the sense of models seeking a transformatory politics. 'Liberal democratic' models, by contrast, are more or less content to analyse the forms of civil society conducive to, or improving of, actually existing liberal democracy.
3 Hume, Smith, Ferguson, Hutcheson and Kames were the most significant of these philosophers, who wrote between circa 1730 and 1780. Of these theorists, Ferguson, in *An Essay on the History of Civil Society* [1767], is the first to use the concept systematically.
4 Keane (1988a) and Arato (1981) have demonstrated that the distinction between civil society and the state – obliterated by Marxist theory in the nineteenth century – first re-emerged, although in a different form, in Central-Eastern European (particularly Polish) thinking.
5 Also, as with Gramsci, civil society for Tocqueville is non-economic, which marks a distinction from the classical (including the Hegelian) idea – a distinction which we also see in contemporary versions.
6 See Keane (1988b 62), Habermas (1992: 452–7; 1994: 8), Cohen and Arato (1992: 25), Held (1996: 316), Giddens (1994: 116), Lefort (1986: 265–6, 278–9).
7 Schwarzmantel points to the use of the word 'atomizing' as an example of the link of this conceptualisation with Arendt's earlier work (Schwarzmantel 1996: 9).

1 'The self-limiting revolution'

1 Kuron wrote in 1980, for example, that the organisation of 'democracy at the lowest primary social level ... should expand so as to include eventually the activities of the whole state administration' (1981b: 37).
2 Kuron provided a similar analysis when he wrote that a democratic order 'can only be attained through democratic means' (1981b: 39).
3 Keane sees the shift in emphasis from the self-limiting 'evolutionist' strategy to that of self-governing republic as motivated by increased radicalisation during 1981 (1998: 22). This analysis is no doubt accurate, but my point is to emphasise also the ways in which these strategies were normatively complementary, the latter commitment being prefigured to some extent in the former.

4 Kolakowski wrote:

> [I]f the motives of private profit in production are eradicated, the organisational body of production – i.e. the state – becomes the only possible subject of economic activity and the only remaining source of economic initiative. This must, not by bureaucratic ambition but by necessity, lead to a tremendous growth in the tasks of the state and its bureaucracy. This is what really happened. The civil society ... is left economically passive and deprived of ... initiative.
>
> (1974: 31)

5 As Kolakowski put it, '... far from promising the fusion of civil with political society, the Marxian perspective ... if put into practice, [leads to] a cancerous growth of quasi-omnipotent bureaucracy, trying to shatter and paralyse civil society ...' (1974: 31).

6 'The urgent question is how society can tame its expanding bureaucracy and not how it can dispense with it' (Kolakowski 1974: 34).

2 'The independent life of society'

1 On the explicit connection made between a 'moral' and a 'political' model of resistance, see Havel (1985: 40), Battek (1985: 104), Benda (1985: 121), Hejdánek (1985: 146), Kusý (1985: 174) and Uhl (1985: 192).

2 Apart from the essays within *On Freedom and Power* that are the subject of attention here, the Czech thinker Václav Benda, in his 1978 essay *The Parallel Polis*, also advances 'strikingly similar' ideas to those contained in Adam Michnik's *The New Evolutionism* (1976) (Garton Ash 1989: 194). Benda 'calls for organised, parallel activities independent of the state, in which the various currents gradually form a broad, unlimited association of people, a community, a *polis*' (Uhl 1985: 192). The notion of a 'parallel polis' is of course reminiscent of the Polish emphasis on a self-organising society constructed outside the party-state.

3 One exception here was Benda, who, owing to his Catholicism, was confident that a 'more essential unity' was possible. However, Benda did accept that 'this unity [is] among people of disparate opinion and background' (1985: 120–1). Uhl is also ambiguous on this point, for, although he recognises the need for the opposition to 'frequently regroup and divide, unite and separate', he is still in search of 'the revolutionary avant-garde' (1985: 197).

4 Scruton also sees Havel's talk of antipolitics as indicative of a generally conservative thinker. Yet, as Jorgensen observes, in agreement with the argument made here, the call to 'antipolitics' in *The Power of the Powerless* is directed at elements 'of Charter 77 (the reform communists, among others) which sought power or influence and those ... who viewed Charter 77 as a revolutionary avant-garde' (1992: 42).

3 'We need to build civil society because we want freedom'

1 Although Cardoso was never a conventional Marxist (if indeed he could be described as having been a Marxist at all), his thinking was clearly heavily influenced by Marxian categories.

2 Other examples of ideological transformation in exile include former Chilean Communist Party Youth Leader, Antonio Leal (who spent his exile in Italy and Hungary). Leal 'attributes his ideological transformations to his immersion in European left debates throughout the 1970s and 1980s'. Similarly, former Chilean congressman and Communist Party member Luis Guastavino claims that 'his

exile experience in Italy was the most influential factor in his ideological transformation' (interviews with Hite 1996: 317, 325).

3 Post-Marxist intellectual developments within Eurocommunism were particularly connected to the Italian Communist party (PCI), for example Norberto Bobbio. As Hite observes of Chilean leftists in Rome, 'the Italian Communist Party ... provided an extremely influential network for those in exile in the 1970s and 1980s' (1996: 322). Former Chilean congressman and Communist Party member Luis Guastavino was particularly influenced by the PCI's openness:

> Now the Chilean Communist Party had lived in complete unanimity, unanimity was an article of faith, and here I was with the PCI divided in half, and the response over the phone from the leader was, 'Fantastic, keep up the debate, the polemics'. I looked at him as if to say that this is a sure way to destroy a party, to permit this so called freedom which isn't freedom, it's what was called and criticised as the freedom to criticise as Lenin wrote, and I remember my aversion to the scene I witnessed. Yet the communist party of Florence, they have the mayorship of Florence, they have tremendous force and hegemony in the social life of Florence. They were contradictions that I lived with constantly. Those ten years in Italy were for me, want it or not, ten years of unconscious learning, there were things I picked up simply from the air I breathed.
>
> (interview in Hite 1996: 325).

4 James Petras provides an alternative and controversial perspective on the shift in left theory. He claims that the ascendancy of 'institutional intellectuals' (through their connections with and – initially in exile – dependency upon Western funding and institutions) explains the abandonment of the orthodox Marxist categories that had previously 'illuminated popular struggles' (Petras 1990). The direction of the argument here, however, is that while exposure to changes on the European left were influential on Latin American leftists, this was neither the only impetus for change (direct experience of military rule being crucial also) nor a purely strategic and self-interested appropriation of theory as Petras claims.

5 In Chile, for example, the military coup of 1973 prompted a number of Chilean leftists to look, for the first time, at the 'effects, both visible and latent, of authoritarianism on Chilean culture and society' (Hite 1996: 301). See here Jose Joaquin Bruner (1981) and Pilar Vergara (1983).

4 The idea of civil society in the theory–practice of Latin American new social movements

1 Slater's approach reflects that the Latin American new social movement debate is not synonymous with post-structuralism as sometimes appears to be the case in Western discourses. Whereas for Slater and others writing in a Latin American context the 'war of position' had discernible (socialist) ends, for post-structuralists like Laclau and Mouffe (1985) political struggle itself is effectively nonsequential. Thus their 'war of position' is arguably 'only between antagonistic meanings – a process of semiotic disruption and change' (Artz 1997: 94).

5 Civil society and theories of democratisation in Eastern Europe

1 Adam Michnik too, despite his earlier contribution to the Polish opposition's radical model of civil society, now claims that the crucial issue is simply between those who prefer 'what Popper calls "the open society", and those who prefer a closed society' (1991a: 101). Indeed, many earlier radicals appear now to accept

a liberal democratic reading of civil society as constituting a sphere of negative liberty (see Michnik 1991b: 70; 1995: 8–10; Konrád 1990: 189; 1992: 36–7; Kis 1995: 18; Arato 1994: 10).

6 Civil society and theories of democratisation in Latin America

1 The watershed of 1989 does not apply so neatly to the democratisation literature on Latin America, for the simple reason that democratic transitions in the region began earlier in the 1980s. Yet as a heuristic device, by which to point up that the ascendancy of the liberal democratic model of civil society is only a recent phenomenon, 1989 remains a useful signifier. Indeed, in this section I look at just one work pre-1989, because it is only since this point that the democratisation literature on Latin America begins to mention civil society extensively.

7 Models of global civil society

1 Bohman, writing within the same Kantian tradition, argues that in the 'cosmopolitan public sphere', the emergence of which parallels the development of international civil society, 'the public opinions of world citizens can be made known and recognized in such a way that even the supreme political authorities of the state cannot avoid acknowledging them' (1997: 181).

2 Stephen Gill, whose work is close to Cox's, also sees counter-hegemonic action through transnational links in civil society as more promissory than actual: '[E]merging global civil society ... might then provide the political space and social possibility to begin to mobilize for the solution to deep-seated problems of social inequality, intolerance, environmental degradation and the militarization of the planet' (1991: 311).

3 This non-hierarchical mode of coordination represents the 'postmodern' alternative to the steering role allocated by Gramsci to his Modern Prince – the Communist Party (Cox 1999: 15).

8 'An echo that turns itself into many voices'

1 Although the EZLN formed a civilian arm in 1996 (the Frente Zapatista de Liberación Nacional – FZLN), this organisation does not endorse political parties and is not itself one. Its establishment followed the EZLN's invitation for civil society without party affiliation to organise.

2 This uncompromising commitment to autonomy from the state and its agencies is by no means uncontested in Chiapas, however. One long-time peasant leader protests:

> Marcos is always talking about 'civil society', but who does he think we are? He dismisses us as compromised by the relations we have had with the state [agencies] to get the things that peasants need. He appeals over the head of people here to civil society in the rest of Mexico and abroad, as if people further away from Chiapas have not made their own compromises!
>
> (interview in Hellman 2000: 10)

3 In the Mexican context, the concept of civil society – and on a reading close to that offered within Zapatismo – seems to have taken root following the earthquake. Writing in 1987, Monsiváis observed that:

> The earthquake raised the term to the height of its glory. And on the 22nd September it starts to be commonly used, at first as a synonym for 'society'

> without any additional organizational emphasis or meaning. But by the beginning of October practice dominates: civil society is self-generated community power and solidarity ...
>
> (cited in Esteva 1999: 159)

4 Elsewhere, Marcos writes that in a more 'just' and 'human' international order, 'there will have to be a prominent place for international and national NGOs ...' (2001: 202).

9 Theorising the democracy of civil society

1 This conciliatory view of public and private appears to be a more general feature of contemporary civic republicanism. Although republicans do not want to obliterate the distinction between public and private, they see the boundaries of the political in much broader terms than liberals. Paul Hirst, for example, contends that:

> If core activities of central concern to the life of the citizen ... are not to remain dominated by top-down administration ... then the whole of society and not just the state needs to be viewed politically, as a complex of institutions that require a substantial measure of public and popular control ... That is, civil society must no longer be viewed as a 'private' sphere, it needs to take on elements of 'publicity' in the original sense of the term.
>
> (1996: 101)

2 With regard to possibilities for self-management in the market sphere, republican civil society theory is also akin to theories of market socialism in failing to specify adequately the forms of social ownership. In particular, how would capital be allocated?

> Workers may manage their enterprises but they still require capital to prosper. Is capital to be distributed on market principles and if it is by whom? If not by private banks then by collectively owned investment banks and who, if not the state, is likely to take control of these? By what calculus could the state allocate capital? If not the same ruthless calculus of profitability that contemporary capitalist economies run then how? If the state is to have that much power how on earth is it to be brought within the bounds of legitimate democratic control?
>
> (Goldblatt 1996: 968)

Bibliography

Alvarez, S. (1994) 'The (trans)formation of feminism(s) and gender politics in democratizing Brazil', in J.S. Jaquette (ed.) *The Women's Movement in Latin America*, Oxford: Westview.

Alvarez, S. and Escobar, A. (1992) 'Conclusion: theoretical and political horizons of change in contemporary Latin American social movements', in A. Escobar and S. Alvarez (eds) *The Making of Social Movements in Latin America*, Oxford: Westford.

Alves, M. (1989) 'Interclass alliances in the opposition to the military in Brazil: consequences for the transition period', in S. Eckstein (ed.) *Power and Popular Protest: Latin American social movements*, Berkeley, CA: University of California Press.

Anderson, D. (1996) 'Bringing civil society to an uncivilised place', in C. Hann and E. Dunn (eds) *Civil Society: Challenging western models*, London: Routledge.

Arato, A. (1981) 'Civil society against the state: Poland 1980–81', *Telos* 47: 23–47.

—— (1989) 'Civil society, history and socialism: reply to John Keane', *Praxis International* 9, 1: 133–52.

—— (1990) 'Revolution, civil society and democracy', *Praxis International* 10, 1: 24–39.

—— (1994) 'The rise, decline and reconstruction of the concept of civil society, and directions for future research', in A. Bibic and C. Graziano (eds) *Civil Society, Political Society, Democracy*, Ljubljana: Slovenian Political Science Association.

Archibugi, D. (1998) 'Principles of cosmopolitan democracy', in D. Archibugi, D. Held and M. Köhler (eds) *Reimagining Political Community*, Cambridge: Polity.

—— (2000) 'Cosmopolitical democracy', *New Left Review* 4, July/Aug: 37–150.

Arendt, H. (1958a) *The Origins of Totalitarianism*, London: George Allen and Unwin.

—— (1958b) *The Human Condition*, London: The University of Chicago Press.

—— (1963) *On Revolution*, London: Faber and Faber.

Artz, B.L. (1997) 'Social power and the inflation of discourse: the failure of popular hegemony in Nicaragua', *Latin American Perspectives* 24, 1: 92–113.

Ashenden, S. (1999) 'Questions of criticism: Habermas and Foucault on Civil society and resistance', in S. Ashenden and D. Owen (eds) *Foucault contra Habermas*, London: Sage.

Assies, W. (1994) 'Urban social movements in Brazil: a debate and its dynamics', *Latin American Perspectives* 21, 2: 81–105.

Autonomedia (1995) *Ya basta! Documents on the New Mexican Revolution*, New York: Autonomedia.

Barrig, M. (1994) 'The difficult equilibrium between bread and roses: women's organizations and democracy in Peru', in J.S. Jaquette (ed.) *The Women's Movement in Latin America*, Oxford: Westview.

Barros, R. (1986) 'The left and democracy: recent debates in Latin America', *Telos* 68: 49–70.

Battek, R. (1985) 'Spiritual values, independent initiatives and politics', in V. Havel *et al.* (eds) *The Power of the Powerless: Citizens against the state in Central–Eastern Europe*, London: Hutchinson.

Bauman, Z. (1999) *In Search of Politics*, Cambridge: Polity.

Bence, G. (1981) 'Interview with Bence', *Telos* 47: 145–6.

Benda, V. (1985) 'Catholicism and politics', in V. Havel *et al.* *The Power of the Powerless: Citizens against the state in Central–Eastern Europe*, London: Hutchinson.

Benda, V., Simecka, M., Jirous, I.M., Dienstbier, J., Havel, V., Hejdnek, L. and Simsa, J. (1988) 'Parallel polis, or an independent society in Central and Eastern Europe: an inquiry', *Social Research* 55, 2: 211–47.

Bermeo, N. (1992) 'Democracy and the lessons of dictatorship', *Comparative Politics* 24, 3: 273–93.

—— (1997) 'Myths of moderation: confrontation and conflict during democratic transitions', *Comparative Politics* 29, 3: 305–22.

Bernhard, M. (1993) 'Civil society and democratic transition in East Central Europe', *Political Science Quarterly* 108, 2: 307–26.

Bibic, A. (1994) 'Democracy and civil society', in A. Bibic and C. Graziano (eds) *Civil Society, Political Society, Democracy*, Ljubljana: Slovenian Political Science Association.

Bibic, A. and Graziano, C. (1994), 'Introduction', in A. Bibic and C. Graziano (eds) *Civil Society, Political Society, Democracy*, Ljubljana: Slovenian Political Science Association.

Blaug, R. (1997) 'Between fear and disappointment: critical, empirical and political uses of Habermas', *Political Studies* 45, 1: 100–17.

—— (1999) *Democracy, Real and Ideal: Discourse ethics and radical politics*, Albany, NY: State University of New York Press.

—— (2000) 'Blind hierarchism and radical organizational forms', *New Political Science* 22, 3: 379–95.

Bohman, J. (1997) 'The public spheres of the world citizen', in J. Bohman and M. Lutz-Bachman (eds) *Perpetual Peace: Essays on Kant's cosmopolitan ideal*, London: MIT Press.

Borda, O.A. (1992) 'Social movements and political power in Latin America', in A. Escobar and S. Alvarez (eds) *The Making of Social Movements in Latin America*, Oxford: Westford.

Boron, A. (1995) *State, Capitalism and Democracy in Latin America*, London: Lynne Rienner.

Bozoki, A. and Sukosd, M. (1993) 'Civil society and populism in the Eastern European transitions', *Praxis International* 13, 3: 226–44.

Bruner, J.J. (1981) *La cultura autoritaria en Chile*, Santiago: FLACSO.

Burbach, R. and Nunez, O. (1987) *Fire in the Americas: Forging a radical agenda*, London: Verso.

Calderon, F., Piscitelli, A. and Reyna, J. (1992) 'Social movements: actors, theories, expectations', in A. Escobar, and S. Alvarez (eds) *The Making of Social Movements in Latin America*, Oxford: Westford.

Canovan, M. (1985) 'Politics as culture: Hannah Arendt and the public realm', *History of Political Thought* 6, 3: 617–42.

—— (2001) 'Sleeping dogs, prowling cats and soaring doves: three paradoxes in the political theory of nationhood', *Political Studies* 49, 2: 203–15.

Cardoso, F.H. (1986) 'Democracy in Latin America', *Politics and Society* 15, 1: 23–41.
—— (1989) 'Associated-dependent development and democratic theory', in A. Stepan (ed.) *Democratizing Brazil*, Oxford: Oxford University Press.
Cardoso, R. (1992) 'Popular movements and the consolidation of democracy in Brazil', in A. Escobar and S. Alvarez (eds) *The Making of Social Movements in Latin America*, Oxford: Westford.
Carr, B. (1993) 'Mexico: the perils of unity and the challenge of modernization', in B. Carr and S. Ellner (eds) *The Latin American Left*, London: Latin America Bureau.
Castaneda, J.G. (1994) *Utopia Unarmed*, New York: Vintage Books.
Cerný, V. (1985) 'On the question of Chartism', in V. Havel *et al. The Power of the Powerless: Citizens against the state in Central–Eastern Europe*, London: Hutchinson.
Chandler, D. (2000) 'International justice', *New Left Review* 6, November/December: 55–60.
—— (2001) 'New rights for old: cosmopolitan citizenship and the critique of state sovereignty', unpublished paper.
Chilcote, R.H. (1990) 'Post-Marxism: the retreat from class in Latin America', *Latin American Perspectives* 17, 2: 3–24.
Chinchilla, N.A. (1992) 'Marxism, feminism, and the struggle for democracy in Latin America', in A. Escobar and S. Alvarez (eds) *The Making of Social Movements in Latin America*, Oxford: Westford.
—— (1994) 'Feminism, revolution and democratic transitions in Nicaragua', in J.S. Jaquette (ed.) *The Women's Movement in Latin America*, Oxford: Westview.
Chuchryk, P.M. (1994) 'From dictatorship to democracy: the women's movement in Chile', in J.S. Jaquette (ed.) *The Women's Movement in Latin America*, Oxford: Westview.
Cohen, J.A. and Arato, A. (1984) 'Social movements, civil society and the problem of sovereignty', *Praxis International*, 4: 266–83.
—— (1992) *Civil Society and Political Theory*, Cambridge, MA: MIT Press.
Coraggio, J.L. (1985) 'Social movements and revolution: the case of Nicaragua', in D. Slater (ed.) *New Social Movements and the State in Latin America*, Amsterdam: CEDLA.
Coutinho, C.N. (1979) 'A democracia como valor universal', *Encontros com a Civilazacao Brasileira* 9: 33–47.
Cox, R. (1983) 'Gramsci, hegemony and international relations: an essay in method', *Millennium* 12, 2: 162–75.
—— (1999) 'Civil society at the turn of the millennium: prospects for an alternative world order', *Review of International Studies* 25: 1–28.
Cuninghame, P. and Ballesteros Corona, C. (1998) 'A rainbow at midnight: Zapatistas and autonomy', *Capital and Class* 66: 12–22.
Curry, J.L. (1994) 'A reconsideration of the realities of "civil society" in the light of postcommunist society' in A. Bibic and C. Graziano (eds) *Civil Society, Political Society, Democracy*, Ljubljana: Slovenian Political Science Association.
Dahl, R.A. (1989) *Democracy and its Critics*, London: Yale University Press.
Dahrendorf, R. (1990a) *Reflections on the Revolution in Eastern Europe*, London: Chatto and Windus.
—— (1990b) 'Roads to freedom: democratization and its problems in east central Europe', in P. Volten (ed.) *Uncertain Futures: Eastern Europe and democracy*, New York: Institute for East–West Security Studies.

De Angelis, M. (2000) 'Globalization, new internationalism and the Zapatistas', *Capital and Class* 70: 9–35.

Diamond, L. (1994) 'Rethinking civil society: towards democratic consolidation', *Journal of Democracy*, 5, 3: 5–17.

Diamond, L. and J. Linz, (1989) 'Introduction: politics, society, and democratization in Latin America', in L. Diamond, J. Linz and S. Lipset (eds) *Democracy in Developing Countries*, Vol. 4: *Latin America*, London: Lynne Rienner.

Dos Santos, T. (1979) 'La viabilidad de capitalismo dependiente y la democracia', *America Latina: Estudios y Perspectivas* 1: 33–53.

Ehrlich, S. (1994) 'Introductory remarks', in A. Bibic and C. Graziano (eds) *Civil Society, Political Society, Democracy*, Ljubljana: Slovenian Political Science Association.

Ekiertz, G. (1991) 'Democratization processes in East Central Europe: a theoretical reconsideration', *British Journal of Political Science*, 21: 285–313.

Ellner, S. (1993) 'The changing status of the Latin American left in the recent past', in B. Carr and S. Ellner (eds) *The Latin American Left*, London: Latin America Bureau.

Ely, J. (1992) 'The politics of civil society', *Telos* 93: 173–78.

Escobar, A. (1992) 'Culture, economics, and politics in Latin American social movements', in A. Escobar and S. Alvarez (eds) *The Making of Social Movements in Latin America*, Oxford: Westford.

Escobar, A. and Alvarez, S. (1992) 'Introduction: theory and protest in Latin America today', in A. Escobar and S. Alvarez (eds) *The Making of Social Movements in Latin America*, Oxford: Westford.

Esteva, G. (1999) 'The Zapatistas and people's power', *Capital and Class* 68: 153–82.

Evers, T. (1985) 'Identity: the hidden side of new social movements in Latin America', in D. Slater (ed.) *New Social Movements and the State in Latin America*, Amsterdam: CEDLA.

Falk, R. (1995) *On Humane Governance: towards a new global politics*, University Park, PA: Pennsylvania University Press.

—— (1998) 'The UN and cosmopolitan democracy', in D. Archibugi, D. Held and M. Köhler (eds) *Reimagining Political Community*, Cambridge: Polity.

Federowicz, M. (1993) 'The actors and mechanisms of systemic changes in the economy', *Sisyphus* 9, 2: 91–9.

Ferguson, A. [1767] (1966) *An Essay on the History of Civil Society*, D. Forbes (ed.), Edinburgh: Edinburgh University Press.

Fine, R. (1997) 'Civil society: theory, enlightenment and critique', *Democratization* 4, 1: 7–28.

Foucault, M. (1989) *Foucault Live*, S. Lotringer (ed.), translated by J. Johnston, New York: Semiotext(e).

Frankel, B. (1997) 'Confronting neoliberal regimes: the post-marxist embrace of populism and realpolitik', *New Left Review* 226: 57–92.

Frentzel-Zagorska, J. (1992) 'Patterns of transition from a one-party state to democracy in Poland and Hungary', in R.F. Miller (ed.) *The Development of Civil Society in Communist Systems*, Sydney: Allen and Unwin.

Garreton, M.A. (1989) 'Popular mobilization and the military regime in Chile: the complexities of the invisible transition', in S. Eckstein (ed.) *Power and Popular Protest: Latin American social movements*, Berkeley, CA: University of California Press.

Garton Ash, T. (1989) *The Uses of Adversity: Essays on the fate of Eastern Europe*, New York: Random House.

Gellner, E. (1994) *Conditions of Liberty: Civil society and its rivals*, London: Hamish Hamilton.
—— (1995) 'The importance of being modular', in J.A. Hall (ed.) *Civil Society: Theory, history, comparison*, Cambridge: Polity.
Ghils, P. (1992) 'International civil society: international non-governmental organizations in the international system', *International Social Science Journal* 133: 417–31.
Giddens, A. (1994) *Beyond Left and Right*, Cambridge: Polity.
Gill, S. (1991) 'Reflections on global order and sociohistorical time', *Alternatives* 16, 3: 305–20.
Goldblatt, D. (1996) Book review, *Political Studies* 44, 5: 967–9.
Gramsci, A. (1971) *Selections from the Prison Notebooks*, London: Lawrence and Wishart.
Habermas, J. (1992) 'Further reflections on the public sphere', in C. Calhoun (ed.) *Habermas and the Public Sphere*, Cambridge, MA: MIT Press.
—— (1994) 'Three normative models of democracy', *Constellations* 1, 1: 1–10.
—— (1996) *Between Facts and Norms: Contributions to a discourse theory of law and democracy*, Cambridge: Polity.
Hagopian, F. (1993) 'After regime change', *World Politics* 45, 3: 464–90.
Hájek, J. (1985) 'The human rights movement and social progress', in V. Havel *et al.* (eds) *The Power of the Powerless: Citizens against the state in Central–Eastern Europe*, London: Hutchinson.
Hankiss, E. (1990) *East European Alternatives*, Oxford: Oxford University Press.
Havel, V. (1985) 'The power of the powerless', in V. Havel *et al.* (eds) *The Power of the Powerless: Citizens against the state in Central–Eastern Europe*, London: Hutchinson.
—— (1988) 'Anti-political politics', in J. Keane (ed.) (1988) *Civil Society and the State: New European perspectives*, London: Verso.
—— (1996) 'Interview', *Journal Of Democracy* 7, 1: 3–10.
Hegadus, G. (1981) 'Interview with Hegadus', *Telos* 47: 47–8.
Hejdánek, L. (1985) 'Prospects for democracy and socialism in Eastern Europe', in V. Havel *et al.* (eds) *The Power of the Powerless: Citizens against the state in Central–Eastern Europe*, London: Hutchinson.
Held, D. (1993) 'Democracy: from city-states to a cosmopolitan order?', in D. Held (ed.) *Prospects for Democracy*, Cambridge: Polity Press.
—— (1995) *Democracy and the Global Order: From the modern state to cosmopolitan governance*, Cambridge: Polity.
—— (1996) *Models of Democracy*, 2nd edition, Cambridge: Polity.
Heller, A. (1991) 'The concept of the political revisited', in D. Held (ed.) *Political Theory Today*, Cambridge: Polity.
Hellman, J.A. (1992) 'The study of new social movements in Latin America and the question of autonomy', in A. Escobar and S. Alvarez (eds) *The Making of Social Movements in Latin America*, Oxford: Westford.
—— (2000) 'Real and virtual Chiapas: magic realism and the left', *Socialist Register*, 161–81.
Hirst, P. (1991) 'The state, civil society and the collapse of Soviet communism', *Economy and Society* 20: 217–42.
—— (1996) 'Democracy and civil society', in P. Hirst and S. Khilnani (eds) *Reinventing Democracy*, Oxford: Basil Blackwell.
Hite, K. (1996) 'The formation and transformation of political identity: leaders of the Chilean left, 1968–1990', *Journal of Latin American Studies* 28: 299–328.

Holloway, J. (1998) 'Dignity's revolt', in J. Holloway and E. Peláez (eds) *Zapatista! Reinventing Revolution in Mexico*, London: Pluto Press.

Holloway, J. and Peláez, E. (1998) 'Introduction: reinventing revolution', in J. Holloway and E. Peláez (eds) *Zapatista! Reinventing Revolution in Mexico*, London: Pluto Press.

Howarth, D. (2001) 'An archaeology of political discourse? Evaluating Michel Foucault's explanation and critique of ideology', *Essex Papers in Politics and Government*, Colchester: University Of Essex.

Huber, E. (1995) 'Assessments of state strength', in P.H. Smith (ed.) *Latin America in Comparative Perspective*, Oxford: Westview.

Huntington, S. (1989) 'The modest meaning of democracy', in R.A. Pastor (ed.) *Democracy in the Americas: Stopping the pendulum*, London: Holmes and Meier.

Hutchings, K. (1999) *International Political Theory*, London: Sage.

Isaac, J. (1998) *Democracy in Dark Times*, New York: Cornell University Press.

Jaquette, J.S. (1994) *The Women's Movement in Latin America*, Oxford: Westview.

Jelin, E. (1995) 'Building citizenship: a balance between solidarity and responsibility', in J.S. Tulchin (ed.) *The Consolidation of Democracy in Latin America*, London: Lynne Rienner.

Johnston, J. (2000) 'Pedagogical guerrillas, armed democrats, and revolutionary counterpublics: examining paradox in the Zapatista uprising in Chiapas Mexico', *Theory and Society* 29: 463–505.

Jorgensen, K. (1992) 'The end of anti-politics in Central Europe', in P.G. Lewis (ed.) *Democracy and Civil Society in Eastern Europe*, London: Macmillan.

Kaldor, M. (1999) 'Transnational civil society', in T. Dunne and N.J. Wheeler (eds) *Human Rights in Global Politics*, Cambridge: Cambridge University Press.

Keane, J. (1985) 'Introduction', in V. Havel *et al.* (eds) *The Power of the Powerless: Citizens against the state in Central–Eastern Europe*, Armonk, NY: M.E. Sharpe.

—— (1988a) 'Despotism and democracy', in J. Keane (ed.) *Civil Society and the State: New European perspectives*, London: Verso.

—— (1988b) *Democracy and Civil Society*, London: Verso.

—— (1998) *Civil Society: Old images, new visions*, Cambridge: Polity.

—— (1999) *Václav Havel: A political tragedy in six acts*, London: Bloomsbury.

Keck, M.E. (1989) 'The new unionism in the Brazilian transition', in A. Stepan (ed.) *Democratizing Brazil*, Oxford: Oxford University Press.

King, P. and Villanueva, F.J. (1998) 'Breaking the blockade: the move from jungle to city', in J. Holloway and E. Peláez (eds) *Zapatista! Reinventing Revolution in Mexico*, London: Pluto Press.

Kis, J. (1981) 'Interview with Kis', *Telos* 47: 146–7.

—— (1995) 'Interview with Janos Kis', *Constellations* 2, 1: 12–20.

Köhler, M. (1998) 'From the national to the cosmopolitan public sphere', in D. Archibugi, D. Held and M. Köhler (eds) *Reimagining Political Community*, Cambridge: Polity.

Kolakowski, L. (1971) 'Hope and hopelessness', *Survey* 17: 42–8.

—— (1974) 'The myth of human self-identity: unity of civil and political society in socialist thought', in L. Kolakowski and S. Hampshire (eds) *The Socialist Idea: A reappraisal*, London: Cox and Wyman.

Konrád, G. (1984) *Antipolitics*, London: Quartet.

—— (1990) 'Chance wanderings: reflections of a Hungarian writer', *Dissent* 37, 2: 189–91.

—— (1992) 'What is the charter?', *East European Reporter* 5: 32–40.

Korbonski, A. (1994) 'Civil society and democracy in Poland: problems and prospects', in A. Bibic and C. Graziano (eds) *Civil Society, Political Society, Democracy*, Ljubljana: Slovenian Political Science Association.

Krizan, M. (1987) ' "Civil Society" and the modernisation of Soviet type societies', *Praxis International* 7, 1: 90–110.

Kumar, C. (2000), 'Transnational networks and campaigns for democracy', in A.M. Florini (ed.) *The Third Force: The rise of transnational civil society*, Washington, DC: Carnegie Endowment for International Peace.

Kuron, J. (1981a) 'Not to lure the wolves out of the woods: an interview with Jacek Kuron', *Telos* 47: 93–7.

—— (1981b) 'What next in Poland?', *Dissent* 28, 1: 34–9.

Kusý, M. (1985) 'Chartism and real socialism', in V. Havel *et al.* (eds) *The Power of the Powerless: citizens against the state in Central–Eastern Europe*, London: Hutchinson.

Laclau, E. and Mouffe, C. (1985) *Hegemony and Socialist Strategy: Towards a radical democratic politics*, London: Verso.

Lamounier, B. (1989) 'Brazil: inequality against democracy', in L. Diamond, J. Linz and S. Lipset (eds) *Democracy in Developing Countries*, Vol. 4: *Latin America*, London: Lynne Rienner.

Lefort, C. (1986) *The Political Forms of Modern Society*, Cambridge: Polity.

Levine, D.H. (1989) 'Venezuela: the nature, sources, and future prospects of democracy', in L. Diamond, J. Linz and S. Lipset (eds) *Democracy in Developing Countries,* Vol. 4: *Latin America*, London: Lynne Rienner.

Lewis, P.G. (1993) 'Democracy and its future in Eastern Europe', in D. Held (ed.) *Prospects for Democracy*, Cambridge: Polity.

Linklater, A. (1998) *The Transformation of Political Community*, Cambridge: Polity.

Linz, J. and Stepan, A. (1989) 'Political crafting of democratic consolidation or destruction: European and South American comparisons', in R.A. Pastor (ed.) *Democracy in the Americas: Stopping the pendulum*, London: Holmes and Meier.

Lipschutz, R.D. (1992) 'Reconstructing world politics: the emergence of global civil society', *Millennium* 21, 3: 389–420.

Lorenzano, L. (1998) 'Zapatismo: recomposition of labour, radical democracy and revolutionary project', in J. Holloway and E. Peláez (eds) *Zapatista! Reinventing Revolution in Mexico*, London: Pluto Press.

Lowy, M. (1986) 'Mass organisations, Party and State: democracy in the transition to socialism', in R. Fagen *et al.* (eds) *Transition and Development: Problems of third world socialism*, New York: Monthly Review Press.

Lukes, S. (1985) 'Introduction', in V. Havel *et al.* (eds) *The Power of the Powerless: citizens against the state in Central–Eastern Europe*, London: Hutchinson.

Mainwaring, S. (1987) 'Urban popular movements, identity and democratization in Brazil', *Comparative Political Studies* 20, 2: 131–59.

—— (1989) 'Grassroots popular movements and the struggle for democracy: Nova Iguaca', in A. Stepan (ed.) *Democratizing Brazil*, Oxford: Oxford University Press.

—— (1992) 'Transitions to democracy and democratic consolidation: theoretical and comparative issues', in S. Mainwaring, G. O'Donnell and J. Valenzuela (eds) *Issues in Democratic Consolidation: The new South American democracies in comparative perspective*, Indiana: University of Notre Dame Press.

Mainwaring, S. and Viola, E. (1984) 'Political culture and democracy: Brazil and Argentina in the 1980s', *Telos* 61: 17–52.

Mainwaring, S. O'Donnell, G. and Valenzuela, J. (1992) 'Introduction', in S. Mainwaring, G. O'Donnell and J. Valenzuela (eds) *Issues in Democratic Consolidation: The new South American democracies in comparative perspective*, Indiana: University of Notre Dame Press.

Marcos (Subcommandante Insurgente) (2001) *Our Word is Our Weapon*, J. Ponce de Leon (ed.), London: Seven Stories.

Marx, K. (1977) 'On the Jewish question', in D. McLellan (ed.) *Karl Marx: Selected writings*, Oxford: Oxford University Press.

Melucci, A. (1989) *Nomads of the Present: Social movements and individual needs in contemporary society*, J. Keane and P. Mier (eds), London: Hutchinson Radius.

Michnik, A. (1981) 'What we want to do and what we can do', *Telos* 47: 66–74.

—— (1985) *Letters From Prison and Other Essays*, Berkeley, CA: University of California Press.

—— (1991a) 'The three cards game: an interview with Adam Michnik', *Telos* 89: 95–102.

—— (1991b) 'The presence of liberal values', *East European Reporter* 4: 66–74.

—— (1995) 'Interview with Adam Michnik', *Constellations* 2, 1: 5–11.

Miller, R.F. (1992) 'Civil society in communist systems: an introduction', in R.F. Miller (ed.) *The Development of Civil Society in Communist Systems*, Sydney: Allen and Unwin.

Milosz, C. (1985) 'Foreword', in A. Michnik, *Letters from Prison and Other Essays*, Berkeley, CA: University of California Press.

Mische, A. (1993) 'Post-communism's "lost treasure": subjectivity and gender in a shifting public place', *Praxis International* 13, 3: 242–67.

Moises, J.A. (1982) 'What is the strategy of the "new syndicalism" ', *Latin American Perspectives* 9, 4: 55–73.

Morawski, W. (1993) 'Economic change and civil society in Poland', in P.G. Lewis (ed.) *Democracy and Civil Society in Eastern Europe*, London: Macmillan.

Munck, R. (1990) 'Farewell to socialism?', *Latin American Perspectives* 17, 2: 113–21.

Narojek, W. (1994) 'The making of democratic order and market economy: social engineering for democratic transformation', *Polish Sociological Review* 1, 105: 5–15.

Nowak, L. (1991) *Power and Civil Society: Towards a dynamic theory of real socialism*, Westport, CT: Greenwood Press.

O'Donnell, G. (1973) *Modernization and Bureaucratic Authoritarianism*, Berkeley, CA: University of California Press.

—— (1979) 'Tensions in the bureaucratic–authoritarian state and the problem of democracy', in D. Collier (ed.) *The New Authoritarianism in Latin America*, Princeton, NJ: Princeton University Press.

—— (1989) 'Transitions to democracy: some navigation instruments', in R.A. Pastor (ed.) *Democracy in the Americas: Stopping the pendulum*, London: Holmes and Meier.

O'Donnell, G. and Schmitter, P. (eds) (1986) *Transitions from Authoritarian Rule: Tentative conclusions about uncertain democracies*, London: Johns Hopkins University Press.

Oxhorn, P. (1994) 'Where did all the protesters go? Popular mobilization and the transition to democracy in Chile', *Latin American Perspectives* 21, 3: 49–68.

Pakenham, R.A. (1992) *The Dependency Movement*, Cambridge, MA: Harvard University Press.

Passerin d'Entreves, M. (1992) 'Hannah Arendt and the idea of citizenship', in C. Mouffe (ed.) *Dimensions of Radical Democracy*, London: Verso.

Pateman, C. (1987) 'Feminist critiques of the public/private dichotomy', in A. Phillips (ed.) *Feminism and Equality*, Oxford: Blackwell.

Pearce, J. (1996) 'How useful is "civil society" as a conceptualisation of democratisation processes? With reference to Latin America', in L. Broadhead (ed.) *Issues in Peace Research 1995–96*, Bradford: University of Bradford, Department of Peace Studies.

—— (1997) 'Civil society, the market and democracy in Latin America', *Democratization* 4, 2: 57–83.

Pelczynski, Z.A. (1988) 'Solidarity and the rebirth of civil society', in J. Keane (ed.) *Civil Society and the State: New European perspectives*, London: Verso.

Petras, J. (1990) 'The metamorphosis of Latin America's intellectuals', *Latin American Perspectives* 17, 2: 102–12.

Piccone, P. (1996) 'The tribulations of left social criticism', *Telos* 107: 139–68.

Przeworski, A. (1986) 'Some problems in the study of the transition to democracy', in G. O'Donnell, P. Schmitter and L. Whitehead (eds) *Transitions from Authoritarian Rule*, London: Johns Hopkins University Press.

—— (1992) 'The games of transition', in S. Mainwaring, G. O'Donnell and J. Valenzuela (eds) *Issues in Democratic Consolidation: The new South American democracies in comparative perspective*, Indiana: University of Notre Dame Press.

Reidy, D. (1992) 'Eastern Europe, civil society and the real revolution', *Praxis International* 12, 2: 168–81.

Reilly, C. (1995) 'Public policy and citizenship', in C. Reilly (ed.) *New Paths to Democratic Development in Latin America*, London: Lynne Rienner.

Remmer, K.L. (1991) 'New wine or old bottlenecks?', *Comparative Politics* 23: 479–92.

Risse, T. (2000) 'The power of norms versus the norms of power: transnational civil society and human rights', in A.M. Florini (ed.) *The Third Force: The rise of transnational civil society*, Washington, DC: Carnegie Endowment for International Peace.

Rose, N. (1993) 'Government, authority and expertise in advanced liberalism', *Economy and Society* 22, 1: 283–305.

—— (1996) 'The death of the social? Refiguring the territory of government', *Economy and Society* 25, 3: 327–56.

Rose, N. and Miller, P. (1992) 'Political power beyond the state: problematics of government', *British Journal of Sociology* 43, 2: 173–205.

Ruml, J. (1985) 'Who really is isolated?', in V. Havel *et al. The Power of the Powerless: Citizens against the state in Central–Eastern Europe*, London: Hutchinson.

Rupnik, J. (1988) 'Totalitarianism revisited', in J. Keane (ed.) *Civil Society and the State: New European perspectives*, London: Verso.

Sakamoto, Y. (1991) 'Introduction: the global context of democratization', *Alternatives* 16, 2: 110–23.

Saward, M. (1998) *The Terms of Democracy*, Cambridge: Polity.

Schecter, D. (2000) *Sovereign States or Political Communities? Civil society and contemporary politics*, Manchester: Manchester University Press.

Schmitter, P.C. (1995) 'Transitology: the science or the art of democratisation', in J.S. Tulchin (ed.) *The Consolidation of Democracy in Latin America*, London: Lynne Rienner.

Schwarzmantel, J. (1996) 'Civil society and democracy: what is the connection?', paper presented at the conference on 'The Emergence of Civil Society: a precondition or a problem for democracy?', The University of Warwick.

Scruton, R. (1988) 'The new right in Central Europe', *Political Studies* 36, 3: 449–62.

Seligman, A. (1992) *The Idea of Civil Society*, Princeton, NJ: Princeton University Press.

Shaw, M. (1994a) 'Civil society and global politics: beyond a social movements approach', *Millennium* 23, 3: 647–67.

—— (1994b) *Global Society and International Relations*, Cambridge: Polity.

—— (1999) 'Global voices: civil society and the media in global crisis', in T. Dunne and N.J. Wheeler (eds) *Human Rights in Global Politics*, Cambridge: Cambridge University Press.

Silva, G.R. (1988) 'Crisis, democracy, and the left in Peru', *Latin American Perspectives* 15, 3: 77–96.

Skapska, G. (1997) 'Learning to be a citizen: cognitive and ethical aspects of post-communist society transformation', *Democratization* March: 143–67.

Slater, D. (1985) 'Introduction', in D. Slater (ed.) *New Social Movements and the State in Latin America*, Amsterdam: CEDLA.

Smolar, A. (1996) 'From opposition to atomization', *Journal of Democracy* 7, 1: 24–38.

Splichal, S. (1994) 'Civil society and media democratization in East-Central Europe', in A. Bibic and C. Graziano (eds) *Civil Society, Political Society, Democracy*, Ljubljana: Slovenian Political Science Association.

Stepan, A. (1989) 'Introduction', in A. Stepan (ed.) *Democratizing Brazil*, Oxford: Oxford University Press.

Swidlicki, A. (1981) 'The struggle for the media in Poland', *Telos* 47: 113–24.

Szakolczai, A. and Horvath, A. (1992) 'The discourse of civil society and the self-elimination of the party', in P.G. Lewis (ed.) *Democracy and Civil Society in Eastern Europe*, London: Macmillan.

Sztompka, P. (1991) 'The intangibles and imponderables of the transition to democracy', *Studies in Comparative Communism* XXIV, 3: 295–311.

Tarkowska, E. and Tarkowski, J. (1991) 'Social disintegration in Poland: civil society or amoral familism?', *Telos* 89: 103–9.

Tempest, C. (1997) 'Myths from Eastern Europe and the legend of the West', *Democratization* March: 132–44.

Tesar, J. (1981) 'Totalitarian dictatorships as a phenomenon of the twentieth century and the possibilities of overcoming them', *International Journal of Politics* 11, 1: 85–100.

Tocqueville, A. de (1962) *L'Ancien Regime*, Oxford: Basil Blackwell.

—— (1968) *Democracy in America*, London: Fontana.

Touraine, A. (1987) *Actores Sociales y Sistemas Politicas en America Latina*, Santiago: PREALC.

Uhl, P. (1985) 'The alternative community as revolutionary avant-garde', in V. Havel *et al.* (eds) *The Power of the Powerless: Citizens against the state in Central–Eastern Europe*, London: Hutchinson.

Valenzuela, J. (1992) 'Consolidation in post-transitional settings', in S. Mainwaring, G. O'Donnell and J. Valenzuela (eds) *Issues in Democratic Consolidation: The new South American democracies in comparative perspective*, Indiana: University of Notre Dame Press.

Vergara, P. (1983) 'Las transformaciones del estado chileno bajo el regimen militar', in *Chile 1973–1980*, Santiago : FLACSO.

Villas, C.M. (1988) 'Popular insurgency and social revolution in Central America', *Latin American Perspectives* 15, 1: 55–77.

Vink, N. (1985) 'Base communities and urban social movements – a case study of the metal-workers' strike 1980, Sao Bernardo, Brazil', in D. Slater (ed.) *New Social Movements and the State in Latin America*, Amsterdam: CEDLA.

Vohryzek, J. (1985) 'Thoughts inside a tightly-corked bottle', in V. Havel *et al.* (eds) *The Power of the Powerless: Citizens against the state in Central–Eastern Europe*, London: Hutchinson.

Von Beyme, K. (1994) 'The last ideology of the old intelligentsia', in A. Bibic and C. Graziano (eds) *Civil Society, Political Society, Democracy*, Ljubljana: Slovenian Political Science Association.

Walker, R.B.J. (1994) 'Social movements/world politics', *Millennium* 23, 3: 669–700.

Wapner, P. (1995) 'Environmental activism and world civic politics', *World Politics* 47, 3: 311–40.

Weffort, F. (1989) 'Why democracy?', in A. Stepan (ed.) *Democratizing Brazil*, Oxford: Oxford University Press.

Whitehead, L. (1989) 'The Consolidation of fragile democracies', in R.A. Pastor (ed.) *Democracy in the Americas: Stopping the pendulum*, London: Holmes and Meier.

Wojcicki, K. (1981) 'The reconstruction of society', *Telos* 47: 98–103.

Wood, E.M. (1995) *Democracy Against Capitalism*, Cambridge: Cambridge University Press.

Index